# BASEBALL'S
# DREAM
# TEAMS

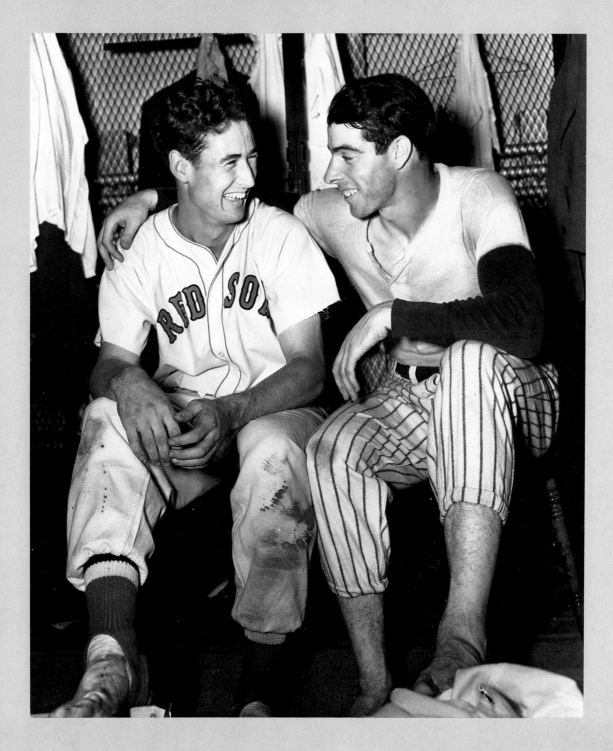

# BASEBALL'S
# DREAM TEAMS

### THE GREATEST MAJOR LEAGUE PLAYERS DECADE BY DECADE

**Lloyd Johnson**

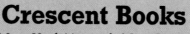
**Crescent Books**
New York/Avenel, New Jersey

This 1994 edition published by
Crescent Books,
distributed by Outlet Book
Company, Inc.,
a Random House Company,
40 Engelhard Avenue
Avenel, New Jersey 07001

Produced by
Brompton Books Corp.
15 Sherwood Place
Greenwich, CT 06830

ISBN 0-517-10306-0

Printed and bound in China

Updated and revised 1994

8 7 6 5 4 3 2 1

Page 1: *Perennial American
League All-Stars, Ted
Williams and Joe DiMaggio
relax in the locker room at
Briggs Stadium after the 1941
All-Star game. With two out
in the bottom of the ninth,
"The Splendid Splinter"
belted a game-winning three-
run homer.*

Page 2: *Fernando Valenzuela
unleashes a pitch. This
dream team left-hander of
the 1980s won both Rookie of
the Year and Cy Young
honors in 1981.*

This page: *The L.A. Dodgers'
Maury Wills slides safely into
third for his 104th stolen base
of the 1962 season – the year
he shattered the major league
steal mark of 96 set by Ty
Cobb in 1915. Wills is the
dream team shortstop of the
1960s.*

# CONTENTS

Left top: *The Royals' third baseman George Brett readies himself to make a play. Brett's .390 batting average in 1980 helped his team to the World Series, and earned him the MVP Award.*

Left bottom: *Boston's Jim Rice at the plate. For 16 years the big slugger played left field and some DH for the Red Sox. Rice won the American League MVP Award in 1978 with his league-leading 213 hits, 15 triples, 46 homers and 139 RBI.*

Right top: *The Yankees' stellar first sacker Don Mattingly takes the throw in a pick-off attempt. Mattingly, who hits well for both average and power, turned in an MVP season in 1985 when he belted a league-leading 48 doubles and 145 RBI.*

Right bottom: *Carl Yastrzemski at bat. The future Hall of Famer played a brilliant left field for the Red Sox from 1961 until 1983, when he yielded the position to newcomer Jim Rice.*

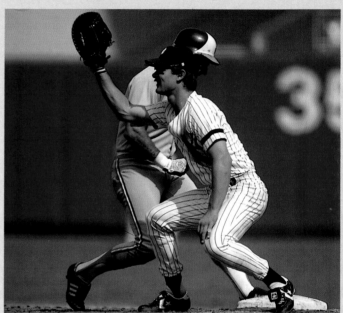

# INTRODUCTION

Walter Johnson, Christy Mathewson, Honus Wagner, Babe Ruth and Ty Cobb, the first five inductees into the Baseball Hall of Fame, embody the greatest skill, the most talent, and the toughest competitive spirit in baseball. Not many living fans of the national pastime ever saw the first five inductees play, yet most would agree that they represent baseball's highest achievements. What if they had played on the same team? What spectacular, dizzying heights might have been attained? That would indeed have been a dream team.

On the following pages the past and present stars of major league and Negro League baseball have been selected for All-Star teams for each decade of the twentieth century. Many of these performers played before radio and television brought baseball into America's living rooms. The names of some of those early players are well known, such as Frank Chance, George Kelly and Mel Ott. Others — Hippo Vaughn and Wally Schang, for example — were excellent ballplayers whose names have been obscured by time. The players' statistics, records, honors and other data used in making selections have been drawn only from the relevant decade. To be considered for a position on a decade's dream team, a player must have played at least 800 games, excepting catchers, who usually platooned until the 1930s. The player must have spent at least five seasons as a regular during the decade.

To facilitate the analysis of players, a database of statistics by decade was prepared. Statistics make a forum for comparative analysis. An abundance of major league statistics, beginning with the 1876 National League (NL) and continuing through the present season, exist in publications such as *The Baseball Encyclopedia, Total Baseball* and *The Baseball Register*. Studies by such renowned baseball analysts as Bill James, John Thorn and Pete Palmer have weighed the effects of factors like park size, pitching distance and rule changes on the whole body of baseball statistics. Even though their new statistical analyses have not produced a new pantheon of stars, use of their formulae has made the choice of the dream team players more scientific and more open to critical analysis.

Offensive ability is a strong criterion for selection. It can weight the choice of one player over another whose main contribution is fielding or team play. There is a bias toward those who scored and drove in runs, and a detectable lean toward players with 10 full seasons. As a case in point, two players, Sam Rice of the 1920s Washington Senators and Pete Rose of the 1970s Cincinnati Reds, had over 2000 hits for those respective decades. Both were selected over players who had more slugging ability. A batter who averages 200 hits per season will make the dream team anytime.

First choice and alternate dream team members were selected for each position, for left- and right-handed pitcher, and for designated hitter. Choosing an alternate in addition to the dream team starter gives the book bench depth. Honorable Mention players are those who were in contention.

JOHNSON, WASHINGTON

Above: *Walter Johnson, the Washington Senators' pitching ace from 1907 to 1927. This dream team right-hander of the 1910-1919 decade tossed a major league record 110 shutouts in his career and was elected to the Hall of Fame in 1936.*

TONY LAZZERI

BIG LEAGUE CHEWING GUM

Above: *Tony Lazzeri played for the Yankees for most of his 14-year career — from 1926 to 1937. For his ability to advance baserunners, Lazzeri became known as "Poosh 'Em Up." The second baseman batted in more than 100 runs seven times.*

Below: *Cleveland's future Hall of Famer Bob Feller on the mound on September 26, 1946. "Rapid Robert" turned in a sparkling performance that season, leading the league in wins (26), games (48), strikeouts (348) and shutouts (10). Bob Feller is the dream team right-hander of the forties.*

Below: *Ernie Banks played shortstop and first base for the Cubs his entire 19-year career. This future Hall of Famer and dream team shortstop of the fifties hit more than 40 homers four times, and turned in back-to-back MVP performances in 1958 and 1959.*

Bottom: *The Yankees' Mickey Mantle at bat in 1956, the year he won the Triple Crown. During Mantle's 18-year career with New York, he led the league in round-trippers four times, in runs six times, and in walks five times. "The Commerce Comet" was elected to the Hall of Fame in 1974.*

Each chapter's beginning is comprised of The Setting, that puts the decade in context within baseball history; The Game Strategy section; and a section describing factors that influenced player performance in that decade.

The Setting relates each decade to its contemporary framework. Baseball, as with most of life, does not occur in a vacuum. Consider this: in the 1930s, the St. Louis Cardinals were in the midst of a long road trip and had just finished a late night game in Boston. The hour was too late, and the time too short to wash and dry their woolen uniforms before they arrived in New York to play the next game. The Cardinals appeared on the field in absolutely filthy apparel. New York sportswriters claimed that the Cards looked like gas-house workers. Sure enough, they became known as the Gas House Gang. In today's world of high-speed transportation and polyester uniforms, the players always look spiffy – at least at the beginning of the game.

The Game Strategy portion describes the tactics employed by managers of the period. Strategy affects player performance, which is reflected in statistics. Stolen bases, home runs, triples and strikeouts are statistics that strategic maneuvers have caused to fluctuate from 1900 to the present.

The factors most influencing player performance are rule changes, equipment development, extraneous circumstances, and ballpark effect. Minor ballpark changes – moving a fence, or blocking out the center-field bleachers, for instance – can translate into major performance adjustments. In 1947 Pittsburgh officials installed a chain-link fence at Forbes Field, decreasing the depth of left field by 30 feet. The press first called the area Greenberg Gardens, then Kiner Corner. Ralph Kiner hit 23 home runs pre-fence, 51 post-fence. He led the NL in homers for seven straight seasons.

Above: *Babe Ruth, pictured with the black armband worn to mourn the death of manager Miller Huggins, September 26, 1929. This dream team right fielder of the twenties, who still holds all-time records for home run percentage, walks and slugging average, was a legend in his own time.*

Changes in equipment, especially in the baseball itself, influence player peformance. The very definition of the "Dead Ball Era," 1900-1919, is related to the public's concept of baseball construction.

Changes in baseball rules may define an entire era of play. The era of the high strike, 1963-1968, allowed Boston's Carl Yastrzemski to lead the American League (AL) in batting with a .301 average in 1968. Other rule changes are not so pronounced in their effects. The ever-changing sacrifice fly rule altered the batting averages of only those players who hit long fly balls with a runner on third and less than two outs.

Extraneous circumstances can lead to actions that will seriously alter a player's performance, and therefore, his statistics. Bob Feller would easily have been a 300-game winner if World War II had not disrupted his career. Player strikes and the trimming of rosters during the Depression both affected seasonal totals: one reduced the number of games played, and the other increased the number of at-bats and innings played during the season. When Willie Mays moved to San Francisco with the Giants, he found that the new park had been built so that the prevailing wind blew to right field. Mays altered his swing to become a right field home run hitter while at home in Candlestick Park.

Of course, there are other things that affect a ballplayer's performance. Before getting into the dream team selections, a word about the arbitrator would be appropriate. There is an old joke that goes like this: Satan once challenged God to a baseball game. St. Peter, who accepted on behalf of God, rubbed his hands in delight, thinking of fielding a team consisting of Ruth, Gehrig, Cobb, Simmons, Foxx, Collins and the like. But God cautioned St. Peter, saying, "You may have all the ballplayers, but he has all the umpires."

Likewise, the reader will find no umpires here, but instead will see and read about some of the greatest performers ever to play the game of baseball.

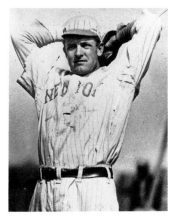

Above: *Christy Mathewson winds up. The future Hall of Fame right-hander pitched for the New York Giants from 1900 to 1916. Among his great achievements is his World Series performance in 1905, when he pitched three shutouts in six days.*

LEFT FIELD

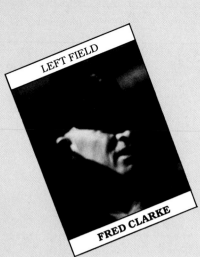

**FRED CLARKE**

CENTER FIELD

**GINGER BEAUMONT**

SHORTSTOP

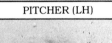

**HONUS WAGNER**

SECOND BASE

**NAPOLEON LAJOIE**

THIRD BASE

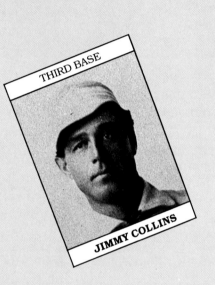

**JIMMY COLLINS**

PITCHER (LH)

**RUBE WADDELL**

PITCHER (RH)

**CHRISTY MATHEWSON**

CATCHER

**ROGER BRESNAHAN**

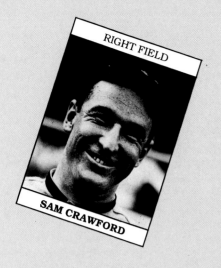

RIGHT FIELD

SAM CRAWFORD

# THE GREATEST PLAYERS
## OF THE
# FIRST DECADE
## 1900-1909

FIRST BASE

FRANK CHANCE

## ALTERNATE DREAM TEAM

| | | | |
|---|---|---|---|
| **Pitcher** | Cy Young (rh)<br>Eddie Plank (lh) | **Third Baseman** | Harry Steinfeldt |
| | | **Shortstop** | None |
| **Catcher** | John Kling | **Left Fielder** | Mike Donlin |
| **First Baseman** | Harry Davis | **Center Fielder** | Jimmy Sheckard |
| **Second Baseman** | Johnny Evers | **Right Fielder** | Elmer Flick |

## HONORABLE MENTION

| | | | |
|---|---|---|---|
| **Pitcher** | Joe McGinnity<br>Mordecai Brown<br>Orval Overall<br>Ed Reulbach<br>Sam Leever<br>Deacon Phillippe<br>Vic Willis<br>Ed Walsh<br>Addie Joss<br>Jack Chesbro<br>Chief Bender<br>Bill Donovan | **First Baseman**<br><br>**Second Baseman**<br><br>**Third Baseman**<br><br>**Shortstop** | Fred Tenney<br>Jake Beckley<br><br>Miller Huggins<br>Jimmy Williams<br><br>Bill Bradley<br><br>Bobby Wallace<br>Fred Parent<br>Joe Tinker<br>Bill Dahlen |
| **Catcher** | Red Dooin<br>Ossie<br>  Schreckengost | **Left Fielder**<br>**Center Fielder**<br>**Right Fielder** | Topsy Hartsell<br>Fielder Jones<br>"Wee Willie" Keeler<br>Socks Seybold |

# THE SETTING

Players were nicknamed "Turkey Mike," "Iron Man," "The Tabasco Kid," "Old Eagle Eye," and "Miner." Streetcars pulled by horses took fans to baseball games in ballparks surrounded by rickety wooden grandstands. Attendance of games ran to 20,000, with the overflow fans standing along the outfield. At crowded weekend games, fans had to stand behind ropes in center field – usually more than 500 feet from home plate.

The rowdy National League opened the new century by dropping Washington, Louisville, Baltimore and Cleveland teams to form an eight-team major league. There were rumors that a second major league would be formed. Ban Johnson, an energetic sportswriter from Cincinnati, and president of the Western League, was frequently named in conjunction with the new league. At the same time, nineteenth-century Chicago star Cap Anson and *Sporting Life* editor Francis Richter were involved in an attempt to renovate the moribund American Association and make it a major league. It was Johnson, with his dedication to cleaning up the atmosphere in which baseball was played, who carried the day. The American League emerged as an independent minor league in 1900, then declared itself a major league in 1901. Johnson solicited the support of such shrewd operators as Clark Griffith and Connie Mack in his plan to administer a league which would not condone the rowdiness, umpire-baiting, and bottle-throwing typical at baseball games of the time. With his new American League, Johnson brought decency back to baseball.

# GAME STRATEGY

Runs were expensive and outs were cheap. Bunting, sacrificing, and moving the runner up constituted the playing style of the day. Teams would score once or twice, then fiercely protect the lead as daylight faded and the worn, discolored baseballs became particularly difficult to see. At bat, hitters tended to face the pitcher in an open stance with the bat extended over the plate, gripped with their hands spread apart. The hitter punched, slapped or shoved the ball; whatever it took to move the baserunner.

Autocratic managers – master strategists – dominated their teams. Only four managers won pennants in the National League during the first decade of the twentieth century: Ned Hanlon with Brooklyn, Fred Clarke of Pittsburgh, John McGraw with New York, and Chicago's Frank Chance. All but Hanlon are in the Baseball Hall of Fame. In the new American League, Clark Griffith of Chicago, Connie Mack with Philadelphia, Boston's Jimmy Collins, Fielder Jones of Chicago, and Hugh Jennings with Detroit won pennants. All but Jones are in the Hall of Fame.

# FACTORS INFLUENCING PLAYER PERFORMANCE

The ball consisted of a rubber center wound with string and wool, then wrapped with a hand-stitched horsehide cover. The ball was so dead that batters had terrible difficulty hitting it into the outfield. First basemen of the era frequently recorded 20 or more of the 27 putouts in a nine-inning game.

The foul strike rule, adopted by the NL in 1901, and by the AL in 1903, made every foul ball a strike unless there were already two strikes on the batter. Up to then, a batter was not charged a strike when he hit a foul ball. The new rule drove batting averages down. In 1900 NL hitters averaged .279; in 1901, .267. The AL hit .275 on average in 1902, and .255 in 1903. The institution of the foul strike was the most important factor influencing player performance in the decade. Batters, with their defensive posture at the plate, were easy outs for such control specialists as Christy Mathewson or Cy Young.

Equipment changes included the introduction of shin guards, the use of a more heavily padded catcher's mask, and experimentation with a pneumatic batting helmet that featured air pumped into rubber tubes. Shin guards and the more protective mask enabled catchers to effectively block the plate, which made scoring runs even more difficult. The new mask and shin guards became part of the catcher's standard equipment, but the idea of the pneumatic batting helmet was quickly deflated.

The spitball, which broke sharply downward as it reached the batter's strike zone, was introduced to the big leagues by Elmer Stricklett, a journeyman hurler who taught the pitch to Big Ed Walsh during spring training with the Chicago White Sox. The spitball is similar to the split-finger fastball in that it dips in the critical last five feet in front of the plate. This pitch, and the foul strike rule, made batting much more difficult than it had been in the 1890s.

New rules and equipment changes aside, the most remarkable factor about the decade of 1900 to 1909 was the variety of people who played the game. Whereas baseball players had formerly been homogenous in background, the new century brought a new mix of men. Detroit Tiger outfielder Davy Jones is quoted in *The Glory of Their Times*: "The players were more colorful, drawn from every walk of life. We had stupid guys, smart guys, tough guys, mild guys, crazy guys, college men, slickers from the city and hicks from the country." It was a trend that continued through the century.

# THE POSITIONS

## PITCHER

The years 1900 to 1909 were the Golden Years of Pitching. Ballparks were spacious, the ball was dead, and batters choked up to punch or slap at it. Competition for the dream team pitchers of the decade was keen. The pitcher's mound in the 1900s was loaded with talent.

New York Giants hurler "Iron Man" Joe McGinnity once pitched and won three doubleheaders in one month. He and ace Christy Mathewson formed the heart of the New York pitching staff. The Giants faced stiff competition from the Chicago Cubs and Pittsburgh Pirates throughout the decade.

Chicago featured a trio of Cubs who could cause the stoutest batsman's heart to quiver. They were Mordecai Brown, who threw the three-finger pitch similar to the split-finger fastball; Orval Overall, who had an ERA under 2.00 for three consecutive seasons; and Ed Reulbach, whose won-lost percentage was .719 for the decade, and who once threw two nine-inning shutouts in a doubleheader.

The Pittsburgh staff was formidable, helping the Pirates win three pennants during these 10 years. They were Sam Leever, "The Goshen Schoolmaster," who taught a little respect with his 167-72 won-lost record for the decade; Deacon Phillippe, who was tough and stingy, winning 20 or more games five times, and averaging less than one walk per game for three seasons; and Vic Willis, who won 20 or more games six times in 10 seasons.

AL pitchers were just as tough on batters as their NL counterparts. White Sox pitcher Ed Walsh had a lifetime ERA of 1.82. He threw a spitball that was described as approaching the plate and just disintegrating. Walsh won 40 games in 1908.

Cleveland's ace, Addie Joss, had a lifetime ERA of 1.89. Joss met Walsh in an October match in the midst of the 1908 American League pennant race. Walsh allowed four hits and struck out 15 batters. One run scored on a single, a two-base error, and a passed ball as Walsh's slippery toss eluded his catcher. Joss pitched a perfect game. It still stands as the only perfect game in a pennant race.

New York Highlander Jack Chesbro was known as "Happy Jack." His 41 wins in 1904 failed to amuse him, however, since his wild pitch in the first game of the season-ending doubleheader allowed Boston to score the winning run and take the pennant.

Philadelphia A's stoic right-handed ace Chief Bender was manager Connie Mack's money pitcher. The Chippewa did not disappoint Mack; he picked up six World Series wins in 10 starts and helped the A's to three World Series titles.

Tiger hurler Wild Bill Donovan pitched the Bengals to three consecutive pennants and had one 25-4 season.

All this considered, New York's **Christy Mathewson** and Philadelphia's **Rube Waddell** emerge as the decade's best pitchers. Boston's Cy Young and Philadelphia's Eddie Plank are dream team alternates.

As good as Cy Young was from 1900 to 1909 – he had 230

*Dream team right-hander Christy Mathewson hurled his way to 235 wins for the decade, leading the league in wins three times. His talent was not lost on the Giants, who went to the World Series four times with his help.*

wins – Christy Mathewson was better, with 235 victories. Mathewson was the college-educated football star and Renaissance man who, as class president at Bucknell, sang in the school glee club. Tall, blond and good-looking, Mathewson (and his bride) shared an apartment with New York manager John McGraw and his wife. McGraw rode Mathewson's good right arm and the fadeaway pitch to three pennants during the decade. In the 1905 World Series, Mathewson tossed three shutouts in six days, giving up a total of 14 hits, and only one walk. He was never greater than during the 1908 NL pennant race: 37 wins, 56 games, 391 innings pitched, 259 strikeouts, and a 1.43 ERA.

Left: *Rube Waddell, dream team southpaw, led the league in strikeouts seven times during the decade, and turned in four consecutive 20-plus win seasons for the Philadelphia A's. He was elected to the Hall of Fame in 1946.*

Above: *Cy Young (right) poses with Bill Carrigan (left) and Larry Lajoie. Alternate dream team right-hander, the "Ohio Cyclone" was never the best pitcher at any time during his impressive career. His stamina and consistency through 22 years of pitching will never be equalled, however; he holds all-time career records for wins, losses, complete games and innings pitched.*

ciation, and at Philadelphia in the American League. When Waddell wasn't chasing fire engines, wrestling alligators, leading a brass band down the avenue, or playing professional football, he was striking out batters at a record clip.

Waddell fanned 349 batters in 1904. Despite missing the 1905 World Series because of an arm injury sustained while wrestling a teammate, Waddell's performance was ample reward for the risk Manager Mack took on him. Waddell chalked up 131 victories in six years; he had four consecutive 20-win seasons. His legendary showmanship – once, in an exhibition game, he called in the outfielders and struck out the side, and this was many years before Satchel Paige made a living doing it – drew fans to AL games at a crucial time when the success of the new league was in doubt.

By 1908 even Mack was unable to endure any more Waddell pranks, and he sold the eccentric left-hander to the St. Louis Browns. The first time that he faced his old Athletic teammates, he whiffed 16 of them to set an AL record that lasted until Cleveland Indians' Bob Feller mowed down 17 in 1936. In 1914 Waddell died from an illness contracted by standing, armpit deep, in freezing water for hours, passing sandbags to people who were trying to repair a burst dike. He had been just passing through Kentucky, saw the trouble, and decided to stop and help.

In the Golden Years of Pitching the alternate dream team hurlers, Cy Young and Eddie Plank, make a formidable duo. Cy Young had won 268 games in the 1890s, but he jumped from the NL St. Louis Cardinals to the Bostons in the new American League for a pay raise of $500. His change paid off. The "Ohio Cyclone" won 230 games during the decade.

In command of four pitches: a fastball, an overhand curve, a sidearm curve and a "tobacco ball," Young also possessed extraordinary control. He once pitched an entire 20-inning game without giving up a base on balls. As overpowering as the great Cy Young seemed to be, he was never the best pitcher in baseball at any time during his career (Amos Rusie, Kid Nichols, Christy Mathewson, Addie Joss, Ed Walsh and Walter Johnson were his contemporaries), yet he won more games (511), pitched more innings (7356), and completed more games (751), than anyone else in major league history. It is appropriate that the annual award for the best pitcher in each league memorializes him.

"Gettysburg" Eddie Plank of the Athletics was, in many ways, the opposite of his teammate Rube Waddell. But his pitching was similar and almost as good. Together they formed the greatest left-handed pair in the history of baseball. Plank came straight from Gettysburg College to the big leagues, where he stayed for 17 years and won 327 games. Known as a fidgety pitcher, he would drive batters insane messing with his uniform, pawing the mound, talking to the ball ("only nine more to go"), shaking off signs, and doing everything except pitching. When he finally delivered he was good, with a fastball and sidearm curve that won 186 games during the decade. In fact he won 20 or more games eight times. Plank's left-handed victory record of 327 stood until Warren Spahn passed the mark in 1963. Plank's shutout total of 69 is the most for a left-handed pitcher.

"Gettysburg" Eddie brought respectability to being a southpaw. At the turn of the century, many superstitious managers refused to employ a portsider. Rube Waddell and nineteenth-century pitchers Frank Killen and Matches Kilroy were examples of the brilliance, but also of the unreliability, that a manager might expect from a left-handed chucker. Plank and Giants' rookie "Hooks" Wiltse changed that myopic view. Wiltse won his first 12 games in the majors, and Plank pitched winning baseball for 17 years.

The decade's best left-handed hurler, Rube Waddell, was a likeable, overgrown kid who sported a terrific fastball, a biting curve, and exceptional control of his pitches. Control of his actions was another matter; he once turned cartwheels from the mound after defeating Cy Young in a 20-inning contest. Waddell was so uneducated and so unpredictable that only Connie Mack was willing to take a chance on him. Mack was Waddell's manager twice, at Milwaukee in the American Asso-

# CATCHER

Catcher was a position in transition during the first 10 years of the century. The close score in games and the emphasis on moving the runner and stealing bases added importance to the catcher's ability to throw. New and sometimes tricky pitches made the receiver's role crucial to the success of the pitcher. Some star pitchers made sure that their own catchers went with them from team to team. With the introduction of sturdier equipment, the catcher could block the plate and expect to be injury-free and available for the game the next day. The 100-game catcher became a reality by the end of this first decade.

Below: *Selected on the basis of his batting and leadership, Roger Bresnahan is the decade's dream team catcher. The stocky future Hall of Famer played with* *four teams during the decade, including the world champion New York Giants of 1905. Bresnahan tried his hand in the outfield and at four other infield positions.*

Two catchers, the Giants' Roger Bresnahan and John Kling of the Cubs, stand out from the others. The Philadelphia Phillies' Red Dooin was a weak hitter – .235 was his average for the decade – but caught more than 100 games in four of his 15 seasons. The Athletics' Ossie Schreckengost was a better hitter – .267 was his decade average – but was not as enduring. He caught 100 games in a season only once, in 1905 when the Athletics won the pennant. In the early years of the century, when ball clubs saved money by bunking two players to a bed, Schreckengost was best known for a clause in his contract prohibiting roommates from eating soda crackers in bed.

The question of whether Kling was better than Bresnahan was as hotly debated in the 1900s as today. Roger Bresnahan was a throwback to the old days when the catcher would also play other positions. He was one of the only two players to pitch and catch in the same game (never mind the publicity stunts of Bert Campaneris and Cesar Tovar). Bresnahan is credited with the introduction of shin guards and the heavily padded mask for catchers, as well as the pneumatic batting helmet, which he wore in spring training while recovering from a serious beaning.

In 1909 Giants manager John McGraw traded Bresnahan to St. Louis in exchange for pitchers. Bresnahan became a good manager himself, building the last-place Cardinals into pennant contenders by 1911. While with St. Louis, Bresnahan worked as manager for major league baseball's first female team owner, Helene Robison Britton.

John Kling was thought to have the best throwing arm and sharpest wit of any catcher in the decade. The Cubs, with Kling behind the plate, led the NL in ERA seven times in nine years. Kling was an excellent handler of pitchers but a weaker offensive player than Bresnahan, who out-hit Kling .285 to .274 during the decade, out-slugged him .382 to .359, and had a 68 point advantage in on-base percentage.

In retirement in his native Kansas City, Missouri, Kling ran a pool hall and sports emporium and was part-owner of the Kansas City Blues baseball team. Contemporaries outside of New York considered Kling to be the best catcher of his era, but later sportswriters chose **Roger Bresnahan** for the Hall of Fame on the basis of his batting and leadership. That's why he makes the first team here. Kling is the alternate.

# FIRST BASE

The men who played first base during this decade were thought of as fielders whose duties were to catch the ball and throw it to the correct base. As batters, they tended to be good at getting on base and scoring runs. Competition for the dream team first base job is among the Cubs' star Frank Chance, nicknamed "The Peerless Leader" for his ability to guide the Cubs to victory; the Athletics' Harry Davis, who was a top slugger in the earliest years of the AL; Fred Tenney of the Giants, who played more games at first than did the other candidates, but was so weak with the stick that his slugging average (.299) was 57 percentage points below his on-base percentage, and Hall of Fame member Jake Beckley, whose best years had been in the National League prior to 1900. "Old Eagle Eye" Beckley could still hit the ball though; he had a .307 average for the decade with the Browns.

**Frank Chance** is the first choice. He hit .299 for the decade; only Beckley hit for a higher average. Though Chance was out-slugged by Davis and Beckley, he played the style of the decade – get on base (.379 OBA) and steal second (357 stolen bases), thereby saving an out – better than his con-

*Dream team first sacker Frank Chance warms up in the on-deck circle (above) and on the field (right). "The Peerless Leader" played for the Cubs for 15 of his 17 years in the majors. He also managed the Cubs from 1905 through 1912, taking them to the World Series four times during that span. A speedy baserunner, crafty base-stealer, and a no-nonsense manager, Frank Chance was elected to the Hall of Fame in 1946.*

temporaries. Moreover, Chance was the manager and a tough hombre who did not take back talk or put up with disobedience. He led the Cubs to four pennants in five years, including a record 116 victories, never equaled even in these days of 162 games in a season. Defensively, Chance anchored an infield immortalized in poetry by Franklin P. Adams' "Tinker to Evers to Chance." Despite his relatively high totals of bases on balls, stolen bases, batting average, and OBA, Frank Chance's main attribute was his leadership. He governed the Cubs in a blustery, no-nonsense manner that sometimes required him to use his fists as well as his brain.

The alternate for first base is Harry Davis, the stalwart performer for Connie Mack's Athletics. Davis led the AL in home runs four consecutive years, and was one of the decade's most feared power hitters, with a slugging percentage of .423. His 66 home runs led all other players, at any position, for the 1900-1909 period. Bill James chose Davis as the decade's most underrated player in the *Bill James Historical Baseball Abstract*. He played on six pennant winners for Philadelphia over his 22-year career.

## SECOND BASE

At the turn of the century, second base was a slugger's position, not a position for nimble double-play artists as in the 1980s. In fact, few infield combinations could turn double plays (the Cubs infield became famous for double plays, yet they averaged fewer than 100 per season from 1900-1909).

The best second baseman of the decade was undoubtedly **Napoleon "Larry" Lajoie**, who stood head, shoulders and batting average above the crowd of skillful second basemen. John Evers of the Cubs, Miller Huggins of the Cardinals, and Jimmy Williams of the Highlanders and later the Browns, were Lajoie's worthy opponents.

The handsome French-Canadian was born in Woonsocket, Rhode Island. He decimated the 1901 AL pitching to the tune of .426, still the AL batting record. For good measure, Lajoie also led in runs, hits, doubles, home runs, RBIs, OBA and slugging average. Known for his grace and style as a second sacker, Lajoie was easily the dream team's top second baseman during the decade, with a .347 batting average and .488 slugging percentage for those ten years.

The infant American League announced in 1901 that it would participate in organized baseball as a major league, and that league officials intended to sign National League stars. Most of the players who jumped to the new league were past their primes and wanted to make more money before retiring. Lajoie, who jumped from the NL Philadelphia Phillies to the AL Philadelphia Athletics, was one of the few contract jumpers whom the NL went after – that is, the only one that they wanted back. The Phillies went to court to prevent Lajoie from playing with the Athletics. When a restraining order was issued to prevent Lajoie from playing anywhere in Pennsylvania, AL officials arranged for Lajoie to go to Cleveland.

Lajoie's popularity in Cleveland led to the team being called the "Naps" in his honor. He also lent his name to the *Larry Lajoie Baseball Guide*, and he was among the first professional athletes to make extra money by endorsing tobacco and athletic products. A savage line-drive hitter, Lajoie could literally break third baseman's legs with hard hit balls. "Hot corner" guardians usually took a step backward when the graceful French-Canadian took his place at bat. Lajoie once suffered blood poisoning due to a spike wound in his foot. To accommodate the injury he altered his stocking – and baseball history – by cutting the toe and heel from the colored sock, thereby creating the stirrup sock that is worn today.

The dream team alternate at second base is a difficult choice among two Hall of Famers, John Evers and Miller Hug-

gins, and the man who played more games at second than did any other player in the decade, Jimmy Williams. Williams, while appearing in almost twice as many games as Miller Huggins, had fewer walks and stolen bases. He hit .005 better than Huggins and out-slugged him by .059 points. However, Miller Huggins is in the Hall of Fame for his managing, not his ball playing. Williams and Huggins more or less cancel each other, and the vote goes to the player whose statistics fall in between the two, Johnny Evers.

Disliked by umpires, taunted by rivals, and barely tolerated by his teammates, pint-sized John "The Crab" Evers carried a rule book in his back pocket and a burning desire to excel in his heart. The rule book figured in the most dramatic pennant race of the decade. The hated Giants lost a game and the 1908 NL pennant to Chicago when Evers spotted Fred Merkle's failure to touch the bag as the game ended. Evers had protested the same play in Pittsburgh 19 days earlier.

Evers was also resourceful. When the Giants acquired deaf-and-dumb hurler Dummy Taylor, manager John McGraw encouraged the Giants to learn the deaf-and-dumb sign language. McGraw's third base coaches would frequently spell out "bunt" or "steal" with the sign language. Evers, one of the decade's smarter players, studied the sign language and became a proficient conversationalist. The Giants, for some time, could not imagine how Evers was getting their signs. Evers and McGraw once became embroiled in animated conversation in sign language, and Evers threw a finger out of joint replying to McGraw in a brilliant flash of repartee.

Left: *Nap Lajoie, who played for Cleveland most of the decade, is the dream team second baseman. In 1901 Lajoie turned in a Triple Crown year, batting .422 with 14 round-trippers and 125 RBI.*

Below: *A representation depicts Nap Lajoie batting, for Philadelphia, against New York. An all-around player, Lajoie's graceful efficiency on the field was equalled by his offensive skill.*

Horner
Photo

Above: *Dream team second baseman alternate Johnny Evers played for the Cubs from 1902 through 1913. Note the choked-up batting grip, which was prevalent at a time when slap-hit singles to advance baserunners was an important element of game strategy.*

Above right: *Jimmy Collins, the obvious third baseman dream team selection, poses with his bat. An innovative fielder, skillful hitter and successful manager, Collins played six years for each Boston club, and finished his career in 1908 with the A's.*

# THIRD BASE

Third base was a position in transition in the early years of the twentieth century. With the foul-strike rule making bunting more difficult, the hot corner became a variable defensive position. Jimmy Collins of the AL Boston club revolutionized third base play. Before his time, most third sackers anchored themselves to the bag. Collins was one of the first to play in toward home plate or back of third base, depending upon the situation. His bare-handed snap throws on bunts are now standard operating procedure for third basemen.

For these innovations in the field, and for his batting prowess, **Jimmy Collins** receives this decade's honor as the dream team third baseman. He out-hit his closest competitors, Bill Bradley and Harry Steinfeldt, by almost 20 points. Collins jumped to the newly formed American League to join the Boston team as player/manager in 1901, and hit .332 for

the second-place finishers. In 1903 and 1904, he managed Boston to AL pennants.

Challenged by Pittsburgh's owner, Barney Dreyfus, to a championship series of games, Collins played and managed his team to a thrilling come-from-behind victory, five games to three, over the NL Pirates. The year was 1903, and the games constituted the first modern World Series.

While Collins is the obvious dream team selection, the choice for alternate third baseman of the decade, between Cleveland's Bill Bradley and the Cubs' Harry Steinfeldt, is much more difficult to make. Bradley had his best years, 1902-04, in the AL before it became competitive. Steinfeldt not only anchored the Tinker-Evers-Chance infield that helped win four pennants, but led the NL in hits and RBIs during the 1906 season, and ranked highly for three consecutive seasons as a clutch hitter. Bradley averaged .004 points better than Steinfeldt over the decade and out-slugged him, but loses out to Steinfeldt in on-base percentage. Bradley led the AL in fielding four times, Steinfeldt two times, yet Steinfeldt had the highest single-season fielding average of .967. The Cubs' standout drove in 90 more runs in 400 fewer at-bats during the decade. In a very close call, Steinfeldt gets the nod because of playing on four pennant winners and being a clutch hitter who drove in runs. The teams Bradley played for never won a pennant during his 14-year career.

As good as the Cubs were, they did not start to win pennants until Steinfeldt arrived in 1906 in a trade with the Reds for Hans Lobert and Jake Weimer. His .471 average led all hitters in the 1907 World Series sweep of the Tigers.

# SHORTSTOP

During the first decade of the twentieth century, the players at the shortstop position continued the nineteenth-century style of play. The shortstop was considered the best player on the team and, being the only fielder not tied down to a bag, was given free range to position himself where he thought he could provide the most help.

Amicable Honus Wagner was a star shortstop of the first magnitude. His peers were Bobby Wallace of the Browns, who played 25 seasons and is in the Hall of Fame, the Boston Pilgrims' Fred Parent, who was the last survivor of the 1903 World Series when he died in 1972, the Cubs' Joe Tinker, who rode a poem and the ability to hit Christy Mathewson pitches into the Hall of Fame, and National Leaguer Bill Dahlen, who was, by this time, past his prime. While the four second- place contenders for the dream team were good players, and two were Hall of Famers, **Honus Wagner** was far and away the best. He out-hit and had an OBA over 80 points better than the second-best shortstop of the decade. He out-slugged the runner-up by 150 points. Despite playing the same number of games, Wagner scored 400 more runs than his greatest rival. For these reasons, no alternate shortstop was selected for the dream team. There was only one Honus Wagner and he had no real competitors.

In three minor league seasons and 17 consecutive years in the majors, Wagner never batted below .300. An eight-time NL

*The incomparable Honus Wagner played for Pittsburgh for most of his 21-year career, from 1900 to 1917. During the decade "The Flying Dutchman" led the league in stolen bases five times and in batting average seven times. Wagner's six RBI in the 1909 World Series paced the Pittsburgh victory over Detroit. The dream team shortstop was elected to the Hall of Fame in 1936.*

batting champion, Wagner's 3430 hit total remained the benchmark until Stan Musial topped him in 1962. For the decade, Wagner scored 1013 runs, knocked in 956, blasted 1850 hits with 377 doubles, had a batting average of .351, and a slugging average of .508. He is the decade leader in all of the previous categories.

In 1909 Detroit and Pittsburgh met in the World Series. Ty Cobb and Wagner were batting champions of their leagues. A photographer, sensing an historic moment, asked the two to pose at home plate. They adopted hitting postures and looked at each other's batting grips. Both champions were self-taught and employed the same distinctive grip with hands a palm-width apart.

The bowlegged Wagner never had formal instruction on the art of baseball. His huge hands, desire to play, and raw power were ample substitutes. So great was his abandon in play that he often scooped up dirt and pebbles and would throw them with the ball to first base. John McGraw considered him the best player he had ever seen.

# LEFT FIELD

At the turn of the century left fielders generally played shallow – as did the other outfielders – and were expected to turn and catch fly balls with their backs to the infield. On many occasions the left fielder was able to force the runner at second, or to throw out a runner at the plate who tried to score from second on a base hit. The left-field position required a fleet, sure-handed, quick-witted player who could also hit and run.

The three candidates for left fielder on the 1900 to 1909 dream team are Pittsburgh's player and manager Fred Clarke, Cincinnati and New York show-stopper "Turkey" Mike Donlin, and Philadelphia A's diminutive towhead "Topsy" Hartsell.

Fred Clarke was a sure-handed, speedy outfielder, and an excellent hitter with surprising power for a man weighing only 160 pounds. During the decade he scored 887 runs with 133 triples, and had a .302 batting average.

Mike Donlin was married to Broadway actress Mabel Hite, and spent two and one half years during this decade travelling with her vaudeville act. But during the remaining years, he played baseball, and he was very, very good. His decade batting average was .338 and his .474 slugging average was exceeded only by Honus Wagner and Larry Lajoie, the decade's two top stars.

Topsy Hartsell was the lead-off man for the Athletics, and led the AL in bases on balls five times, in runs scored once, and in stolen bases once, as he hit .279 for the decade.

**Fred Clarke** is the top choice for the left-field position, since he was a model of consistency at bat and in the field. Donlin was erratic both on and off the field. Hartsell was a good ballplayer with a talent for getting on base, but he was not in Clarke's league as an all-around player, nor does he compare favorably with Donlin as a hitter.

Clarke's real talent lay in his ability to manage players. After spring training on his Kansas ranch, the Pirates would sally forth, year after year, to battle Chicago and New York, two teams that usually had Clarke's Pirates out-manned. Nevertheless, he won four pennants in 10 years. The 1902 team finished a record 27 and a half games ahead of the Brooklyn Superbas. Clarke led the NL colors into the first modern World Series in 1903. The older league suffered quite a shock when the upstart Boston Pilgrims soundly whipped them. Due to injuries on his pitching staff, Clarke had only one pitcher, Deacon Phillippe. The Deacon won three but tired and lost two. Clarke never complained, but surely felt the humiliation of losing to an upstart league because he had only one pitcher available.

Mike Donlin is the alternate selection. Had he played every year in the decade, Donlin would probably be the top choice for left fielder. But missing part of 1906, and all of 1907, 1909 and 1910, he could hardly be expected to make the first string on this team. "Turkey Mike" was John McGraw's type of player: he strutted wherever he went. When McGraw needed an outfield stick, he remembered Donlin, the brash youngster who had played for him in St. Louis and Baltimore. In 1904 Donlin came to the Giants from the Reds, where he had hit .351 the previous season, finishing second behind powerful Honus Wagner. Turkey Mike did not disappoint McGraw in 1905 and 1908; he had slugging averages over .450. Love for Mabel Hite led the ballplayer from the diamond to the stage. He sat out 1907 and 1909-10 to pursue a secondary career in vaudeville.

Below: *Pittsburgh's Fred Clarke slides home safely. Dream team left fielder for the decade, Clarke managed for most of his 21-year playing career, winning four pennants. The future Hall of Famer could pound out the extra-base hit, and hit for average.*

# CENTER FIELD

In the 1900s, center field was an immense expanse of territory that only jackrabbits and very fast ballplayers could cover. At Boston's Huntingon Park the center-field barrier was more than 635 feet from home plate. One of the greatest ever to patrol center field, Ty Cobb, is not eligible for the position in this decade because he played fewer than 600 games. That leaves three whose playing styles typify the dead ball era, Fielder Jones, Jimmy Sheckard and Ginger Beaumont. One might say that White Sox manager Jones was born to play ball; Fielder was his given name. He managed the White Sox and was the top defensive center fielder of his era. Jimmy Sheckard of the Superbas, and later the Cubs, played on five pennant-winning teams during the decade, had a high OBA, and was an excellent fielder. The Pirates' center fielder, Ginger Beaumont, led the NL in hits four times, and hit .308 in a decade dominated by pitching.

**Ginger Beaumont** is the top choice for the dream team since he out-scored, out-hit, and drove in more runs than Sheckard or Jones, while playing fewer games. Beaumont and his teammate Fred Clarke were always near the top of the NL in fielding, and formed the nucleus of the tough Pirate squads of the decade.

Alternate Jimmy Sheckard was known as a heads-up ballplayer on the Brooklyn pennant-winning teams of 1900-01, where he learned baseball from his teammates Ned Hanlon, Hugh Jennings, Willie Keeler, Fielder Jones and Joe Kelley. Later Sheckard took his abilities to draw bases on balls, score runs, and hit in the lead-off position to the Cubs, who won three pennants during the decade. Sheckard's base-stealing prowess was highly respected by his contemporaries. His greatest feat came in the second decade of the century, when he announced to the league that he was going to draw walks, then proceeded to set the 1911 NL record of 147 bases on balls.

# RIGHT FIELD

During the 1900s right field was populated with heavy hitters. Some could drive the ball into the next county. The selection for this position is a dream to make; there are three members of the Hall of Fame and a home run champion to choose from. The candidates are Baltimore Oriole and New York Highlander "Wee Willie" Keeler, Philadelphia Athletics slugger Socks Seybold, Cleveland Nap Elmer Flick, and Detroit Tiger Sam Crawford.

Willie Keeler, whose batting philosophy was "hit 'em where they ain't," averaged .345 over 19 years of major league baseball. By the end of the decade, he was clearly on the downhill side of a Hall of Fame career. It included a record eight consecutive seasons of 200 or more hits, from 1894 to 1901. Keeler was 31 years old when he jumped to the Highlanders in 1903, where he hit .300 or better for four seasons, but then hit .234 and .263.

Socks Seybold once held the AL home run record with 16 in 1902. He was tied for third place with Honus Wagner for the decade's home run title. The A's replaced him in 1908, however, when his slugging prowess ceased to compensate for ineptitude in the field.

**Sam Crawford** is the dream team right fielder. For eight years Wahoo Sam (he was born in Wahoo, Nebraska) Crawford played beside Ty Cobb, hit behind him, pinch-hit for him, and was overshadowed by him. Supposedly the two did not get

along well, but together they once made a highly successful hold-out against Tigers' owner Frank Navin, and years later Tyrus the Terrible campaigned relentlessly to add Crawford to the Hall of Fame. The hard-hitting right fielder did not need Cobb's help. Crawford is the all-time triples leader with 312. He was a slugger, leading the NL in home runs in 1901, and leading the AL in homers twice, in 1908 and 1914.

Elmer Flick is the dream team alternate, instead of Willie Keeler or Socks Seybold. Although Keeler matched Flick with .311 for the decade batting average, Flick out-slugged Keeler and Seybold and reached first at a better percentage. Flick is in the Hall of Fame. He is best known for winning the 1905 AL batting title with a .306 mark when the league average was only .241. Flick was so good that in 1907, Detroit offered to swap their young, fiery-tempered outfielder Ty Cobb for him, even up. Cleveland turned the Tigers down, preferring to keep Flick, who had hit .302 that year. Unfortunately, injuries prematurely ended his career.

Opposite: *Ginger Beaumont poses in the outfield. The dream team center fielder played for Pittsburgh and the Boston Nationals during the decade. In 1903 Beaumont's league-leading 209 hits and 137 runs helped Pittsburgh to the first World Series, where they lost to Boston in eight games.*

Left: *A cartoon of the day depicts heavy-hitting dream team right fielder Sam Crawford, who played for Detroit for most of his career. Overshadowed by teammate Ty Cobb, Crawford emerged as the all-time leader in triples. "Wahoo Sam" was elected to the Hall of Fame in 1957.*

Above: *The small but speedy Elmer Flick poses with his bat. Right fielder alternate choice, Flick led the league in many batting categories during the decade, and was elected to the Hall of Fame in 1963.*

LEFT FIELD

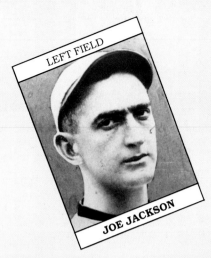

**JOE JACKSON**

CENTER FIELD

**TY COBB**

SHORTSTOP

**HONUS WAGNER**

SECOND BASE

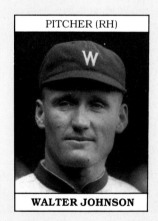

**EDDIE COLLINS**

THIRD BASE

**FRANK BAKER**

PITCHER (LH)

**HIPPO VAUGHN**

PITCHER (RH)

**WALTER JOHNSON**

CATCHER

**WALLY SCHANG**

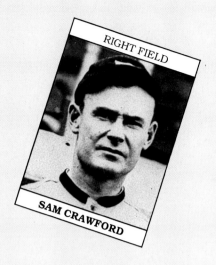

RIGHT FIELD

SAM CRAWFORD

FIRST BASE

HAL CHASE

# THE GREATEST PLAYERS OF THE

# SECOND DECADE

## 1910-1919

## ALTERNATE DREAM TEAM

| | | | |
|---|---|---|---|
| **Pitcher** | Grove Cleveland Alexander (rh) | **Third Baseman** | Heinie Groh |
| | Babe Ruth (lh) | **Shortstop** | John Lloyd |
| **Catcher** | Ray Schalk | **Left Fielder** | Zack Wheat |
| **First Baseman** | Jack Daubert | **Center Fielder** | Tris Speaker |
| **Second Baseman** | Larry Doyle | **Right Fielder** | Gavvy Cravath |

## HONORABLE MENTION

| | | | |
|---|---|---|---|
| **Pitcher** | Eddie Cicotte | **Shortstop** | Everett Scott |
| | Carl Mays | | Dave Bancroft |
| | Bob Shawkey | | Rabbit Maranville |
| | Joe Bush | | Roger Peckinpaugh |
| | Herb Pennock | | Donie Bush |
| | Rube Marquard | | Ray Chapman |
| **Catcher** | Bill Rariden | **Left Fielder** | Duffy Lewis |
| **First Baseman** | Stuffy McInnis | | Sherry Magee |
| | Ed Konectchy | **Center Fielder** | Edd Roush |
| **Second Baseman** | Larry Lajoie | | Max Carey |
| | Miller Huggins | **Right Fielder** | Harry Hooper |
| | Del Pratt | | |
| **Third Baseman** | Heinie Zimmerman | | |
| | Buck Weaver | | |
| | Eddie Foster | | |
| | Larry Gardner | | |

# THE SETTING

The second decade of the twentieth century began with high spirits. United States President William Howard Taft, a former amateur baseball player during the 1860s in the Cincinnati area, opened Washington's 1910 baseball season with a ceremonial first pitch. From 1909 to 1915 new concrete and reinforced steel stadiums in Chicago, New York, Philadelphia, Pittsburgh, Boston, Detroit, Brooklyn and Washington were built to accommodate surging fan interest. The shiny new stadiums attested to the growing popularity of baseball, and to the owners' optimism for the game as a spectator sport.

Improved communication helped make baseball an integral part of American society. Western Union had begun telegraphing game scores on a regular basis in 1908. Along with technological advances came a new breed of newspaper writers. The 1911 freshman group of baseball writers included Heywood Hale Broun, Sid Keener, Fred Lieb, Grantland Rice and Damon Runyon. These men brought an educated sophistication to major league baseball writing.

Ballplayers were increasingly aware of their special position in society. Some, such as Larry Lajoie and Ty Cobb, pursued money-making ventures, endorsing products from tobacco cards to signature bats. The A's and Giants tried to strike the 1911 World Series opener in order to receive a share of film revenues as the Series was slated to be taped in its entirety for the first time. (The filming was cancelled.)

Advances in technology and new prosperity in the second decade of the twentieth century were combined with the tensions of imminent war and its accompanying inflation, to create a volatile atmosphere of uncertainty. Against this backdrop the baseball community struggled to understand these changes and their effects on the game.

# GAME STRATEGY

The hit-and-run play, stealing bases, and going from first to third on a single became ploys of the master strategists of the day. Giants manager John McGraw re-introduced the old nineteenth-century Baltimore Orioles' hit-and-run game. McGraw had hired old-time baserunning star Arlie Latham to teach baserunning and base-stealing to the Giants. They responded to Latham's tutelage by stealing an average of more than 300 bases a season from 1910 to 1913.

Not all the teams were successful with the hit-and-run, base-stealing strategy of this decade. Catchers shot down runners at a record clip. Federal League catcher Bill Rariden had 215 and 238 assists in 1914 and 1915. Six of the top ten all-time leaders in assists among catchers flourished in the teens, the other four played during the 1890s, the decade McGraw and Latham were imitating. Ty Cobb stole 96 bases in 1915, but was caught 36 times. The Boston Red Sox won the 1915 pennant with only a 47 percent success rate for stolen bases.

# FACTORS INFLUENCING PLAYER PERFORMANCE

Factors that had tremendous impact on players in the decade were the cork-center baseball, the rise of individual stars, a players' union, and the new Federal League.

The cork-center baseball replaced the old vulcanized rubber-center baseball for AL balls manufactured by Reach, and for NL balls made by Spalding, in 1911. The hitters rapped a more tightly wound, more resilient ball. The AL batting average rose from .243 in 1910 to .273 in 1911. The NL average jumped from .256 in 1910 to .272 in 1912. Along with the increase in averages came the emergence of individual stars.

Individual play became easier to measure with new statistics such as Earned Run Average, double plays, and passed balls. Strikeouts and bases on balls became official statistics in the National League, but not the American League. Caught stealing was recorded for a couple of years. These statistics meant a new method of emphasizing individual performance, which in turn led to salary demands and to individual awards.

In 1911 the Chalmers Company offered an automobile to the leading batter in each league. In the AL, Detroit's Ty Cobb and Cleveland's Napoleon Lajoie vied for the car in one of the most exciting and controversial batting races in baseball history. Lajoie seemingly edged out Cobb with eight hits on the last day of the season. Despite the fact that most league newspapers, who kept their own statistics, showed Lajoie to be the winner, the official AL statistics gave the title to Cobb. The Chalmers Company presented both Cobb and Lajoie automobiles. A full 72 years later, *The Sporting News* and the Society for American Baseball Research announced that they had discovered three games for that season whose statistics were never entered in the record book. Those additional figures showed that Lajoie had won the title, .384 to .383.

Another factor influencing player performance in the years 1910 to 1919 was the institution of the Federal League. When it announced that it would become the third major league in 1914, there were a lot of discontented ballplayers eager to change leagues. The fact that player salaries had failed to keep up with the war-time economy escaped most of the baseball world. The Federal League antagonized established team owners by offering large sums of money to some of the star players. Salary disputes caused bitterness between players and owners.

Ty Cobb and Sam Crawford used the threat of the Federal League in a spring training holdout to obtain a $20,000 per year contract for Cobb and a four-year contract for Crawford, who was 38 years old. Walter Johnson was offered $20,000 by the Federal League before he inked a contract with the Washington Senators for a similar amount. The rumor was that Senators' owner Clark Griffith lacked the funds to honor the contract, so other American League owners contributed money to pay Johnson. Connie Mack sold his star player, Eddie Collins, to the Chicago White Sox rather than let him go to the Federal League.

The Baseball Players Fraternity was a union founded in 1912, in response to an incident involving Ty Cobb. During a game at Highlander Park in New York, an abusive heckler kept after Cobb until the hot-tempered outfielder charged into the grandstand to assault him. It turned out that the heckler was physically disabled, which added fuel to AL President Ban Johnson's argument that Cobb should be suspended indefinitely. His teammates felt that Cobb was justified in his actions — as court records showed that the heckler had a long history of verbal-abuse arrests — and they voted to strike as long as Cobb stayed suspended.

The Baseball Players Fraternity, founded by former player David Fultz, was seen as a means to resolve problems that might lead to wildcat strikes. Popular in its first three years, the union proved to be powerless to stop pay cuts and player releases when the Federal League collapsed in 1915, and it did not survive the decade.

## PITCHER

It was the age of control, and the pitcher controlled the game. Since he had no fear of home runs, the pitcher could throw strikes at any time. Batting stars were not inclined to walk, they wanted to hit the new cork-center baseball. As more batters put wood on the ball, the pitcher became a fifth infielder, backing up plays and initiating pick-off plays with snap throws.

The Giants' Christy Mathewson saw a batch of young, strong-armed hurlers coming along, such as the Phillies' rookie who pitched like a veteran, Grover Cleveland Alexander, and the Senators' fireballing ace Walter Johnson. Other right-handed pitchers included the Red Sox' Eddie Cicotte and Carl Mays, and the Athletics' Bob Shawkey and Joe Bush.

Cicotte and Mays both had shadows cast over their careers. Cicotte, who threw the impossible-to-hit "shine ball," was banished from baseball for life because of his role in compromising the integrity of the 1919 World Series. Mays, surly and occasionally foul-tempered, threw a submarine pitch with a discolored ball in waning daylight that struck Cleveland Indians shortstop Ray Chapman in the temple and killed him.

Shawkey and Bush were just kids when they pitched for the Athletics in the 1914 World Series. Both would pitch in additional Series with Boston and New York. They were good pitchers, but neither was in a class with Walter Johnson or Grover Cleveland Alexander.

There were no sophisticated measuring devices during Walter Johnson's career, but his fastball was considered to be in a class by itself. So was Sir Walter. Naming **Walter Johnson** the number one right-handed pitcher for the teens was one of the easiest choices in the book. Using a sweeping sidearm delivery, the Big Train fanned 2219 hitters between 1910 and 1919. His 74 shutouts for those years were more than any pitcher before or since. During the teens, he won 265 games (417 altogether — second only to Cy Young on the all-time list) despite hurling for a losing team, and he enjoyed 10 successive seasons of 20 or more victories.

Grover Cleveland Alexander rated the alternate spot over a retiring Christy Mathewson. Over the decade, Alexander hurled 70 shutouts, a total topped only by Johnson. Alexander parlayed an easy pitching motion with pinpoint control to win 235 games for the decade, on his way to a National League record 373 victories during his career. He is tied with Christy Mathewson as the leading NL career winner. Alexander's four one-hitters in 1915 and his 16 shutouts in 1916 are still major league highs. His seventh-inning strikeout of the Yankees' Tony Lazzeri with the bases loaded was one of the most dramatic moments ever, and clinched the 1926 World Series for the Cardinals.

The left-handed phenoms for the decade were Boston's Babe Ruth, Philadelphia's Herb Pennock, Mathewson's Giants teammate, Rube Marquard, and the Cubs' James "Hippo" Vaughn.

Marquard, though a Hall of Fame member, had an up-

*Walter Johnson winds up for the pitch. "The Big Train" pitched for Washington his entire 21-year career. Second on the all-time list for wins, and first for shutouts (with 110), Johnson is the shoo-in for dream team right hander. For nine of the ten years between 1910 and 1919, the future Hall of Famer led the league in strikeouts.*

and-down decade. He won 73 games from 1911 through 1913, then won only 67 games in the remaining six years.

Pennock, also a Hall of Fame pitcher, rose to prominence during the 1920s as the ace of the New York Yankee staff. During the teens he was not a regular starter, although he pitched for five pennant-winning teams.

Like Harvey Haddix, left-handed hurler James "Hippo" Vaughn is remembered for one outstanding game – the double no-hitter – somewhat obscuring the fact that he pitched a number of excellent games over a long period of years. One of the best pitchers during the World War I period, **Hippo Vaughn** is the dream team choice for left-handed pitcher for 1910 to 1919. In seven years with the Cubs, he won 20 or more games five times, 10 once, and 17 once.

In 1918 he was 22-10 to lead the NL in wins, he was tops in ERA at 1.74, and he led the league in strikeouts and innings pitched. In the World Series that year, he pitched three complete games and gave up only three earned runs, yet his record was 1-2.

Babe Ruth was an American original – baseball's greatest slugger and the most celebrated athlete of his time. He is the dream team alternate selection as left-handed pitcher.

Fresh out of St. Mary's Industrial School in Baltimore, Ruth debuted as a pitcher for the Boston Red Sox, winning 89 games over six seasons before he was sold to the Yankees for $125,000 in 1919. He led the American League in shutouts and ERA in 1916 and in complete games in 1917. His 27 and two thirds scoreless innings in World Series play remained the record until 1962 when Whitey Ford surpassed the mark.

Yet his hitting was so impressive that he became a part-time outfielder in 1918, and won his first home run crown, with 11 in 95 games. In 1919 he crushed 29 homers, breaking a record that had stood for 35 years.

Above: *Grover Cleveland Alexander, right-handed dream team alternate, hurled his way to six 20-plus win seasons over the decade. From 1910 to 1919 he led the league in wins five times, in ERA four times, in innings pitched six times, in strikeouts five times, and in shutouts six times – including his 1916 mark of 16 shutouts, which still stands as the major league record.*

Left: *Dream team southpaw James "Hippo" Vaughn follows through after a pitch. Vaughn pitched for the Cubs for most of the decade, turning in his best season performance in 1918, when he helped carry the team to the World Series. That year Vaughn's 22 wins, 1.74 ERA, 148 strikeouts and eight shutouts led the league.*

# CATCHER

The catcher was prone to more aches and pains than other position players and therefore was not expected to catch every day. A valuable receiver was one who could field and throw well enough to play effectively at other positions. Maybe it was that throwing and fielding ability that enabled catchers from this era to pile up extraordinary assist totals. Then on the other hand, maybe the high numbers of assists were simply due to inept baserunning.

The three top candidates for the dream team are Wally Schang of the Athletics and Red Sox; Bill Rariden of the Braves, Giants, Reds and the Federal League; and Hall of Famer Ray Schalk with the White Sox.

Rariden can be eliminated quickly because his hitting ability did not compare to Schang's or Schalk's. Rariden's high assist totals – 214 in 1914 and 238 in 1915 – occurred in the Federal League where baserunning was even worse than in the American League.

**Wally Schang** was selected over Schalk as best catcher of the decade. Schang was a better hitter than Schalk. He over-hit him by 23 points, and out-slugged him by 54 points, during the decade. On top of hitting well, Schang was a winning ballplayer. Three teams won pennants after having traded for him. He played on seven pennant winners during his career. Schang caught a variety of outstanding, gifted pitchers, including Chief Bender, Eddie Plank, Jack Coombs, Herb Pennock, Joe Bush, Carl Mays, Ernie Shore, Bob Shawkey, Urban Shocker, Waite Hoyt, Babe Ruth, Hub Leonard, George Earnshaw and Lefty Grove. Schang had 154 assists in 100 games in 1914.

Ray Schalk was the standout alternate selection. Despite

Top left: *A young Babe Ruth takes practice swings. Dream team alternate lefty, Ruth's stellar pitching helped the Red Sox to two World Championships.*

Left and above: *Dream team catcher Wally Schang in action. Schang played for the A's and Red Sox and appeared in three World Series during the decade; in 1915 and 1916 he even tried his hand in the outfield and at third.*

# FIRST BASE

During the 1910s, the first base position was in transition from a defensive one to an offensive one. Since more runs were needed to win the game in the 1910s than in the previous decade, managers looked for methods to achieve more offense. They soon discovered that a heavy hitter at first base increased the club's chances to score runs, but they were always afraid to sacrifice the snappy-throwing infielder who assisted in so many putouts.

The four top first basemen of the period were Hal Chase of the Highlanders, Reds, and Giants; Jake Daubert of the Dodgers; Stuffy McInnis of the Athletics and Red Sox; and the well-travelled Ed Konectchy of the Cardinals, Pirates, Braves, Dodgers and the Federal League.

The position had no standout performer. Chase had the ability to be great, but lacked the drive for consistent achievement. Daubert was a strong on-base hitter who, with Zack Wheat, formed a formidable 1-2 punch for the Dodgers. He led the league in hitting twice. Stuffy McInnis was chosen by Bill James in the *Historical Baseball Abstract* as the decade's top first baseman. McInnis played on five pennant winners during the decade while never leading the league in any offensive category. Konectchy hit well with some power. He led the National

his diminutive size, he proved his mettle by catching 100 games for 11 seasons in a row, including seven during the teens. He led the league in putouts eight consecutive years, 1913 to 1920, and also led five consecutive years in total chances, 1913 to 1917.

Schalk's contemporaries considered him an outstanding defensive catcher. His mental and physical agility made him a defensive standout, and he was the first receiver to back up plays at first and third. He even made putouts at second base. He caught four no-hitters.

Schalk was one of the untarnished White Sox during the infamous 1919 World Series. His frustration with Black Sox pitchers Eddie Cicotte and Lefty Williams was well documented and may have been a factor in his selection for the Hall of Fame, because Schang was a better all-around catcher.

League in doubles in 1911.

In a close contest, **Hal Chase** was chosen as the 1910-1919 dream team first baseman because of his combination of batting and fielding skills. For the decade, his .414 slugging average was tops among first basemen. By winning the National League batting crown in 1916 he became the only player who threw left and batted right to win a major league batting title.

Chase was known for his fielding ability, yet statistics do not prove him to be a great fielder. Old photos show him playing close in, on the infield grass, when no one is on base. It appeared as though he dared the batter to try to hit one by him. Chase fielded bunts on the third base side of the diamond, yet when batters attempted to swing away at the hard-charging Chase, he would catch the batter's line drive and turn it into an easy double play.

Runner-up to Chase was Jake Daubert, who won back-to-back National League batting titles in 1913 and 1914. He was a lifetime .303 hitter, and hit .301 for the decade as he scored 727 runs – 50 more than Konectchy. Daubert led the NL in triples in 1918 and slugged .403 for the decade.

Daubert was a better than average fielder. In fact, statistics show that he fielded the position better than Chase did. During the 1919 season, Daubert took the time to teach a sore-armed pitcher, Rube Bressler, how to play first base, and Bressler was able to play in the Big Leagues until 1933.

*Far left: Runner-up dream team first baseman Jake Daubert fields his position. Daubert played for the Dodgers for all but the last year of the decade, when he was traded to Cincinnati for Tommy Griffith. Daubert's .301 decade batting average included two batting titles.*

*Left: White Sox catcher Ray Schalk was a tough competitor. Dream team alternative Schalk, who led the league in putouts eight straight years, was elected to the Hall of Fame in 1955.*

*Right: Dream team first baseman Hal Chase, who played for five teams during the decade – including a stint on the Federal League – hustled on the field and was a threat behind the plate. In 1916 his .339 batting average led the league.*

# SECOND BASE

Second base was still a power position during the 1910s. Second basemen frequently out-slugged first basemen. Most of the action took place within the infield, as opposed to outfield or pitcher-catcher play. The second baseman was expected to work with the other infielders as a unit. This teamwork – such as backing up plays and rundowns – was extremely important because of the number of putouts and assists made in the infield during the average game in 1910-1919.

The group of top-notch second basemen included two playing managers, Cleveland's Larry Lajoie and St. Louis' Miller Huggins, both of whom played fewer than 1000 games during the decade. Other dream team candidates are Eddie Collins of the Athletics and White Sox, "Laughing Larry" Doyle of the Giants, and Del Pratt of the Cardinals and Yankees.

Larry Lajoie was at the end of his illustrious career. He was still skillful enough to hit .321 for the decade, but the power had faded. He participated in the decade's most exciting hitting contest as he battled Ty Cobb to the last game of the 1910 season for the batting title.

Miller Huggins' specialty had always been drawing walks, and he was still doing that in the 1910s. He scored 506 runs in

802 games with 571 bases on balls. When Huggins decided to retire as a player, he bought Del Pratt to replace himself.

Pratt out-hit his manager by 12 points and out-slugged him by 72 points for the decade. Pratt was consistently a top fielder as well as good hitter who led the NL in RBIs in 1916.

The top choice, **Eddie Collins** was a great player in the prime of his career, which lasted 25 seasons. Signed in 1906 at the age of 19 by Connie Mack, Collins used a choke-up grip batting style to spray the ball to all fields. In the teens, he hit at a .326 clip with an on-base percentage of .419, a decade mark exceeded only by Ty Cobb and Tris Speaker.

Collins, known as "Cocky," had almost no power, but he played at a time when power was not essential to a successful career. Batting second, he drove in over 80 runs three times during the decade. He scored 991 runs in the 10-season span while stealing 829 bases. Twice Collins stole six bases in one game. He was one of the few base-stealers of the early years who played in the infield.

In late 1914, A's manager Connie Mack sold Collins and his three-year contract to the Chicago White Sox for $50,000. Cocky would lead the Sox to two pennants, but his large contract became the focal point of dissension on the club. It was this clique who threw the 1919 World Series.

The alternate for second baseman was "Laughing Larry" Doyle. He hit .289 for the decade and slugged .417. Only Collins scored more runs, had more hits, and knocked in more runs as a second baseman in the teens.

Doyle was the heart of the Giants' pennant winners of 1911-13. He stole 113 bases, led the 1913 NL in triples, as well as batting in 1915 with a .320 mark. He was never an outstanding gloveman; he let his bat prove his worth to the Giants. Doyle was quoted as proudly remarking, "It's great to be young, and a Giant."

# THIRD BASE

Third base was a position where a manager might try to hide a good hitter who was a defensive liability. While the decade's offensive strategy of bunt, run and bunt, hit and run, and steal, made one think that infield play, particularly at the corners, would be an important aspect of the game, this hypothesis did not appear to be true. Managers played any kind of player they wanted at third base.

Two of the decade's best known third basemen, Heinie Zimmerman of the Cubs and Giants, and Buck Weaver of the White Sox, did not play regularly at third until too late in the decade to be considered for the dream team.

The qualified players were Frank "Home Run" Baker of the Athletics and Yankees, Heinie Groh, whose bottle bat graced the Giants' and Reds' bat racks, Eddie Foster of the Senators, and Larry Gardner of the Red Sox.

Larry Gardner hit .284 for the decade with a team that won three pennants and three World Championships, but he never scored or drove in 90 runs in a season.

Eddie Foster hit only .264 and was not in Baker's or Groh's class. He spent the decade with teams mired in the second division.

Opposite: *Future Hall of Famer Eddie Collins, known as "Cocky," played with the A's and the White Sox during his 25-year career. This speedy, dream team second baseman stole a record 14 bases in the six World Series in which he appeared during the decade.*

Below: *Frank "Home Run" Baker takes a cut. This dream team third baseman had extraordinary range on the field and power at the plate. He was a clutch hitter who batted .307 over his 13-year career, and averaged .363 in six World Series contests.*

**John Franklin "Home Run" Baker** was the undisputed king of third base during the 1910s. He was the third baseman in Connie Mack's famous $100,000 infield. Baker's two home runs in the 1911 World Series were game winners, and gave him his nickname. He was the AL home run leader for four consecutive years, totaling 93 over a 13-year career, with 12 in 1913 being his top mark. He led the AL in RBIs twice, 1912 and 1913, and batted .309 for the decade with a .442 slugging percentage. Baker swung a bat weighing 52 ounces – 20 ounces heavier than the average bat in use today.

Baker sat out the 1915 season in protest of Mack's breaking up the Athletics by selling teammates Eddie Collins and Jack Barry, and releasing Eddie Plank, Chief Bender and Jack Coombs. He also wanted his newly signed three-year contract torn up and rewritten for more money. Mack sold the sulking star to the struggling Yankees, giving that franchise a quality player to build their future upon. Baker, who looked and hit like the modern Jack Clark, had better range on the field than any other third baseman in the Hall of Fame.

Heinie Groh, the second-best third baseman for the decade, was famous for his bat. Shaped like a big milk bottle, its handle ballooned into a thick barrel, which he held high over his right shoulder. Groh felt that his odd bat gave him better control on bunts.

Groh led the NL in doubles and OBA in 1917 and 1918. He hit .294 for the decade, leading the league in hits in 1917 and runs scored in 1918. He led all decade third basemen in on-base percentage.

Altogether, Groh played in five World Series and on seven pennant winners, including three during the 1910s. He was one of the outstanding players on the 1919 Cincinnati team that upset the White Sox. Many Reds went to their graves refusing to admit that the Sox had thrown the Series. Groh and his teammates believed they had whipped them soundly.

Left: *Honus Wagner slides home safely. Dream team shortstop for consecutive decades, the stalwart Wagner led the league in hits (178) in 1910, and in batting average (.334) in 1911. His .296 average topped the decade's shortstops.*

Above: *Honus Wagner at the plate.*

Opposite: *John Henry Lloyd, the decade's alternate shortstop, was considered the finest in the Negro Leagues. He could also hit – .327 against white big leaguers and .340 against black pros. He became a Hall of Famer in 1976.*

# SHORTSTOP

It was a time of change for the shortstop position. Earlier shortstops had been the all-around best players on their teams. Hitting was an important part of the game, and managers wanted a slugger in the shortstop role. The trend, however, was toward a top notch fielder who was not necessarily the best hitter on the team.

The shortstops under consideration for the dream team represent both sides of the transition from emphasis on hitting to fielding. Hall of Famers Honus Wagner of the Pirates and John Lloyd of the Negro Leagues typify the old concept of the shortstop being the best player on the field. A batch of talented youngsters, Everett Scott of the Red Sox, Hall of Famers Dave Bancroft of the Phillies and Rabbit Maranville of the Braves, the Yankees' Roger Peckinpaugh, the Tigers' Donie Bush, and the Indians' Ray Chapman, proved to be slick-fielding shortstops who were not as good at the plate as their older counterparts.

Dave Bancroft and Rabbit Maranville both played on one pennant winner during the decade, and both contributed to their teams' efforts in ways that cannot be measured by statistics. Bancroft was a sparkplug on the field; a fiery team leader with great instincts for the game. When traded to the Giants, his new teammates asked Bancroft if he wanted to go over their signs. He replied, "I don't have to, I know them already." Maranville teamed with John Evers on the Boston Braves in 1914 to lead the league in double plays — many more than Tinker to Evers to Chance ever made — and push the Braves from last place on July 4th to the pennant by season's end.

Donie Bush scored 958 runs during the decade, making his mark fourth best over all, behind Ty Cobb, Eddie Collins and Tris Speaker. Bush has never been considered an outstanding defensive shortstop, although he was a premier lead-off man. After his playing days, he went to Indianapolis and became involved with the minor league team there, eventually owning it. The ball field in Indianapolis, Bush Stadium, is named for him.

Roger Peckinpaugh was a liability at the bat early in his career, but gradually improved to be average. In 1914, at age 23, he became manager of the New York Yankees, the youngest man ever to manage a major league team.

Everett Scott, who would later set the consecutive games record that Lou Gehrig would surpass, began his career by starting for the Red Sox. The Sox won three World Series Championships in Scott's first five years. He was a good fielder, but extremely weak at the plate.

Ill-fated Ray Chapman was beaned by a pitch from submariner Carl Mays, and is major league baseball's only fatality on the field. Despite Chapman's .303 batting average at the time of his death, Cleveland actually improved without him. The inspired play of his replacement, Joe Sewell, led the Indians to the 1920 pennant. Chapman was a better than average fielder and had a .284 batting average for the decade.

Scott, Bancroft, Maranville, Peckinpaugh, and Bush were weak sticks; all of them hit under .250 for the decade. Chapman was not as good a hitter as Honus Wagner or John Lloyd. Wagner still had power and was an inspiring leader. Lloyd was reputed to be the best of early black stars. He hit the New York Giants' pitching well in Cuba during the 1911 winter season.

Many baseball veterans, including John McGraw, considered Honus Wagner to be the greatest all-around player in baseball. Despite his awkward appearance and age, the Pittsburgh Pirates' shortstop was a sensational hitter, a brilliant baserunner and a flawless fielder. Wagner had to be convinced

not to retire before the 1908 season, and he went on to lead the NL in hits in 1910, batting average in 1911, and RBIs in 1912, the year he was rated as the top player in the league.

Wagner's .296 average topped the decade's shortstops. In addition, he led them in triples, home runs, on-base percentage, and slugging percentage. Not bad for a doddering old man who had retired more times than John McGraw won pennants. The kindly Wagner was always ready to help a rookie with his batting or fielding. He provided an example of excellence for players from 1898 to 1917. Even at the end of his career, **Honus Wagner** is the best choice for dream team shortstop of the 1910s.

John "Pop" Lloyd of the Negro Leagues is the alternate. He was a tall man, six feet two inches, with long arms, and was considered the finest shortstop to come out of the Negro Leagues. He was called "el Cuchara," the scoop, by admiring Cuban fans. In addition to his smoothness afield, he also swung a mean bat, consistently hitting for high average. He played for the Philadelphia Giants, the Lincoln Giants, the Chicago American Giants and the Brooklyn Royal Giants. He later managed for more than 10 seasons in the Negro Leagues.

During the 1910s, Lloyd hit .327 against white big leaguers and .340 versus black professionals. Against semipro teams in 1911 and 1912, he reportedly hit .475 and .376.

In 1913 Lloyd managed the New York Lincoln Giants to a 101-6 season. After the season the Lincoln Giants played a series with the Earle Mack (Connie's son) All-Stars. The Lincolns won 7-3, lost 1-0, and then defeated Chief Bender 2-1 to take the series. Later that year, the Lincolns routed the Philadelphia Phillies and Grover Cleveland Alexander 9-2.

Lloyd personified the best qualities of an athlete, both on and off the field. He helped younger players and taught them dedication to the game.

# LEFT FIELD

Managers wanted to put outstanding hitters in the outfield, and not be concerned about their fielding and throwing abilities. This plan was thwarted by the new cork-center baseball. Base hits were ricocheting off the walls of the new parks, and runners traversed the bases as though on a merry-go-round. The main objective of the defense became to throw out runners. Managers tried to find left fielders who could hit and throw.

The candidates for dream team left fielder are Hall of Famer Zack Wheat of the Brooklyn Dodgers, Joe Jackson of the Cleveland Indians and Chicago White Sox, Duffy Lewis of the Boston Red Sox and New York Yankees, and Sherry Magee of the Philadelphia Phillies, Boston Braves and Cincinnati Reds.

Sherry Magee was the batter responsible for the establishment of the sacrifice fly as an official statistic. Early in his career Phillies manager Bill Murray noticed that Magee would attempt to hit the ball to the outfield with a runner on third and less than two outs. The runner would tag up and score on the long fly ball. Magee accomplished what he tried to do, but his batting average suffered. League officials consulted with Murray and established the sacrifice fly as a statistical category in 1908.

Duffy Lewis was an integral part of what many Bostonians consider the greatest outfield ever assembled – Lewis in left, Tris Speaker in center, and Harry Hooper in right. With Lewis agilely patrolling "Duffy's Cliff", a 10-foot embankment in front of the left-field fence, Boston romped to pennants in

Above: *Brooklyn's Zack Wheat, our alternate left fielder, was a fine hitter, averaging .299 for the decade (.355 in 1918), with 51 homers and, in 1916, a slugging percentage of .461.*

Opposite: *Dream team left fielder Shoeless Joe Jackson. Only Cobb bettered Joe's .354 decade batting average. But for the Black Sox scandal, Joe would be in the Hall of Fame.*

1912, 1915 and 1916. Duffy was an outstanding fielder, but he was a weaker batsman than Jackson, Wheat or Magee.

Shoeless Joe Jackson was a sure-fire Hall of Famer until he reached into his pocket and pulled out $5000. Unfortunately for baseball fans, he did not return the money and was banned from baseball for life because of his participation in the throwing of the 1919 World Series. Nevertheless, **Joe Jackson** was selected as the dream team left fielder for the 1910s – what a hitter he was.

Jackson averaged .354, second only to Cobb, during the decade. He was also behind Cobb in triples, 148, but had far more than any other left fielder. Despite playing fewer games than the other candidates, Jackson had more runs scored, hits and triples, with higher batting average, OBA and slugging percentage than the others. He led the AL in triples in 1912, in hits and doubles in 1913, and in triples again in 1916 and 1920.

Jackson, from North Carolina, drawled one of baseball's most famous understatements, "Ah hit .408 and .395 but ah didn't win the title. This is a mighty tough league." He was an outstanding fielder as well. In 1911 to 1913 he averaged 30 assists per game.

Zack Wheat, one of the game's most likeable players, was also one of its deadliest hitters. He was selected as the dream team alternate for left field. Wheat led the NL with a .335 average in 1918. His hitting paced the Brooklyn Dodgers to pennants in 1916 and 1920 as he led the league with a .461 slugging percentage. He hit .299 for the decade and was second, among left fielders, to Jackson in hits, triples and batting average. During the decade, Wheat smashed 51 home runs, second among left fielders behind Sherry Magee, who had 61. Wheat was also a very good fielder, recording one of the highest lifetime range factors among left fielders.

Left: *There would be only one choice for dream team center fielder, the legendary Georgia Peach, Ty Cobb, player of the decade and probably of all time. He batted .420 in 1911 and .410 in 1912 and finished the decade with an average of .387, 1050 runs scored and batting titles in every year but one. He also stole 577 bases (96 in 1915) and batted in 852 runs.*

Opposite top: *Tris Speaker (right), dream team alternate center fielder, made more assists than any other outfielder, and he batted an average .343 for the decade. With him (left) is Gavvy Cravath, our alternate choice for right field. During the decade he led the National League in home runs five times and tied one other year.*

Opposite bottom: *The dream team choice for right field is Sam Crawford, who batted .313 and slugged .459 for the decade. His 312 lifetime triples are a major league record. He was inducted into the Hall of Fame in 1957.*

# CENTER FIELD

Tris Speaker tried to redefine the center-field position by playing unusually close to second base. His attempt to bring the center fielder into infield play failed because Speaker had a unique ability. He could go back on a ball better than any other center fielder, and others were reluctant to position themselves as Speaker did, for fear of missing plays.

The dream team candidates are four Hall of Fame members: Ty Cobb of the Tigers; Tris Speaker of the Red Sox and Indians; Edd Roush of the White Sox, Giants, Reds and the Federal League; and Max Carey of the Pirates.

Max Carey built his reputation as a superb outfielder and scientific base-stealer. He led the NL in chances accepted nine times, including five times during the 1910s. Carey holds several NL career records for fielding.

Carey led the league in steals five times during the 1910s, and was the decade's third greatest base-stealer overall, behind Ty Cobb and Eddie Collins.

Edd Roush was the National League's premier center fielder of his day and one of its most feared hitters. Using a 48-ounce bat, he led NL hitters in 1917 and 1919, and averaged .314 for the decade. Stubborn and independent, he was a regular holdout with the Reds, a device he used to avoid spring training.

The dream team center fielder for the 1910s, is **Ty Cobb**, a man many historians feel was the greatest baseball player of all time. He was certainly the most competitive.

On a steamy Georgia afternoon, Cobb dragged his minor league roommate Nap Rucker out of the bath tub and declared that he wanted to use it first. Cobb explained to the startled Rucker, "I have to be first."

Cobb's batting accomplishments during the teens were legendary. He led all other players with a batting average of .387, nine batting titles in 10 years, two .400 seasons, 1050 runs scored, 852 RBIs, 160 triples, 577 stolen bases, an on-base percentage of .452, and a slugging average of .541. Cobb was the player of the decade. His 96 steals in 1915 was the major league record for almost 50 years.

Born of Scotch-English parents in Banks County, Georgia, Tyrus was raised in the genteel South. His uncle taught

him to trade cotton futures at age 14. Cobb pursued money-making ventures during his baseball career and became a millionaire after he retired from baseball.

Tris Speaker, the dream team alternate, revolutionized outfield play by positioning himself in shallow center field. His unique position resulted in his recording more assists, 450, than any other outfielder. Twice he threw out a record 35 AL baserunners in a single season. He averaged 25 assists per season during the decade. While his fielding put him in a class by himself, his batting skill was considerable.

Speaker compiled a .343 average with the top mark of 367 doubles for the decade. His .484 slugging average was fourth best for all players during the teens. He captured the batting title with a league-leading .386 in 1916.

Speaker still holds several career batting and fielding records. He hit more doubles than any other player, and he holds the AL record for putouts, assists, total chances and double plays.

# RIGHT FIELD

In the 1910s the team slugger was sent to right field where he could do the least harm. Gone were the days when the right fielder would play close in, and throw out runners at first on ground balls between the first and second basemen. There were too many left-handed hitters, and too many long hits to play up close.

The 1910s dream team candidates for right fielder are Hall of Famers Sam Crawford of the Tigers and Harry Hooper of the Red Sox, and home run hitter Gavvy Cravath of the Phillies.

Harry Hooper was the lead-off hitter and right fielder for the 1912, 1915, 1916 and 1918 World Champion Red Sox. He owned a great throwing arm and he perfected the sliding catch. Hooper is remembered for his sensational barehanded grab of a potential home run in the final game of the 1912 World Series. He was not in the same class with Crawford and Cravath, however, as a hitter.

**"Wahoo" Sam Crawford**, the dream team first pick, was one of the hardest hitters of the dead ball era. He was a big, powerful slugger, and many of his long drives resulted in triples. He still holds the major league record with 312 three-baggers, leading the league in 1910 and 1913-1915.

After the cork-center baseball was introduced, Crawford averaged 107 RBIs per season over the next six years. He batted .313 and slugged .459 during the decade. Not possessing great speed, his 170 steals attest to his baserunning prowess. He could still hit when he retired from the majors 36 hits short of 3000. Two years later he hit .360 in the Pacific Coast League.

Born a generation too soon, Gavvy Cravath was the home run king in the dead-ball years immediately preceding the Babe Ruth revolution. Cravath is the dream team alternate for right fielder. In a seven-year span, 1913-1919, the Phillies' outfielder led the NL in home runs five times, and tied for the lead once. A short right-field target in Philadelphia's Baker Bowl helped quite a bit, but Gavvy, a right-handed batter, deserves credit for knowing what to do with it.

Cravath was unsuccessful in two earlier trials with the AL Yankees, and didn't get to the Phillies until 1912, when he was 31 years old. A genial practical joker, he kept his teammates loose with his jokes, and opposing pitchers uptight with his power-laden bat. In 1915 he helped the Phillies to a pennant with a league-high 115 RBIs and 24 homers, a twentieth-century high at that time.

LEFT FIELD

**HARRY HEILMAN**

CENTER FIELD

**TRIS SPEAKER**

SHORTSTOP

**JOE SEWELL**

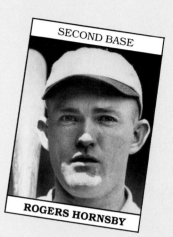

SECOND BASE

**ROGERS HORNSBY**

THIRD BASE

**PIE TRAYNOR**

PITCHER (LH)

**EPPA RIXEY**

PITCHER (RH)

**DAZZY VANCE**

CATCHER

**GABBY HARTNETT**

RIGHT FIELD

BABE RUTH

FIRST BASE

JIM BOTTOMLEY

# THE GREATEST PLAYERS OF THE
# TWENTIES

## ALTERNATE DREAM TEAM

| | | | |
|---|---|---|---|
| Pitcher | Burleigh Grimes (rh)<br>Herb Pennock (lh) | Third Baseman | Fred Lindstrom |
| | | Shortstop | Travis Jackson |
| Catcher | Bob O'Farrell | Left Fielder | Goose Goslin |
| First Baseman | George Sisler | Center Fielder | Ty Cobb |
| Second Baseman | Frank Frisch | Right Fielder | Sam Rice |

## HONORABLE MENTION

| | | | |
|---|---|---|---|
| Pitcher | Waite Hoyt<br>Ted Lyons<br>Urban Shocker<br>Bob Shawkey<br>Art Nehf | Third Baseman | Joe Dugan<br>Willie Kamm |
| | | Shortstop | Roger Peckingpaugh<br>Rabbit Maranville |
| Catcher | Earl Smith<br>Eugene Hargrave<br>Muddy Ruel | Left Fielder | Zack Wheat<br>Al Simmons<br>Heinie Manush |
| First Baseman | Lou Gehrig<br>George Kelly | Center Fielder | Max Carey<br>Edd Roush |
| Second Baseman | Bucky Harris<br>Eddie Collins | Right Fielder | Ross Youngs<br>Kiki Cuyler |

# THE SETTING

The age of the pitcher was over and the age of the slugger was beginning. Post-war prosperity and the booming home runs of a manchild named Ruth combined with headline-grabbing Jack Dempsey to bring America into the Golden Age of Sports. This was the decade that New York City came to the forefront as a sports mecca.

The 1919 World Series scandal that resulted in eight members of the Chicago White Sox being banned from baseball for life, failed to have the anticipated long-term debilitating effect on the national game. Instead, tremendous interest and optimism brought baseball followers to games in record numbers. Single-game attendance records were smashed when the 1923 Yankees opened Yankee Stadium before an immense crowd of 63,000 fans.

Federal Judge Kenesaw Mountain Landis was hired by the American and National Leagues and the National Association to rule over organized baseball and to guide the resolution of its problems. The Commissioner became part of the scene at major league ballparks; time would show that Landis was a baseball fan as well as its chief executive.

# GAME STRATEGY

Play tactics during the 1920s moved away from hit-and-run, advance the runner, and steal runs one at a time, toward power hitting. Successful teams like the New York Yankees, New York Giants, St. Louis Cardinals, Philadelphia Athletics and Chicago Cubs adopted the new style. Heavy hitters would swing from the heels with a thin-handled war club to whip the ball out of the playing field for a home run. Proponents of the earlier strategy – the Washington Senators and Pittsburgh Pirates, for example – enjoyed some success in the middle of the decade. By 1929, though, it was apparent to every baseball fan that teams needed the home run slugger to compete successfully.

The abundance of home runs led to high-scoring innings. The opposing team's task became stopping the big inning. Managers, seeking remedies, turned to the relief pitcher and the relief pitcher's best friend, the double play.

It was Firpo Marberry who made the relief pitcher a respectable contingent of the pitching staff. He was instrumental in the 1924 Washington Senators World Championship season when, as a rookie, he started 15 games and relieved in 35 more to fashion an 11-12 record with 15 saves. His continued bullpen success began to wean managers away from the standard practice of rushing the team's best pitcher into the late innings of a close game. Managers without a Marberry-type reliever continued to bring in the ace in late innings. The Athletics' Lefty Grove won 87 games, 10 in relief, and saved 24 others in a five-year span. The 1927 Yankees featured bullpen ace Wilcy Moore, who won 19 games and saved 13 others. He was 6-4 as a starter; the other victories came in relief.

# FACTORS INFLUENCING PLAYER PERFORMANCE

A new, more tightly-wound baseball, sweeping rule changes, and thin-handled bats affected baseball performances in the twenties. In 1920 the baseball was made livelier by the use of Australian wool, which enabled manufacturers to wrap the cork center tighter than ever before. The result was that the ball held its shape better and when hit flew further than the baseball of the previous decade.

The same year, baseball rules underwent a massive overhaul. The National Commission decided to tidy up the game, and they started with trick pitches, primarily the spitball. During the previous decade, both players and health organizations had begun to disdain the use of the spitball. The latter claimed it was a health hazard, while the former saw it as a hitting hazard. Witness spitball master Big Ed Walsh's lifetime ERA of 1.92. When Big Ed was at the end of his career, and was a sore-armed hurler, managers were quick to make use of the situation. The word passed around that spitballs had done irreparable damage to Big Ed's once invincible arm.

As the 1918 influenza epidemic swept the United States and thousands perished, the movement to ban the spitball began in earnest. At the winter meetings in early 1920, the National Commission disallowed intentional discoloring of the ball, the application of foreign substances to the ball, and the intentional damaging or roughening of the cover of the ball. The penalties for committing one of these offenses was immediate removal from the game.

The outlawing of trick pitches coincided with an edict to umpires to remove soiled balls from the games. Shiny, white, tightly-wound baseballs were the object of focus for a new generation of sluggers. Pitchers complained that they could not grip the new balls, and hitters pounded them as never before.

Besides the new, livelier baseball, thin-handled bats contributed to the awesome distances that early 1920s sluggers like Babe Ruth and Rogers Hornsby could send a pitch. Once the handle of the bat was shaved, the resulting big-barrelled club effected a whip-like action that propelled baseballs further than had ever been dreamed possible.

In order to combat the sudden advantage that hitters held over pitchers, the major leagues established a "grandfather's clause" for spitball pitchers. It was agreed that all bona fide spitball pitchers remaining in the game would be exempt from the operation of the rule against the use of the spitball for the balance of their major league careers. Seventeen pitchers were given the okay to use the spitball, while all others were prohibited from it.

The quick pitch gradually fell from favor during this period as well. A hurler using such a pitch would be standing with one foot on the pitcher's rubber while receiving the return toss from the catcher. The pitcher would quickly zip the ball back to the receiver, and past the unsuspecting and unprepared batter.

Several unrelated factors combined to make the decade "the Big Boom Era." Batters gained advantage over pitchers when the spitball and other trick deliveries were outlawed. The ban on trick pitches coincided with a new, harder, tighter baseball and the league directive to remove soiled baseballs from play. Thinner bat handles produced a whip-like action that made it possible to propel baseballs further than ever before. Hordes of fans came to see the dramatic home runs that created a decade of extra-base hits and extraordinary star players.

## PITCHER

Talk about transition, the pitchers of the 1920s had to adjust to life without trick pitches, and life with the livelier ball and new batting techniques. The phenomenal seasons of Babe Ruth in 1920 and 1921, and of Rogers Hornsby in 1922, proved to pitchers that they had to change their methods, or be subject to merciless battering by sluggers.

The decade's list of outstanding pitchers is overloaded with right-handers. The group includes Hall of Fame members Waite Hoyt of the Red Sox and Yankees, Ted Lyons of the White Sox, Dazzy Vance of the Dodgers, and Burleigh Grimes of the Dodgers, Giants and Pirates. Also to be considered are respected starters Urban Shocker with the Browns and Yankees, and Bob Shawkey of the Yankees.

Waite Hoyt's career commenced with trying out for and being rejected by John McGraw and the Giants in 1916, then going across the river to star for the Yankees in six World Series during the 1920s. Hoyt closed his baseball career as a well-respected and entertaining broadcaster for the Cincinnati Reds. He was a top flight pitcher with the Yankees, as his 161-102 decade record shows.

Ted Lyons was a workhorse for the White Sox. He led the AL in victories in 1925 and 1927, in shutouts in 1925 and 1940, and in complete games in 1927 and 1930. He won the AL ERA title in 1942, at the age of 41, with a 2.10 mark. Un-

fortunately, Lyons spent his career with a chronic second-division team, and had few opportunities to pitch in meaningful situations.

Bob Shawkey broke in with Connie Mack and his fabulous $100,000 infield. Shawkey won 106 games and lost 83 during the decade. He retired after the 1927 season, having won only two games for the Yankees, the greatest team of all time. Shawkey managed the Yankees in 1930, in between the stints of Miller Huggins and Joseph McCarthy.

Urban Shocker was an ace pitcher with the Browns, where he won 20 or more games four straight years – including a league-leading 27 in 1921. He joined the Yankees in 1925, and his pitching provided the impetus for three more Yankee pennants from 1926 to 1928. Shocker won 156 games and lost 93 during the 1920s.

The dream team choice for top right-handed pitcher of the 1920s is **Dazzy Vance**. He was the Brooklyn Dodgers' greatest pitcher. Arm trouble delayed his major league career until the age of 31 in 1922, but he won 146 games in the next eight years of the decade.

*For the dream team of the twenties the choice for the right-handed pitcher goes to the Dodgers' Dazzy Vance, who won 146 games between 1922 and 1929, topping the National League in strikeouts seven consecutive times and being named league MVP in 1924. His fire-balling delivery, with its long, low reach, is well illustrated in this photo.*

Left: *Alternate right-handed pitchers for the 1920s dream team is the last legal spitballer, Burleigh Grimes, shown here (right) in 1937 (when he was managing the Dodgers) shaking hands with the Giants' Bill Terry.*

Below: *Alternate left-hander is Herb Pennock, who pitched for the fabulous Yankees of the 1920s. He hurled in three World Series during the decade and had a 5-0 record. For the Yanks, the "Squire of Kennett Square's" winning percentage was .645.*

Opposite: *Cincinnati's Eppa Rixey is the left-hander for the twenties dream team. Rixey won 166 games during the decade, and his 266 lifetime tally was the best for a lefty until the advent of Warren Spahn.*

Combining an 83-inch reach with a high kicking motion, Vance was a fire-balling right-hander who topped the NL in strikeouts seven consecutive seasons. He was the NL Most Valuable Player (MVP) in 1924 when he won 15 straight games, and he recorded a no-hitter against the Phillies in 1925. Vance led the league in shutouts four times, in the ratio of fewest hits to innings pitched four times, and in complete games twice.

The later rule banning alteration of the player's uniform would come about because Vance frayed the ends of his long-sleeved sweatshirt on his throwing arm. His fastballs, fired from behind the flapping shreds of fabric on his wrist, were virtually impossible to see during the 1924 and 1925 seasons.

Gruff, aggressive Burleigh Grimes, the last of the legal spitballers, was the dream team alternate for the 1920s right-handed spot. He won 270 games over 19 seasons for seven major league teams; 190 of his victories occurred during the 1920s. Grimes won 13 straight for the 1927 Giants.

Grimes was known as "Old Stubblebeard" for his habit of not shaving on days he was scheduled to pitch. His grizzled appearance made him seem older than he was. After nine good years with the Dodgers, it seemed that Grimes was finished. But the Giants picked him up and were rewarded with a 19-8 season. They traded him to the Pirates, where in 1928, at age 35, "Old Stubblebeard" led the NL in victories, games, complete games, shutouts and innings pitched. His ERA that season was 2.99. With a new lease on life, he hurled for three straight pennant winners: the Cardinals in 1930 and 1931, and the Cubs in 1932.

Grimes was a winner and a tough competitor. Twice he led the league in wins, four times in complete games, three times in innings pitched, once in winning percentage and once in shutouts.

The decade's top left-handers were Hall of Famers Eppa Rixey of the Phillies and Reds, and Herb Pennock of the Red Sox and Yankees. Art Nehf of the Giants, Reds and Cubs was also in contention.

Art Nehf was the mainstay of the Giants' staff that won four consecutive pennants, from 1921 to 1924. He won 123 games and was 4-4 in World Series play, appearing in 12 Series games altogether. Nehf was a dependable starter, but not the star of the decade.

The left-handed pitcher for the dream team is **Eppa Rixey**. He pitched better under more dire circumstances than either Nehf or Herb Pennock. Rixey was the NL's winningest left-hander until the arrival of Warren Spahn. Rixey, a tall, slender rookie, fresh off the University of Virginia campus in 1912, never spent a day in the minors. Although hurling for a second-division team during many of his seasons, Rixey amassed 166 victories during the decade.

The six-foot, five-inch, 210-pound Rixey led the league with 25 wins in 1922. He showed his toughness by surviving the moribund Reds and proving his durability by hurling 2677 innings, an average of 267 per year during the 1920s.

The alternate left-hander is Herb Pennock, whose genteel upbringing inspired his nickname "The Squire of Kennett Square," and caused a rare miscalculation of talent by Connie Mack. Mack traded Pennock to the Red Sox, thinking that a boy brought up in luxury would never make a ballplayer. Pennock proved him wrong, and Mack admitted that the biggest mistake he ever made was his evaluation of Pennock as a pitcher.

Pennock's smooth, effortless delivery extended his career over 22 major league seasons during which he won 240 games and lost 162. He made the difficult transition directly from high school to the Philadelphia Athletics in 1912. Three years later Mack sold him to the Red Sox; six years after that Pennock became a Yankee.

During the 1920s, Pennock won 162 games, including a 5-0 record in World Series competition as a Yankee. He led the AL in winning percentage in 1923, shutouts in 1928, and innings pitched in 1925. He was a top pitcher who worked for the most powerful team of the decade.

# CATCHER

The catcher had the task of stopping baserunners, who, in the previous decade, had run wild on the basepaths. Even though some teams, notably the 1927 Yankees, still used tandem catching, star catchers were beginning to emerge. During the decade, receivers asserted themselves as team leaders, the "masterminds" of the clubs. The role of the catcher had come full circle, returning to the days when the catchers were the brains behind the good teams.

The dream team catching candidates are Earl Smith of the Giants, Braves, Pirates and Cardinals; Eugene "Bubbles" Hargrave of the Reds; Harold "Muddy" Ruel of the Yankees, Red Sox and Senators; Hall of Famer Charles "Gabby" Hartnett of the Cubs; and Bob O'Farrell with the Cubs, Cardinals and Giants.

Earl Smith played on five National League pennant-winning teams during the 1920s: the Giants of 1921-1922, the Pirates of 1925 and 1927, and the Cardinals of 1928. While he never caught 100 games in any season, Smith was valuable as a part-time catcher and pinch hitter. His decade batting average was .305.

Eugene Hargrave caught 100 games only once, but he won the NL batting title in 1926 with a .353 average. He did not play enough games to be considered more than a platoon player.

Harold Ruel was weak with the stick, but he had a big mitt. While he hit over .300 only once, he led the AL in putouts and assists from 1923 to 1925, in fielding average from 1926 to 1928, and in double plays in 1922, 1924 and 1925. Ruel played in two World Series with the Senators, including their stunning upset of the favored New York Giants in 1924.

The choice for dream team catcher is **Charles "Gabby" Hartnett**. Though he had a lower batting average than Hargrave or Smith, Hartnett slugged .508, better than any catcher. In the 1920s he had almost twice as many home runs, 81, than did Bob O'Farrell. Hartnett chalked up 1254 lifetime assists.

Hartnett was not only a standout catcher; he was also a dangerous hitter. He garnished his .297 lifetime average with 236 home runs. Joe McCarthy, his manager in Chicago, and a

fellow member of the Hall of Fame, said of Hartnett, "He had everything except speed. He was super smart. Nobody ever had more hustle. Nobody could throw with him. There have been few great clutch hitters and he was the best."

Hartnett caught 100 or more games 12 times and set NL career marks for putouts and total chances. As a rookie manager in 1938 he hit a memorable home run in near darkness to beat the Pirates and lead the Cubs to the pennant.

Bob O'Farrell is the alternate dream team catcher, in recognition of his receiving, leadership and clutch hitting. He won the 1926 NL MVP Award as he led the league in putouts, and had career-high totals for games played, at-bats and hits. O'Farrell was one of the top fielding catchers before Hartnett entered the league.

# FIRST BASE

The position called for a player who was a good hitter and fielder at the start of the decade. By its end, the first base slot was filled almost exclusively by home run sluggers. Teams that were competing for the pennant could not afford the luxury of a high-average, on-base man at first base. Managers needed the big basher on first.

Candidates for first base included four Hall of Fame members: Lou Gehrig of the Yankees, George "Highpockets" Kelly of the Giants and Reds, Jim Bottomley of the Cardinals, and George Sisler of the Browns, Senators and Braves.

Opposite: *Dream team catcher is the Cubs' Gabby Hartnett. He slugged .508 in the decade, reaching .591 in 1929 (and a career high of .630 in 1930). According to Cub manager Joe McCarthy, Gabby was the best clutch hitter yet.*

Below: *Cardinal Jim Bottomley, the team's first baseman, hit 146 homers during the decade and for six consecutive years topped 100 RBI (137 in 1929). "Sunny Jim" was league MVP in 1928, when he led the NL in RBI, doubles and triples.*

Right: *The alternate at first base is George Sisler, who played for most of the decade with the Browns. He averaged .346 and in 1920 set a major league record with 257 hits. His 41-game hitting-streak record lasted 19 years until broken by Joe DiMaggio in 1941.*

Lou Gehrig was the premier first baseman in the majors; by 1929 and he had a decade slugging average of .621. Because he was a regular starter for only four seasons and played fewer than 800 games, Larrupin' Lou does not fulfill the criteria for dream team selection until the 1930s.

George Kelly led the NL in home runs in 1921 and in RBIs in 1920 and 1924. The Giants won four pennants with him at first base. Highpockets was not as good a hitter as George Sisler, nor was he as good a slugger as Jim Bottomley.

**"Sunny" Jim Bottomley**, the dream team first baseman, tied with Gehrig for most decade home runs by first basemen, with 146, and out-slugged all other candidates except Gehrig. Bottomley drove in 885 runs in 1062 games. He slugged 83 points higher and bashed 70 more home runs than did George Sisler.

Bottomley earned Frankie Frisch's praise as "the best clutch hitter I ever saw." The graceful first baseman with the sunny disposition drove in 100 or more runs six years in a row, leading the league twice during the 1920s. Sunny set the major league record of 12 RBIs in a single game when he went six for six on September 16, 1924, with two homers and a double against Brooklyn. Bottomley was the loop's MVP in 1928, when he led the league in doubles, triples and RBIs.

Ty Cobb called George Sisler, the dream team alternate first baseman, "the nearest thing to a perfect ballplayer. He can do everything – hit, hit with power, field, run and throw." Sisler broke into baseball as a pitcher, once hurling a 2-1 win against Walter Johnson. But his chief accomplishments came with a bat in his hands. Twice Sisler hit over .400, winning two batting titles, and he put together a 41-game hitting streak in 1922. His 257 hits in 1920 set a major league record.

Sisler, who hit .346 and led the decade's first basemen in triples, suffered from severe sinus problems and played much of the 1924 season while reeling from double vision. Despite that, he hit a remarkable .305.

# SECOND BASE

Even though the position was still dominated by excellent hitters during the 1920s, second base was losing the reputation of being a slugger's position. Managers began to look for second basemen who were good fielders, and could turn the double play, as well as hit and score runs. In 1922 Bucky Harris of the Senators turned 116 double plays. It was the first time that a second baseman ever participated in more than 100 double plays in a season, and a new era of infield play began.

Dream team candidates for second base include four Hall of Fame players: Bucky Harris of the Senators; Eddie Collins of the White Sox and Athletics; Rogers Hornsby of the Cardinals, Giants, Braves and Cubs; and Frank Frisch of the Giants and Cardinals.

Bucky Harris was the Boy Wonder, who as the 27-year old manager, led the Senators to their only World Championship in 1924. His 40 years of service as player, manager and coach were rewarded by selection to the Baseball Hall of Fame in

1975. He was a better than average hitter who was a slick fielder with leadership ability.

Eddie Collins averaged .346 with the fourth highest OBA (.433) for the decade, but he could not hit with power. His 1920s statistics show that he was able to adapt to the changing game.

Rogers Hornsby and Frank Frisch were two of the greatest second basemen in the history of the game. Hornsby's lifetime batting average of .358 ranks him as the best right-handed hitter of all time. Frisch was a leader extraordinaire. He was captain of the New York Giants and manager of the truculent Gas House gang. Later he served on the Hall of Fame Veterans Committee, and dominated there as well.

**Rogers Hornsby**, the dream team number one pick for second base, hit .382 for the decade. It was the second highest 10-year average in baseball history. His decade slugging average, .636, was exceeded only by Ruth's, .739. Hornsby averaged 208 hits, 119 runs and 115 RBIs per season for the entire decade.

During the decade, Hornsby whacked 405 doubles, more than any other hitter at any time. In the 1920s his 250 home

Opposite: *Second base goes to Rogers Hornsby, who had the second highest 10-year batting average (.382) in history. In the twenties only Ruth topped his slugging average of .636.*

Above: *Alternate for second base is Frank Frisch. Starting in 1921 "The Fordham Flash" hit .300 or better for 11 straight years. In 1923 he led the NL with 223 hits.*

runs were topped only by Babe Ruth. Hornsby's .457 OBA for the decade was second to Ruth's, and the fourth highest ever. Hornsby captured seven batting championships – six in a row – averaging better than .400 between 1921 and 1925, during which he batted .397, .401, .384, .424 and .403. His .424 mark set a National League record for the twentieth century. Twice selected as MVP, Hornsby managed the 1926 Cardinals to their first World Championship.

Frank Frisch, the dream team second baseman alternate choice, was unequalled as a clutch performer. "The Fordham Flash" jumped directly from college to the New York Giants, and in 19 seasons he played on eight pennant-winners and six runners-up.

Although out-hit by Eddie Collins by 21 points, Frisch

out-scored Collins by 310 runs and out-slugged him by 22 points. Frisch stole 310 bases during the decade, second only to well known base-stealer Max Carey. The switch-hitting second baseman compiled a string run of 11 straight .300 seasons, and set fielding records for assists and total chances with the Cardinals in 1927. His hard-nosed style typified the St. Louis Gas House Gang, whom he managed in the 1930s.

The Fordham Flash performed under the most pressure that any player ever faced, in 1927. The Cardinals had decided to trade their outspoken second-baseman, Rogers Hornsby, during the 1926 season, when he cursed at the owner and sent him out of the clubhouse after a hard-fought loss. The impending trade deal became complicated when Hornsby led the Cardinals to the pennant and an upset victory over the mighty New York Yankees in the World Series. The Giants gave the Cardinals Frisch and Jimmy Ring for the great Hornsby. Frank Frisch came to a city not only stunned by the news of the trade, but wild with rage and indignation. Frisch weathered the storm to play on four Cardinal pennant-winners, while Hornsby was banished to the Boston Braves after only one season with McGraw and his Giants.

# THIRD BASE

Third base was another position that was changing from a fielder's domain to a slugger's spot. Defending against bunts was no longer particularly important, since the decade was characterized by power hitting. Younger players at the position symbolized the ascendancy of the hitter, whereas the older players still emphasized fielding.

Contenders for the dream team third base position are "Jumping Joe" Dugan of the Athletics, Red Sox, Yankees and Braves; Willie Kamm of the White Sox; and Hall of Famers Pie Traynor of the Pirates, and Fred Lindstrom of the Giants.

Joe Dugan was best known for jumping teams and being traded often. His late season acquisition by the Yankees in 1922 caused such an outcry among AL teams that a trading deadline was established. Dugan was also well known for being Babe Ruth's pal, but evidently they did not work on hitting together. Dugan's batting average for the decade, .291, is lower than Fred Lindstrom's or Pie Traynor's. Jumping Joe was not a power hitter either.

Willie Kamm was a moderately good hitting third sacker who played for a below-average team. He had no power, but drew enough walks to lead all decade third basemen in on-base percentage.

**Harold "Pie" Traynor** is rated as one of the greatest third basemen of all time, and is the top choice for third base on the dream team. His spectacular defensive prowess overshadowed his fine hitting, for he was a consistent .300 batter and 100 RBI man.

Rugged, rangy and handsome, Traynor was the pride of the Pirates in the 1920s and 1930s, and John McGraw considered him to be "the finest team player in the game." Traynor received his nickname because of his fondness for pastry.

Traynor played more games, scored more runs, stole more bases, and had more hits, RBIs, triples and a higher average than any other third baseman during the decade. He was dominant in the field as well. Traynor led the NL in putouts in 1923 and in 1925 to 1927, in double plays in 1924 to 1927, and in assists in 1923 and 1925. In 1925 Traynor led the league's third basemen in putouts, assists, double plays and fielding average, but finished eighth in the MVP voting.

Fred Lindstrom, the dream team alternate, began his professional career as a 16-year-old player with Toledo in 1922. Two years later, with the New York Giants, he was the youngest performer to appear in the World Series. Lindstrom took advantage of the opportunity: he collected four hits in the fifth game of the Series against the Washington Senators, and went on to hit .333 for the seven games.

Lindstrom hit .316 for the decade and slugged .452, highest among third basemen for the decade. Lindstrom had seven .300 seasons, and twice he garnered 231 hits. His lifetime batting mark was .311.

Left: *Pirate Hall of Famer Pie Traynor is the obvious choice for third base. Not only did he hit better than any other third baseman in the 1920s, he led his league in putouts for four years, in double plays for four years and in assists for two years.*

Opposite top: *For shortstop Joe Sewell of the Indians is the clear choice. He led all other shortstops of the twenties in games, hits, runs, doubles and walks, and his hitting topped .300 in nine of the decade's ten years.*

Opposite bottom: *Pie Traynor poses on the field. A team player, Traynor's talent was matched by his hustle.*

# SHORTSTOP

The value of shortstop as a fielding position was finally recognized during the 1920s, when double plays became an important part of a team's defense. In 1919 there were 805 double plays in the AL and 789 in the NL. By 1929 the league totals for double plays were 1196 for the AL and 1177 for the NL.

The decade's top shortstops were Roger Peckinpaugh of the Yankees, Senators and White Sox; and Hall of Famers Rabbit Maranville of the Braves, Pirates, Cubs, Dodgers, Cardinals and Braves again, Joe Sewell of the Indians, and Travis Jackson of the Giants.

Roger Peckinpaugh won the 1925 AL MVP Award. His inspired play drove the Senators to their second consecutive pennant. Despite making several errors in the 1925 World Series, he was a top fielder. His batting was only fair.

Rabbit Maranville was on the downhill side of his long career that led to the Hall of Fame. He could not hit with power, and he had a drinking problem, yet teams still sought him to fill infield gaps. The 1928 Cardinals won the pennant with Rabbit at shortstop. He played in two World Series 14 years apart. His batting was weak and his performance erratic during the decade.

**Joe Sewell** was the run-away favorite over Travis Jackson as the dream team shortstop. Sewell replaced Ray Chapman following his tragic death during the 1920 season, and inspired Cleveland to the pennant. Sewell out-hit Jackson by 27 points with a .322 average, and excelled Jackson's OBA by 50 points with a .393 figure.

Sewell played more games, scored more runs, had more hits, knocked in more runs, smashed more doubles and walked more than any other shortstop during the decade. He was a good hitter, but he was also a durable infielder who led the AL in fielding twice and in putouts and assists four times.

Even though Sewell posted a .312 career batting average, and topped .300 in nine of ten seasons during the decade, he is best remembered for hardly ever striking out. He was fanned only 114 times in his entire 14-year career. He whiffed but three times in both 1930 and 1932, and he struck out only four times in three other seasons.

Travis Jackson, the hustling captain and clutch-hitting shortstop on McGraw's Giants of the 1920s and 1930s, was one of the game's all-time top glove men at the key infield position. His outstanding arm, exceptional range and ability to get rid of the ball quickly earned him star status, and qualify him as the alternate shortstop selection.

A hitter as well as a fielder, Jackson pounded twice as many home runs as did his competitors, and led all shortstops in slugging percentage with .447. At the plate he enjoyed six .300-plus seasons while compiling a .291 career mark. By combining speed and power with his other diamond talents, he helped the Giants to four World Series. He played 1925-27 with an entire infield of future Hall of Fame members.

# LEFT FIELD

The left field position in the 1920s is loaded with five Hall of Famers: Zack Wheat of the Dodgers and Athletics, Al Simmons with the Athletics, Heinie Manush of the Tigers and Browns, Harry Heilmann of the Tigers, and Goose Goslin with the Senators. Any one of the five would be an excellent choice to play left on the dream team. Managers put their hitter with the highest batting average into left field where he could relax and save his energy between batting appearances.

Although Zack Wheat was on the downhill side of his career, he still had enough pop in his bat to average .339 for the decade, but his .384 OBA and .491 slugging percentage trailed those of the other four candidates. Wheat led the Dodgers to the 1920 NL pennant.

"Simmons will never be a hitter," stated the critics in 1924 as they viewed rookie Al Simmons' foot-in-the-bucket batting stance. But the Athletics' outfielder went on to compile more hits than any right-handed AL batter until Al Kaline. Simmons was also a deadly clutch hitter. Many veteran baseball fans consider Simmons the hardest-hitting outfielder ever to play the game. His 253 hits in 1925 is the fourth highest all-time single-season total.

Heinie Manush was consistently among the game's top hitters for more than a decade. His batting average was .338 for the 1920s. Manush won the AL batting crown in 1926 with a .378 mark by going six-for-nine in a doubleheader the final day of the season to overtake Babe Ruth. He missed the 1928 batting title by one point.

**Harry Heilmann** gets the nod as dream team left fielder because of his high decade batting average, .364, and four batting titles during the 1920s. Simmons was ruled out because he was the number one pick for the 1930s. Manush did not have the power of Goose Goslin, therefore the Goose was selected as alternate left fielder.

The line drive hitting Harry Heilmann was rated second only to Rogers Hornsby as the best right-handed hitter of his day. He teamed with Ty Cobb for most of his career to give the Detroit Tigers an awesome slugging combination. Heilmann

Above and opposite: *Dream team alternate for left field is the Senators' hulking Leon "Goose" Goslin, who hit .330 over the decade (with a high of .379 in 1928). He appeared in two Series in the 1920s; in them he had 19 hits, scored 10 runs and batted in three more. He entered the Hall of Fame in 1968.*

Right: *Our first choice for left field goes to Tiger Harry Heilmann, at the time perhaps second to only Rogers Hornsby as a right-handed hitter. His decade average was .364, and "Slug" slugged at .559 during the same period. He leads all other left fielders of the twenties in games, hits, homers, runs, RBI, doubles and walks. He was inducted into the Hall of Fame in 1952.*

won four batting crowns during 1921 to 1927 with marks of .394, .403, .393 and .398 in the odd-numbered years.

Heilmann played more games, scored more runs, had more hits, drove in more runs, ripped more doubles, blasted more home runs, had the highest average with .364 and the highest OBA with .430, and walked more than any other left fielder during the decade. He averaged 113 RBIs per season. His on-base percentage was the fifth highest for all players during the decade. Primarily an outfielder, he was also a fine first baseman.

Goose Goslin was a great clutch hitter whose powerful bat figured in five pennants in a 12-year span – three flags for the Senators and two for Detroit.

Goslin had the second highest RBI total and most triples of any left fielder during the 1920s. The big, lumbering fly-hawk drove in 90 or more runs and batted .300 or higher seven straight seasons. Goose hit .330 for the decade. His 18 and 20 triples were league highs in 1923 and 1925. Goslin led the AL in 1928 with a .379 batting average, and he recorded 2735 career hits, adding 37 more in World Series competition.

# CENTER FIELD

Managers had difficulties adjusting their defensive strategy to the new livelier baseball. Those who did adjust to the long-distance hitting sent speedy, daring flyball catchers into center. The center fielder became the main defense against batters who were capable of driving the ball into the outer reaches of the ballpark. The basis for the old baseball adage of building strength up the middle may have originated in the later years of this decade.

The four dream team candidates are Hall of Famers: Max Carey of the Pirates and Dodgers; Edd Roush of the Reds and Giants; Tris Speaker of the Indians, Senators and Athletics; and Ty Cobb of the Tigers and Athletics.

Above and left: *Ty Cobb is again the choice for center field, but this time as the alternate. Between 1920 and 1928, when he retired, he hit .357, never falling below .300 and reaching .401 in 1922. The picture at the left is just a bit of nostalgia, a memento of those never-to-be-forgotten Ty Cobb spikes.*

Opposite: *Our first choice for center field in the twenties dream team was our alternate for the teens, Tris Speaker. He hit .354 for the decade, with 398 doubles, and he led all center fielders in runs, hits, RBI and several other batting categories. He also led the AL twice in fielding and once in double plays.*

*This installation of greats includes, from left to right, Lou Gehrig, Tris Speaker, Ty Cobb and our inevitable pick for right field, Babe Ruth. The 1920s almost belonged to the Babe. His stats are legend: 1365 runs (467 of them home runs), 1339 RBI, 82 triples, 314 doubles, 1236 walks and so on and on. No other player in history ever had such a fabulous decade.*

57

Max Carey earned his reputation as a superb outfielder and proficient base-stealer as he led the NL in total chances four times during the 1920s. He was the decade's leading base-stealer with 346, including 51 in 53 attempts in 1922. Carey led the NL in stolen bases in 1920, and from 1922 to 1925. His defensive play and base-stealing were outstanding, but his hitting did not rank with the .350 and higher averages of Tris Speaker and Ty Cobb.

Edd Roush was the NL premier center fielder of his day and one of its most feared hitters. He batted .331 for the twenties. Roush's big bat and skillful outfield play kept the Reds competitive until he was traded to the Giants in 1927. He was known as a regular holdout with the Reds, and he once sat out an entire season in a contract dispute with the Giants.

The center-field spot on the 1920s dream team is allocated to the same duo who held it in the previous decade, but in reverse order. **Tris Speaker** is the top choice, and Ty Cobb is the alternate.

Tris Speaker, playing a revolutionary shallow center field, led the league in fielding in 1921 and 1922. At age 37, Speaker led the league in double plays. As impressive as his fielding was, it was his hitting that put him on the dream team.

Speaker's best season was 1923, when he hit .380 and was runner-up to Babe Ruth for RBI honors with 130. He averaged .354 with 398 doubles for the 1920s. His .438 on-base percentage was highest among his peers in center field. Speaker's

doubles total, 398, was the second highest ever for one decade. He led other center fielders in runs scored, hits, RBIs, doubles, OBA and bases on balls during the 1920s.

Speaker still holds several career batting and fielding records. He hit more doubles than did any other player. He also holds the AL records for putouts, assists, total chances and double plays.

Ty Cobb, baseball's fiercest competitor, left the teens with nothing more to prove. He became a playing manager and was

Above: *Ruth poses with manager Miller Huggins* (left), *who led New York to six Series and three world championships in the decade of the twenties. Ruth's contribution to these Series* *was 31 runs, 24 RBI and 12 home runs (for a Series batting average of .352 and slugging average of .742). In the 1928 Series, in 16 at-bats, he got 10 runs and four RBI, batting .625.*

credited with the development of Harry Heilmann and Charlie Gehringer as hitters. As a teacher, he was still his own best pupil. Cobb hit .357 for the decade, including nine straight .300-seasons and a .401 season in 1922. He hit the next to most triples, and stole 126 bases for the decade. He tied with Speaker for the most runs scored and RBIs among the decade center-field candidates.

Cobb finished his career by playing for Connie Mack. He hit .323 as a 42-year-old, part-time outfielder.

# RIGHT FIELD

Babe Ruth defined the role of the right fielder. Previously, a variety of hitters and fielders had played the position; some could field grounders and throw out runners at first base, others could hit but did not concentrate on fielding. Ruth changed baseball's outlook on outfield personnel. By the end of the twenties, all the clubs' front offices wanted a power hitter in right field.

Dream team candidates for right fielder included four Hall of Famers: Ross Youngs of the Giants, Kiki Cuyler of the Pirates and Cubs, Babe Ruth of the Yankees, and Sam Rice of the Senators.

Ross Youngs was the stocky, hard-hitting, hard-running, hard-sliding right fielder of the champion Giants of the 1920s. Aggressive and consistent, he was called "the greatest outfielder I ever saw" by his manager, John McGraw. McGraw had only two players' pictures on his office wall, one was Mathewson and the other Youngs. Ross Youngs hit over .300 in nine of his ten seasons to compile a decade average of .326.

More than a good hitter, Youngs led NL outfielders in assists in three seasons. A great overall player, his life resembled a Greek tragedy. A kidney disorder ended his career in 1926, and resulted in his premature death one year later at age 30.

Kiki Cuyler was one of the NL's outstanding outfielders of the period. A fine hitter, fielder, thrower and baserunner, he batted .333 for the decade. Cuyler also led the circuit in stolen bases three times, and in runs scored twice. He played for three pennant-winning teams in the 1920s.

Babe Ruth was an American original, baseball's greatest slugger and the most celebrated athlete of his time. Fresh out of St. Mary's Industrial School in Baltimore, he debuted as a pitcher for the Boston Red Sox, winning 89 games over six seasons before his sale to the Yankees for $125,000 in 1919. Converted to the outfield because of his prodigious power, he launched his amazing home run career, smashing 467 of his 714 home runs in the 1920s.

Ruth had the greatest decade of any player ever. He scored 1365 runs, drove in 1339, ripped 314 doubles and 82 triples, and walked an amazing 1236 times. His averages can only be called Ruthian: .355 batting, .485 on-base and .739 slugging. His 1920 and 1921 seasons are the greatest seasons of any player in the history of the game. Single-handedly turning the sport of baseball into the industry of baseball by his mass appeal to spectators, **Babe Ruth** is the obvious choice for right field on the dream team.

Durability and consistency made Sam Rice a Hall of Famer and the alternate 1920s dream team right fielder. Although weighing a mere 150 pounds, the Senator's outfielder played for 20 seasons and hit over .300 in all but five. He averaged .322 for his career, and fell only 13 hits shy of the coveted 3000-hit goal. While not a slugger, Rice was a speedster, leading the AL in base thefts with 63 in 1920. In 1925 he batted .350 and had 227 hits, adding 12 more in the World Series.

Rice scored 1001 runs and made 2010 hits for the decade. He had more doubles, triples and stolen bases than did any other right fielder.

Left: *Lou Gehrig congratulates Ruth as he crosses home plate after making his record 60th season home run in the 151st game of 1927. First baseman Gehrig had a fine decade as well. Between 1925 and 1929 he scored 744 runs and batted in 618 more, twice leading the league in RBI. He also twice led in doubles and once in triples. He batted .331 and slugged .615.*

LEFT FIELD

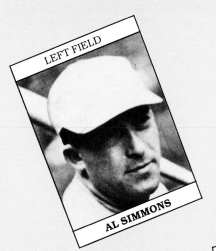

**AL SIMMONS**

CENTER FIELD

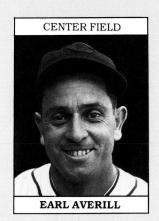

**EARL AVERILL**

SHORTSTOP

**JOE CRONIN**

SECOND BASE

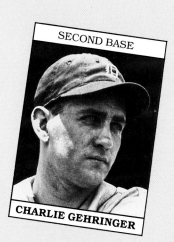

**CHARLIE GEHRINGER**

THIRD BASE

**JUDY JOHNSON**

PITCHER (LH)

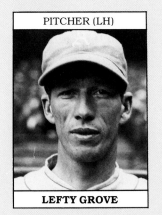

**LEFTY GROVE**

PITCHER (RH)

**SATCHEL PAIGE**

CATCHER

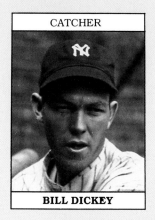

**BILL DICKEY**

60

RIGHT FIELD

MEL OTT

# THE GREATEST PLAYERS OF THE
# THIRTIES

FIRST BASE

JIMMIE FOXX

## ALTERNATE DREAM TEAM

| | | | |
|---|---|---|---|
| **Pitcher** | Dizzy Dean (rh) | **Third Baseman** | Red Rolfe |
| | Carl Hubbell (lh) | **Shortstop** | Arky Vaughan |
| **Catcher** | Mickey Cochrane | **Left Fielder** | Joe Medwick |
| **First Baseman** | Lou Gehrig | **Center Fielder** | James Bell |
| **Second Baseman** | Tony Lazzeri | **Right Fielder** | Chuck Klein |

## HONORABLE MENTION

| | | | |
|---|---|---|---|
| **Pitcher** | Lon Warneke | **Second Baseman** | Billy Herman |
| | Mel Harder | | Buddy Myer |
| | Paul Derringer | **Third Baseman** | Stan Hack |
| | Wes Ferrell | | Joe Stripp |
| | Red Ruffing | | Marv Owen |
| | Lefty Gomez | | |
| | Larry French | **Shortstop** | Luke Appling |
| | | | Dick Bartell |
| **Catcher** | Gabby Hartnett | | |
| | Josh Gibson | **Left Fielder** | Heinie Manush |
| | Al Lopez | | Goose Goslin |
| | Ernie Lombardi | | |
| | Rich Ferrell | **Center Fielder** | Ben Chapman |
| **First Baseman** | Zeke Bonura | **Right Fielder** | Kiki Cuyler |
| | Hank Greenberg | | |
| | Bill Terry | | |
| | Hal Trosky | | |
| | Ripper Collins | | |
| | Buck Leonard | | |

# THE SETTING

The Great Depression hovered around baseball like mist over a pond on a cool summer morning. Team rosters were reduced to 23 players, and Commissioner Landis took a voluntary pay cut, but at least they still had jobs. Many of the fans accustomed to watching the Cardinals, Browns, Reds, Indians and Pirates found themselves unemployed. Attendance declined so far that major league baseball resorted to playing night games. The novelty of nocturnal games proved to be a savior for midwestern minor leagues when it was first tried during the 1930 season. In the majors, Larry McPhail, president of the Reds, initiated night baseball on May 24, 1935, in a game against the Phillies.

Hard times produced hard players. Team photos from the 1930s reveal creased faces, vacant stares and tightly clenched lips. The alternatives to playing ball were grim indeed.

# GAME STRATEGY

Managers continued in the 1930s to search for the power hitter. The big boppers imitated Ruth and uppercut the ball, driving it out of the parks, where fences seemed to be creeping closer. As home run hitting gained in popularity, batting averages declined slightly, as did the numbers of stolen bases and sacrifice hits.

Fear was the motivating factor in society during the Depression, and in baseball it was no different. Fear of the long ball was a major factor in strategy decisions. Pitchers walked Jimmie Foxx and Lou Gehrig over 1000 times each in the 1930s. Yankees southpaw Lefty Gomez tried glasses to aid his failing eyesight. Once on the mound facing the Red Sox, Lefty called time, walked to the dugout, and placed his spectacles on the shelf. "I just got a look at Jimmie Foxx through these things," he explained. "It's enough to scare you to death."

Managers, having fewer pitchers in the bullpen, returned to the earlier strategy of using the ace of the staff in relief. The baseball adage "go with your number one" took effect, as Lefty Grove, Dizzy Dean and Carl Hubbell appeared in 10-15 games of relief in the early 1930s.

# FACTORS INFLUENCING PLAYER PERFORMANCE

The thirties witnessed night baseball, equipment modifications and rule changes that affected the performance of ballplayers.

In the first night game ever held in Brooklyn, Johnny Vander Meer hurled his second consecutive no-hit game. Most batters worried about their ability to see the baseball at night, but the fans had no such qualms. They appeared in record numbers. At a time when weekday games were drawing 700 if the franchise was a winning team, night games during the week drew overflow crowds. In one such overflow crowd in Cincinnati on July 31, 1935, singer Kitty Burke took advantage of the chaos to bat off Paul Dean in a major league game. Her at-bat was disallowed over the vehement protest of Cardinal manager Frank Frisch, who wanted the out to count.

Several rule changes involved equipment modification. Limits were placed on the size of gloves to be used in the field. The rule came about because Hank Greenberg attempted to use a first baseman's mitt in right field. The scrappy, Depression Era ballplayer was always trying to get the edge over the other players. Competitiveness led Brooklyn ace Dazzy Vance to fray his undershirt into strips that dangled around his wrist. Rumor had it that he even tied glass beads to the strips, so that his already overpowering fastball came at the hitter through a maze of dancing lights and flapping fabric. In the 1930s alterations to the standard baseball uniform were finally outlawed.

In other attempts to limit deception, rules were passed making it mandatory that the pitcher's glove be uniform in color, and that glass buttons or polished metal could not be worn on the uniform.

Another rule new to the decade was one that further defined interference. In the early years of the 1900s, third base coaches would often run toward home plate to draw a throw from the defense while the real runner was safely perched on third. In the following years rules continued to be passed limiting and defining interference. The 1930s rule covered coaches in their coaching boxes. The rule change read, "Players and coaches must vacate space if it is needed by a fielder making a play."

The rule that most affected play in the thirties was made in 1931, and dealt with home runs. The new rule read, "A fair ball bouncing into the stands is a two-base hit. If a fair ball passes outside the playing field, the umpire shall decide it fair or foul according to where it leaves the playing field." Prior to this rule, base hits that bounced into the stands in fair territory were home runs.

# THE POSITIONS

## PITCHER

Pity the pitcher during the 1930s. With competition keen for employment, the hurler would frequently face such well known bashers as Gehrig, Foxx, Greenberg, Ott, Medwick, Simmons, Goslin and Gehringer. Dramatic, tension-filled pennant races in 1934, 1935 and 1938, and rosters with fewer players, forced managers to use their aces as relievers in turn-of-the-century style. During this decade of slugging, pitchers such as Wes Ferrell and George Uhle extended their careers by being good hitters.

Right-handers Lon Warneke of the Cubs and Cardinals, Mel Harder of the Indians, Paul Derringer of the Cardinals and Reds, Wes Ferrell of the Red Sox and Indians, Red Ruffing of the Red Sox and Yankees, Dizzy Dean of the St. Louis Cardinals, and the Negro Leagues' Leroy "Satchel" Paige, were stiff competition for dream team picks.

Lon Warneke, the Arkansas Hummingbird, was as fine a

pitcher as a manager could want. During the decade he won 147 games despite virtually no action in 1930 and 1931. In 1932 he led the league in won-lost percentage and shutouts while winning 22 games for the NL champion Cubs.

Mel Harder was consistent, winning 11 or more games in 11 straight seasons, including 20 in 1934 and 22 in 1935. He led the AL in ERA in 1933 and in shutouts in 1934. Harder won 158 games during the 1930s.

Wes Ferrell, in addition to winning 170 games, had two tremendous hitting seasons. In 1931 he batted .319 with nine home runs, 30 RBIs and a slugging percentage of .621. Four years later, he ripped his fellow AL pitchers for a .347 average,

*Future Hall of Famer Satchel Paige demonstrates his fastball for Grover Cleveland Alexander, when he was with the New York Black Yankees in 1941. A living legend in the Negro Leagues, Paige is the number one right-hander of the thirties. Known for his fastball and his hesitation pitch, Paige later pitched in the majors.*

seven home runs and 32 RBIs. He won 20 games six times — five of those times in the 1930s. For all of his hitting and pitching ability, Ferrell had an explosive temper and was often at odds with his teammates and manager.

Paul Derringer won 18 games as a 24-year-old rookie in 1931. He pitched the Cardinals to the pennant and World Championship. Derringer was traded to Cincinnati, then the Siberia of the NL, suffered through the ignominies of 27 losses in one season, and emerged by the end of the decade as the ace of the two-time NL champion Reds' staff. He won 148 games over the decade.

Red Ruffing overcame adversity to achieve pitching stardom. As a youngster he had lost four toes on his left foot in a mining accident, ending his hopes of being a major league outfielder. He switched to the mound and went on to win 273 major league games, including 174 (with four consecutive 20-victory seasons) during the thirties. His big break came when he was traded from the Red Sox to the Yankees. Ruffing's record with Boston was 39-93; with the Yankees it was 231-127.

Not only could Ruffing pitch, he was one of baseball's best hitting pitchers. He hit .285, with 26 home runs and 166 RBIs for the decade. On the pitching front, he led the AL twice in shutouts, once in strikeouts, and once in games won during the thirties.

Warneke, Harder, Ferrell, Derringer and Ruffing were all tough competitors and fine pitchers, but not as winning or as dominating as the dream team right-handed duo of Satchel Paige and Dizzy Dean.

*Above: Jay Hannah "Dizzy" Dean (right) and his brother Paul "Daffy" Dean, pitched together for the Cardinals from 1934 through 1937. During the decade, right-handed alternate dream team choice Dizzy Dean led his league twice in wins, games and shutouts. His amazing 30-7 record in 1934 helped St. Louis to a World Championship.*

*Opposite top: Dream team choice Lefty Grove was the best left-hander of the decade. A fierce competitor, Grove won the American League's MVP Award in 1931, when he led the league in wins (31), winning percentage (.886), ERA (2.06), complete games (27), strikeouts (175) and shutouts (4). He was elected to the Hall of Fame in 1947.*

**Leroy "Satchel" Paige**, the 1930s dream team number one right-handed pick, may have been the greatest pitcher of all time, and was certainly baseball's greatest showman. In his prime, he pitched at least three innings every day, sometimes guaranteeing that he would strike out the first nine hitters. Paige's assortment of pitches included "Old Tom," his fastball, and "Long Tom," his really fastball. The most famous pitch, called "the Hesitation," was so named because Paige would stop in midstride, balancing on his back foot, waiting for the right moment to slip the ball by the nervous batter. This pitch was outlawed in the majors by the time Paige finally made it to the big leagues. Dizzy Dean said of him, "If Satch and I were pitching on the same team, we'd clinch the pennant by July 4th and go fishing until World Series time."

A legend in the Negro leagues, Paige broke into major league baseball as a 42-year-old rookie with the Cleveland

The Great Diz once shut out the Braves without taking a sign from the catcher. He threw all fastballs and had announced his intentions to the startled Boston bench before the game began.

Left-handed contenders for the dream team include Hall of Famers Lefty Grove of the Athletics and Red Sox, Carl Hubbell of the Giants, and Vernon "Lefty" Gomez of the Yankees, plus Larry French of the Pirates and Cubs.

Lefty Gomez baffled the opposition with his fastball and curve, while he entertained his teammates with his wit and good humor. He was a 20-game winner four times during the 1930s, while helping the Yankees to five pennants. Twice he led the AL in won-lost percentage and in ERA, and three times in strikeouts. Lefty set a World Series record by winning six consecutive games. Great as he was, Gomez's 165 wins fell considerably short of Grove's 199 and Hubbell's 188 for the 1930s.

Larry French, a left-handed thrower who was not called "Lefty," won 156 games and pitched his teams to two pennants during the thirties. French was a dependable hurler who would give his manager 27-35 starts every season, but he was not in the same class with Grove and Hubbell.

**Lefty Grove**, the 1930s dream team left-hander, is generally considered as the greatest left-handed pitcher in AL history. Although he did not reach the majors until the age of 25, he still won 300 games by fashioning eight 20-win seasons, including a 30-win season and four 20-win seasons in the thirties. With a temperament as mean as his fastball, he was 31-4 for the 1931 Athletics, compiling a 16-game winning streak.

Grove developed speed and control by throwing rocks as a youngster. He used that speed and control to lead the AL in strikeouts seven consecutive seasons and in ERA nine times (seven times within the 1930s). Grove was not only the decade's best starter, but a darned good relief pitcher with 23 wins in relief and 21 saves.

"King" Carl Hubbell, the dream team alternate left-handed pitcher, was also known as the "Giants' Meal Ticket" during the Depression. Hubbell led the Giants to three pennants and two near-misses in a five-year span during which he averaged 23 victories a season and was twice named Most Valuable Player.

Baffling hitters with a devastating screwball, Hubbell compiled a 46-scoreless inning streak in 1933, and won 16 straight games in 1936. He became famous for his performance in the 1934 All-Star Game when he fanned Ruth, Gehrig, Foxx, Simmons and Cronin in succession. He looked like the quintessential 1930s ballplayer — lean, hollow-cheeked, grizzled and tough.

# CATCHER

No fewer than seven Hall of Fame players caught during the 1930s. The shortest path to the majors during the previous decade had been through the catcher's position, therefore many young, talented hitters chose catching as their ticket to stardom. Mickey Cochrane of the Athletics, Gabby Hartnett with the Cubs, the Yankees' Bill Dickey, and Negro League great Josh Gibson started catching regularly in their early twenties during the 1920s. Al Lopez of the Boston Bees; Ernie Lombardi of the Reds; and Rick Ferrell of the Browns, Red Sox and Senators, were also Hall of Famers who caught during the 1930s. The catching position was loaded with talent during the thirties.

Indians. In his first appearance, against the mighty Yankees, he threw 16 straight strikes. An example of his legendary control was his warm-up method. He would lay a matchbook cover out lengthwise and work on the corners.

Satchel played ball all over the North American continent. One season he pitched for the Dominican dictator Rafael Trujillo's team, whose supporters carried guns and expected a victory every time. Armed with his mad assortment of pitches, Satchel would barnstorm against white teams led by such veterans as Dizzy Dean and Bob Feller once the major league season was finished.

Jerome Herman Dean, or Jay Hannah Dean, depending on the source, was the greatest pitcher of his day. Some fans proclaimed, "Dizzy Dean was a legend in his own time," though some wags preferred to say a "legend in his own mind." The brash fireballer burst upon the major league scene in 1932 and he averaged 24 wins a season over his first five campaigns. He was 30-7 in 1934 when he and his brother Paul led the Cardinals to the World Championship. Diz topped the league in strikeouts four times and he held the single game record of 17. A broken toe suffered in the 1937 All-Star Game led to an arm injury that shortened his career.

In the Depression years, Dean was just the man to represent baseball, and the alternate dream team. His folksy, no-nonsense ways made a lot of sense to a confused and frightened generation. "It ain't braggin', if you can do it," "A lot of folks ain't saying ain't, ain't eatin'," and "It could be that (Bill) Terry's a nice guy when you get to know him, but why bother?"

Above: *Behind the plate, Bill Dickey was known for his intelligent calling of pitches and his rifle arm. Dickey was elected to the Hall of Fame in 1954.*

Inset above: *Yankee catcher Bill Dickey loosens up at spring training in St. Petersburg. Dream team catcher for the decade, Dickey was a consistently good hitter throughout his 17-year career, ending up with a .313 batting average.*

Right: *Mickey Cochrane makes a diving tag. Dream team runner-up catcher, "Black Mike" appeared in five World Series during his 13-year career. The future Hall of Famer was an excellent all-around ballplayer.*

Charles "Gabby" Hartnett had already been a star in the previous decade. His catching and managerial skills led the Cubs to four flags during the thirties. Late in the 1938 season, he hit the famous home run, called the "homer in the gloamin'" that defeated the Pirates and pushed the Cubs to the top. Hartnett hit .303 and slugged .492 for the decade.

Josh Gibson was known as "the Babe Ruth of the Negro League." Next to Satchel Paige, the barrel-chested catcher who generated tremendous batting power with little apparent effort was the biggest attraction in black baseball. He began playing professionally at 18 with the Homestead Grays in 1930, and he also starred for the Pittsburgh Crawfords as Paige's battery mate. A brain tumor led to his untimely death at the age of 35.

Ernie Lombardi was a big, muscular guy, with a banana nose, an easy-going manner and feet of pure lead. His lack of foot speed was legendary. Infielders played shallow on the grass in the outfield and could still throw him out.

Nevertheless, Lombardi was one of baseball's greatest hitting catchers. He led the league in batting twice. He was voted MVP in 1938 as he hit .342. His decade average was .315 with five stolen bases.

Rick Ferrell, known primarily for catching four knuckleball pitchers with Washington in the forties, was on the receiving end of brother Wes to form one of baseball's best sibling batteries. He hit a respectable .292 for the decade.

Al Lopez was elected to the Hall of Fame for his managerial ability as much as for his ballplaying talent. Both were superb. As a catcher his record for most games caught was finally broken in 1987 by Bob Boone.

The 1930s dream team catcher and alternate are **Bill Dickey** and Mickey Cochrane. During the decade writers and fans argued over who was better, Dickey or Cochrane, unaware that seven future Hall of Famers would be catching the decade. The writers never considered anyone else in their class; neither does the dream team.

Bill Dickey, number one choice, was unquestionably one of the game's greatest receivers. An expert handler of pitchers and the owner of a deadly accurate throwing arm, the rangy Yankee backstop was a durable and tireless worker. He set a record by catching 100 or more games 13 years in a row. Dickey also excelled at the plate, batting over .300 in 10 of his first 11 seasons while hitting 202 homers during his career. He played in 38 World Series games.

Mickey Cochrane, runner-up selection, batted .324 for the decade and excelled behind the plate, but he also possessed that special trait – a fierce, competitive spirit – that gave him exceptional leadership qualities. "Black Mike" was the spark of the Athletics' championship teams of 1929, 1930 and 1931, and as player manager he later directed the Detroit Tigers to two league pennants and a World Series title. A beaning in 1937 ended his playing career.

# FIRST BASE

By the 1930s first base had completed the transition from a fielding and contact hitting position to a true power position. Hitting became more important for first basemen than fielding, and first base mitts became quite large.

There were eight first basemen of the decade who were qualified for the dream team; all of them put together tremendous statistics. They were Zeke Bonura of the White Sox, Senators and Giants; Hank Greenberg of the Tigers; Bill Terry of the Giants; Hal Trosky of the Indians; Ripper Collins of the Cardinals; Buck Leonard of the Pittsburgh Crawfords; Jimmie Foxx of the Athletics and Red Sox; and Lou Gehrig of the Yankees.

Zeke Bonura's .312 batting average with a .503 slugging percentage ranked him, believe it or not, near the bottom of the decade's first basemen. He was known for lack of fielding mobility, though statistics show that he caught most everything that came his way.

Hank Greenberg ripped American League hurlers for 206 home runs and 853 RBI in only 822 games during the decade. He made a run at Ruth's home run record, hitting 58 in 1938. With all of his four-baggers he compiled a .617 slugging percentage that was only third best among the decade's first basemen – and third best among the decade's hitters.

Bill Terry, the NL's last .400 hitter, averaged .351 for the period. As manager of the Giants, he led his team into the World Series in 1933, 1936 and 1937. Terry's .510 slugging average was only fifth best among the decade's first basemen.

Hal Trosky put together a fantasy season in 1936 with 45 doubles, 42 home runs, 162 RBI and a batting average of .343. But his accomplishments were dwarfed by all the talent in the AL that year; he finished in tenth place for the Most Valuable Player Award.

James "Ripper" Collins was the top home run hitting NL first baseman during the thirties. He led the league with 35 homers in 1934 as he batted .333 and knocked in 128 runs.

Buck Leonard was the slugger of the Homestead Grays when the team won the Negro League pennant nine times in a

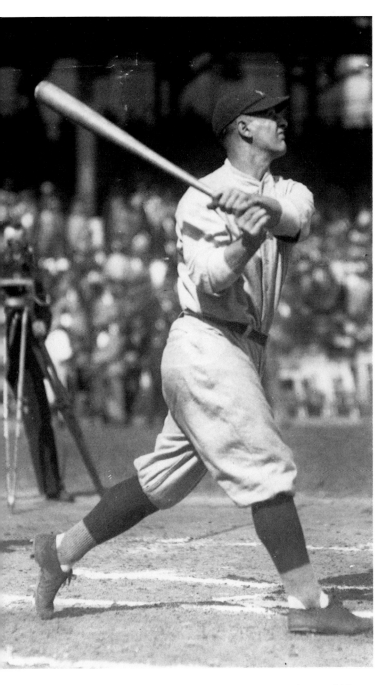

Far left: *Jimmie Foxx belts out his first hit of the 1935 season in a practice game against the New York Giants. Dream team first baseman of the thirties, "The Beast" won the American League MVP Award three times – in 1932, 1933 and 1938. In 1933 Foxx also achieved the Triple Crown, leading the league in batting average (.356), RBI (163) and home runs (48).*

Left: *Yankee Lou Gehrig hits a long ball. During the Iron Horse's brilliant, 17-year career, he led his league in many offensive categories, winning two MVP Awards and winning the Triple Crown in 1934. Gehrig is the dream team first baseman alternate.*

Below: *Lou Gehrig crosses the plate after belting a solo home run in game four of the 1937 World Series. The future' Hall of Famer's 35 RBI and .731 slugging average both rate third on all-time World Series lists.*

row (1937-1945). In any decade but the 1930s, he could have been a dream team starter. Leonard teamed with Josh Gibson to form the Ruth-Gehrig hitting tandem of Negro League baseball. Leonard consistently ranked among the leaders in home runs and batting average, winning the Negro League batting title, with .391, in 1948.

The first base spot for the 1930s dream team goes to **Jimmie Foxx** with Lou Gehrig as alternate. The two players put together the second and third greatest decades of all time, by any player. Only Babe Ruth's 1920s decade was better.

Jimmie Foxx was one of baseball's all-time best power hitters. During the decade of the thirties, he scored 1244 runs, drove in 1403, hit 316 doubles and 415 homers, and drew 1015 bases on balls. He hit .335 and slugged .651 with an on-base percentage of .429.

He belted 534 home runs over 20 seasons, hitting 30 or more a record 12 years in a row. "Double-X" walloped 58 for the A's in 1932, only to miss Ruth's mark when rained out games erased two others. He won the Triple Crown the following year when he repeated as MVP. He had a 50-homer season with the

Red Sox in 1938, but Greenberg's 58 round-trippers cost Foxx a second Triple Crown. Foxx's 175 RBI in 1938 is the fourth-highest single-season total in major league baseball history. His 438 total bases in 1932 is fifth highest on the all-time single-season leaders list.

Lou Gehrig played an amazing 2130 consecutive games. During the thirties, the Iron Horse scored 1257 runs, had 1358 RBI, ripped 328 doubles, 91 triples and 347 home runs, walked 1028 times, and even stole 72 bases. Gehrig actually put up these numbers in nine years.

A product of Columbia University, the big first baseman teamed with Babe Ruth to form the greatest one-two punch in baseball history. The "Iron Horse" drove in 100 runs 13 seasons in a row, and he topped 150 RBI on seven occasions. Gehrig's 184 RBI for 1931 is the second-highest total in baseball and is still the AL record. The following year he became the first twentieth-century player to hit home runs in four consecutive at-bats. His 167 runs scored in 1936 is the fourth-highest single-season total in baseball history. His consecutive games streak is considered an untouchable record.

Left: *Charlie Gehringer demonstrates his fielding style. First choice for dream team second baseman of the thirties, "The Mechanical Man" played for Detroit his entire 19-year career, leading the league in many offensive categories along the way. In 1937, the year he batted a career-high .371, he won the AL MVP Award.*

Above: *Detroit's stellar second baseman, Charlie Gehringer, was elected to the Hall of Fame in 1949.*

Right: *Tony "Poosh 'Em Up" Lazzeri warms up before a game. Alternate dream team second baseman for the decade, Lazzeri was a consistent RBI man and a clutch hitter.*

Overleaf: *Red Rolfe scores for the Yankees during the 1939 World Series.*

## SECOND BASE

The keystone sack was a sparkplug position in the thirties. Teams such as the Washington Senators, St. Louis Cardinals, New York Yankees, Chicago Cubs and Detroit Tigers, who had good-hitting, good-fielding second basemen, won pennants.

Dream team candidates include all-time favorite Charlie Gehringer of the Tigers, Tony Lazzeri of the Yankees, and the Cubs' star Billy Herman, all of whom are in the Hall of Fame, and Buddy Myer of the Senators.

As second baseman with the pennant-winning Cubs of the 1930s, Billy Herman was in a fielding class by himself. He still holds NL fielding records for leading the league in putouts seven times (five times during the thirties), most years with 900 or more chances (again, five times during the thirties), and most putouts in a single game with 11. Herman was no slouch at the plate either. He hit .312 for the decade, but Tony Lazzeri knocked in more runs in fewer games.

Buddy Myer won the AL batting title in 1935. He played in the 1925 and 1933 World Series with the Senators, and hit over .300 six times during the 1930s. Myer was a well respected gloveman, but not a star like Charlie Gehringer.

Quietly and efficiently, **Charlie Gehringer**, the overwhelming choice for dream team second baseman, played out his career with aplomb both in the field and at the plate. His batting swing was the envy of his peers, and he was so smooth in the field that he made even spectacular plays look routine. Gehringer led the second basemen of the decade in games played, runs, hits, RBI, doubles, home runs, batting average, on-base percentage, slugging percentage, stolen bases and bases on balls. His 1865 hits and 400 doubles topped all hitters during the 1930s. His five consecutive seasons with 200 or more hits are still an AL record. Gehringer's 60 doubles, in 1936, constitute the sixth-most on the all-time single-season record list. He led the AL in 1937 when his .371 batting average earned him the Most Valuable Player Award.

Tony Lazzeri, the alternate for second base, was a top slugger, with 787 RBI for the decade. He frequently batted in the fifth position in the powerful Yankee lineup. He drove in 267 more runs than did Billy Herman in 500 fewer at-bats. Lazzeri knocked in over 100 runs seven times in his career, with a high of 121 in 1930. Although not known as a home run hitter, he hit a grand slam in the 1936 World Series. Lazzeri hit .400 and slugged .733 in the 1937 Series against the Giants. Traded to the Cubs in 1938, the quiet Italian faced his former teammates in the Fall Classic that year.

Despite being handicapped with epilepsy, Lazzeri played 12 straight seasons as a New York Yankee regular. He bridged the gap between the Yankee dynasties of the Murderers Row (1926-1928) and the Bronx Bombers (1936-1939).

## THIRD BASE

The powerhouse slugging of the 1930s made the slick-fielding third baseman a relic of an earlier era. The "Hot Corner" was a position in need of adjustment. Some who played third were hitters and some were fielders, but only the aging Pie Traynor combined both talents, and he played too few games in the decade to qualify for the dream team.

The dream team candidates for third baseman are Stan Hack of the Cubs; Joe Stripp of the Reds, Dodgers, Cardinals and Braves; Red Rolfe of the New Yankees; Marv Owen of the Detroit Tigers; and Judy Johnson of the Negro Leagues.

"Jersey Joe" Stripp hit .298 as he led the decade's third base candidates in hits and doubles. He scored a career-high 94 runs with Brooklyn in 1932.

Marv Owen precipitated the decade's most notorious incident when he rammed the ball into Joe Medwick's throat as the Cardinals' left fielder slid, spikes high, into third with a triple during the seventh game of the 1934 World Series. When the Cardinals finished their inning and Medwick appeared in the outfield, fans began to throw fruit at him. The fans caused such a ruckus that play was interrupted until Commissioner Landis removed Medwick from the game.

Owen had a decent batting average, .276, but it was much lower than the averages of his peers.

"Smiling Stan" Hack played on four Cub pennant-winning teams, and hit .348 for the four World Series, but the Cubs lost all four. A lifetime .301 hitter, Hack's average was .300 during the thirties. He stole 100 bases, making him fourth-best among the decade's base thieves. He also drew 466 walks and scored 600 runs during the decade. Hack seldom hit with much power, but he was consistent.

**Judy Johnson**, the dream team top choice, was considered the Negro Leagues' best third baseman of the 1920s and 1930s. An outstanding fielder and a fine clutch hitter, he was a thoughtful student of the game who played with grace and poise. Johnson exerted a steadying influence on his teammates. He was a consistent .300 hitter who led the Hilldale team to three flags in a row prior to starring for the Homestead Grays and the Pittsburgh Crawfords.

Red Rolfe, the dream team alternate, scored 692 runs in only 800 games as he led the league in runs, hits and doubles in 1939. Rolfe led dream team candidates in runs, home runs, on-base percentage and slugging average. He batted over .300 four times, helping the Yankees win six pennants.

A left-handed batter, Rolfe could slice a hit to the opposite field, hit behind the runner or put down a perfect bunt. Noted for his ability in clutch situations, Rolfe hit .300 in four of six World Series. In the 1936 Fall Classic, he hit 10 singles and averaged near .400.

Left: *William "Judy" Johnson, dream team third baseman of the decade, is poised in the hot corner for action. Johnson played in the Negro Leagues from 1921 to 1938, batting around .300 for the Pittsburgh Crawfords in the thirties. He then retired to manage the Homestead Grays.*

Below left: *Alternate dream team third baseman, Red Rolfe slides safely into second base during 1937 World Series action. Rolfe played in six World Series*

*during his ten years with the Yankees. His best year at the plate was 1939, when he led the league in hits (213), doubles (46) and runs (139).*

Below: *Joe Cronin at the plate. Runaway choice for dream team shortstop of the thirties, Cronin began the decade with Washington as the American League's Most Valuable Player. He was traded to the Red Sox in 1934 for Lyn Lary and $225,000, and played out the rest of his 20-year-long, Hall of Fame career with Boston.*

# SHORTSTOP

During the 1930s shortstop advanced from the fielding position of the 1920s to a position of significant offense. Managers wanted players who could do more than field. The shortstops of the decade had strong batting statistics.

The four candidates for dream team shortstop include three Hall of Fame members: Joe Cronin of the Senators and Red Sox, Arky Vaughan of the Pirates, and Luke Appling of the White Sox. Dick Bartell, of the Pirates, Phillies, Giants and Cubs, is also a contender.

A remarkably steady shortstop, Luke Appling also had an uncanny batter's eye. He spent his entire 20-year career with the White Sox, and his average dipped below .300 in only four seasons. While setting fielding records for a shortstop, he was compiling a .311 decade batting average. Appling's ability to foul off pitches he didn't particularly like became his trademark at the plate. He was known as "Old Aches and Pains" because of his imaginary ailments.

"Rowdy Richard" Bartell was a pepperpot who usually batted first or second in the lineup. He hit over .300 four times in the 1930s. In 1933 he tied a record with four doubles in one game. Bartell was at the top of his game in 1936 and 1937. In the former year he hit .298 for the Giants and led all shortstops in assists, double plays and total chances per game. His teammate, Carl Hubbell, was the MVP with 26 victories, but Bartell played every day and may have had more total value.

Above: *Arky Vaughan bangs one the opposite way. Dream team alternate shortstop, Vaughan played for Pittsburgh from 1932 through 1941, and finished his career with four years in Brooklyn. A threat at the plate and solid in the field, Vaughan was elected to the Hall of Fame in 1985.*

Right: *"Bucketfoot Al" Simmons follows through at the plate. Dream team left fielder of the thirties, Al Simmons played for seven clubs during his 20-year career, ending up with a .334 batting average. After participating in four World Series contests, Simmons' .658 slugging average places him fourth on the all-time list.*

**Joe Cronin**, the runaway choice for dream team shortstop, played that position as the AL's All-Star seven times. He was the league's MVP in 1930 when he hit .346 with 126 RBI. The jovial, square-jawed Irishman possessed the determination and toughness to become a wizard with the glove and a powerhouse at bat. He led 1930s shortstops in games played, runs scored, hits, RBI, doubles, home runs, slugging average and bases on balls. His 1036 runs driven in was one of the decade's highest marks. Cronin won a pennant in 1933 as a rookie manager at Washington. Clark Griffith, who was both Cronin's owner and father-in-law, traded him to the Red Sox for Lyn Lary and a quarter of a million dollars – a fantastic amount in the depth of the Depression.

Arky Vaughan was selected as alternate. Among Hall of Fame shortstops, his .318 lifetime batting average (.328 during the thirties) is second only to Honus Wagner's .329. In 1935 Vaughan hit a league-leading .385 for the Pirates, a mark since unequalled by any NL performer. Vaughan led the decade shortstops in triples, batting average and on-base percentage, and he was only one point under Cronin's .476 slugging percentage.

Though not a power hitter, Vaughan hit 19 homers one season and led the league in triples three years. He homered twice in the 1941 All-Star game, the first player to do so.

# LEFT FIELD

Managers fighting for pennants realized that it was necessary to have good defense in left and right fields. The successful teams during the thirties loaded up on sluggers and put them in the left- and right-field positions. Over the years, power hitters instead of fielding specialists tended to be inducted into the Hall of Fame. The dream team candidates were chosen from the elite of Cooperstown.

The four candidates were outstanding hitters for their teams: Heinie Manush of the Browns, Senators, Red Sox, Dodgers and Pirates; Goose Goslin of the Browns, Senators and Tigers; Al Simmons of the Athletics and White Sox; and Joe Medwick of the Cardinals.

Heinie Manush ranked consistently among the game's top hitters for more than a decade. The slashing flyhawk hit .323

for the thirties. Having won the 1926 batting title on the last day of the season, Manush missed the 1928 batting title by one point and was runner-up to Jimmie Foxx in 1932.

A pure hitter, Manush batted over .333 five times during the 1930s, and nine times in a 17-year career. His big bat drove the Senators to the pennant in 1933 when he led the league in hits and triples.

Goose Goslin was a great clutch hitter whose powerful bat figured in three consecutive pennants for two different teams from 1933 to 1935. He was the dream team left fielder of the twenties. Though time had slowed Goslin, the big powerful slugger still batted .301 and slugged .507 for the decade. He drove in 100 or more runs in six of the first seven years of the decade.

As good as Manush and Goslin were, and they were very good, Simmons and Medwick were even better during the 1930s.

Dream team first choice **Al Simmons** went from a rookie with a unique, foot-in-the-bucket stance to become one of the hardest hitting outfielders ever to play the game. He led three other Hall of Famers in runs scored, hits, RBI, triples and home runs. His .325 batting average, .372 on-base percentage and .539 slugging percentage are the second highest for left fielders during the decade. He won AL batting titles in 1930 and 1931, and was voted MVP by *The Sporting News*. He experienced 11 consecutive seasons as a .300 hitter and 100-RBI man. His 253-hit total in 1925 is the fourth-highest all-time for a single season.

The dream team alternate left fielder, Joe Medwick was a notorious bad ball hitter whose competitive spirit typified the rowdy Gas House Gang Cardinals of the 1930s. He batted .337 and slugged .552 for the decade, both top marks for left fielders. Nicknamed "Ducky Wucky" in the minors because of his distinctive, waddling run, Medwick hit 353 doubles — the fourth-highest for all players during the decade. His 1937 season was one of the greatest offensive seasons in NL history. Medwick won the MVP Award and the Triple Crown as he led the loop in 12 departments. Ducky Joe's total of 64 doubles in 1936 is second on the all-time single-season record list. He was traded to the Dodgers in 1940.

# CENTER FIELD

Center field, during this era, resembled golf courses more than ballparks. Distances to some of the major league center-field fences were 468 feet (593 feet to the right-center corner) in Fenway Park, 520 feet (550 feet to the right-center corner) at Braves Field, 515 feet in Shibe Park, 505 feet in the Polo Grounds, 490 feet at Yankee Stadium, and 477 feet to the right-center corner in Ebbets Field. The decade's center fielders had to have fast feet and strong arms. While the position sported several good players such as Terry Moore of the Cardinals and JoJo White of the Tigers, few were able to sustain 10 years of covering the center-field garden.

The candidates for the dream team featured Ben Chapman of the Yankees, Senators, Red Sox and Indians; Hall of Famers Earl Averill of the Indians; and "Cool Papa" Bell of the Negro Leagues. The graceful Joe DiMaggio played only four seasons and fewer than 600 games in the 1930s, and therefore could not be considered.

Ben Chapman was extremely fast. He scored 1009 runs and stole 269 bases, leading the league four times during the decade. Sure-handed as well, Chapman led the AL in assists twice and in double plays once. He left baseball as manager of the Phillies under a cloud of racism when his relentless taunting of Jackie Robinson was not accepted as "just part of the game." Chapman was a good ballplayer, but he was not as good a hitter as Earl Averill, nor as fast a runner as "Cool Papa" Bell.

**Earl Averill,** dream team center fielder, had incredible power for his size — five feet, nine-and-a-half inches and 170 pounds. He joined the Indians in 1929 at the age of 26 after three explosive seasons in the Pacific Coast League, and homered in his first major league at-bat. Averill hit .331 that season, and the following year came within inches of connecting for four home runs in one game. In the 1930s he scored 1102 runs, drove in 1046, ripped 354 doubles, sped to 114 triples, hit 218 home runs, and had an OBA of .393 and a slugging percentage of .537, leading all other center fielders. Averill occupied the gap left by Cleveland's retired legend, Tris Speaker, and adequately filled his shoes.

Left: *Dream team center fielder Earl Averill combined speed and power during his 13-year career. He was elected to the Hall of Fame in 1975.*

Below: *James "Cool Papa" Bell (left), alternate dream team center fielder, in the dugout with manager Jim Taylor. On the basis of his stellar 29-year career, Bell was elected to the Hall of Fame in 1974.*

Left: *Mel Ott, dream team right fielder for the decade, played for the Giants his entire 22-year career. Master Melvin, with his unorthodox but effective batting style, led the Giants to three pennants during the thirties.*

Above: *Chuck Klein receives the 1932 National League MVP trophy. This dream team alternate right fielder followed his MVP year with a Triple Crown in 1933, batting .368 with 28 round-trippers and 120 RBI.*

James "Cool Papa" Bell, the alternate, combined speed, daring and batting skill to rank among the best players ever in the Negro Leagues. His contemporaries rated him the fastest man, especially from first to third, on the basepaths. The switch-hitting center fielder played for the St. Louis Stars, the Pittsburgh Crawfords, the Homestead Grays and the Kansas City Monarchs between 1922 and 1950. Twenty-one of those years he also competed in winter ball. His calm before big crowds and his general outlook on life resulted in his nickname – "Cool Papa."

# RIGHT FIELD

The contest for this position was a two-man horse race, with Kiki Cuyler of the Cubs, Reds and Dodgers finishing a distant third. Giants star **Mel Ott** crushed 308 home runs and slugged .560 for the decade to become dream team right fielder. Phillies' slugger Chuck Klein's 238 home runs and .551 slugging percentage placed him behind Ott as the decade's alternate.

Kiki Cuyler was one of the NL's outstanding outfielders of the era. A fine hitter, fielder, thrower and baserunner, he batted .313 for the decade. In 1930 he scored 155 runs, stole 37 bases, and made 228 hits for a .355 batting average. His 42 doubles was league high in 1934. He slugged .611 for the Cubs in the 1932 World Series.

Mel Ott was a New York Giants' hero for 22 seasons, during which he emerged as one of the game's leading sluggers. As a 16-year-old Boy Wonder in 1925, his size (five-foot-nine, 165 pounds) belied his power. Using an unorthodox batting style in which he lifted his right foot prior to impact, he smashed 511 home runs (at the time a NL record), 308 of them during the 1930s. He led the NL in home runs in 1932, 1934, 1936, 1937 and 1938. He scored 1095 runs, drove in 1135 and walked 956 times during the decade.

Feared at the plate, Ott drew five walks in a game on four occasions. He drew 100 or more bases on balls for seven consecutive years. The homers and walks combined to make Ott a tremendous offensive player. His on-base percentage of .417 and slugging percentage of .560 led other right fielders. His slugging led the Giants to three pennants during the thirties.

Chuck Klein was a powerful hitter who finished with a .325 decade average and 238 homers. His 1930 season with the Phillies is remembered as one of the most remarkable for an individual. He hit .386 with 40 home runs and 170 RBIs, yet failed to lead the league in any of the three categories. Klein was the NL MVP in 1932, and the Triple Crown winner the following season. His 250-hit mark in 1930 is fifth on the all-time single-season record list. He still holds the major league record for assists by an outfielder, with 44 in 1930.

LEFT FIELD

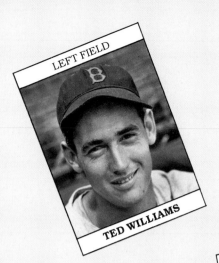

**TED WILLIAMS**

CENTER FIELD

**JOE DIMAGGIO**

SHORTSTOP

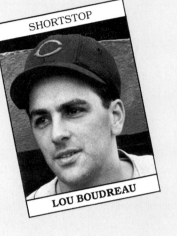

**LOU BOUDREAU**

SECOND BASE

**BOBBY DOERR**

THIRD BASE

**BOB ELIOT**

PITCHER (LH)

**HAL NEWHOUSER**

PITCHER (RH)

**BOB FELLER**

CATCHER

**WALKER COOPER**

RIGHT FIELD

ENOS SLAUGHTER

FIRST BASE

JOHNNY MIZE

# THE GREATEST PLAYERS
# OF THE
# FORTIES

## ALTERNATE DREAM TEAM

| | | | |
|---|---|---|---|
| **Pitcher** | Morton Cooper (rh) Harry Breechen (lh) | **Third Baseman** | Stan Hack |
| | | **Shortstop** | Vern Stephens |
| | | **Left Fielder** | Stan Musial |
| **Catcher** | Josh Gibson | **Center Fielder** | Augie Galan |
| **First Baseman** | Rudy York | **Right Fielder** | Mel Ott |
| **Second Baseman** | Joe Gordon | | |

## HONORABLE MENTION

| | | | |
|---|---|---|---|
| **Pitcher** | Spud Chandler Dizzy Trout | **Shortstop** | Pee Wee Reese Luke Appling Phil Rizzuto Marty Marion Johnny Pesky |
| **Catcher** | Buddy Rosar | | |
| **First Baseman** | Mickey Vernon Phil Cavaretta | | |
| | | **Left Fielder** | None |
| **Second Baseman** | Billy Herman Eddie Stanky | **Center Fielder** | George Case |
| **Third Baseman** | George Kell Ken Keltner | **Right Fielder** | Tommy Holmes |

# THE SETTING

War. Japanese kamikaze infantry charged American trenches, yelling, "To Hell with Babe Ruth!" English-speaking Nazi soldiers dressed in American uniforms infiltrated the Allied Forces and caused great confusion during the Battle of the Bulge, until counter-espionage agents trapped the clever Germans with questions like "Who won the 1938 World Series?" or "Who led the National League in batting in 1942?"

While the political face of the globe changed almost daily, baseball became conservative and static during the 1940s. Only the St. Louis Browns tried to adapt to the war and player shortage by searching for the draft records of 4-F ballplayers. While the Browns stockpiled players who could not be drafted, unprepared managers filled their positions as best they could.

The St. Louis Cardinals brought 40-year-old Pepper Martin out of retirement. Baseball veterans such as Johnny Cooney, Jimmie Foxx and Paul Waner hung on as bit players. Teenagers Carl Scheib and Joe Nuxhall pitched for the Athletics and the Reds.

Baseball was much more than recreation for the home front during World War II. It did its part to preserve the sanity of the nation, but it also contributed flesh and blood – the young men who played the game – to the war effort. Figures published in the *New York Times* in January of 1945 estimated that of the 5800 players in organized baseball on December 7, 1941, 5400 were serving in the military.

These ballplayers were highly sought-after for armed services baseball teams, and many of them – from different major league teams and different leagues – met and became friendly with each other for the first time. This co-mingling of players from all teams had a profound effect on the players' union movement and pension plans of later years.

After the war baseball drifted, feeling that great changes were imminent, but not quite knowing what to do. All this is not to say that wartime baseball had no colorful personalities, no dramatic pennant races and no great performances. It had all three.

# GAME STRATEGY

Strategy was dictated by the quality of players. The prevailing tactic for offense was to wait for the right pitch and uppercut it. As batters waited for their pitches they discovered that they could draw walks. Offense in the forties was characterized by home runs and bases on balls.

New strategic initiatives dominated defense. Relief specialists like Johnny Murphy, Hugh Casey and Joe Page contributed to the history of the fireman's position. Johnny Murphy of the Yankees appeared in games from 1935 to 1943, and was consistently good. He rarely started, and was seldom used in a mop-up role, thus he could be called the first "relief ace."

Hugh Casey of the Dodgers was a big man who liked to throw smoke. His reliever's profile became the prototype for the Red Sox's Dick Radatz and the Yankees' Goose Gossage.

Joe Page, under Yankee manager Casey Stengel's guidance in 1949, proved that a relief pitcher could make a valuable contribution. He saved 27 games and won 13 in relief. Page was used day after day, in key situations, making him the first modern reliever.

# FACTORS INFLUENCING PLAYER PERFORMANCE

Influential factors included regular scheduling of night games, the modification of baseball bats and changes in the rules pertaining to catchers' and batters' interference in plays.

Night baseball became the norm during the wartime era. The result was that more people watched baseball than ever before. Increasing attendance meant more money for the owners. Players witnessed the growing popularity of the national pastime, and wanted to share in the prosperity the game was bringing its management.

In the 1940 rulebook a new regulation stated that baseball bats had to be made from one solid piece of wood. The fact that this rule appeared implies that there had been some issue raised about loaded bats.

The manpower shortage caused teams to become conscientious about players' health and well-being. More squads began to employ full-time trainers to keep their players active and on the field.

As could be expected, baseball rules changed very little during this decade. In addition to the ruling on bats described above, there was a rule that set curfews for night games. The rule change with the most effect on player performance was the one that further defined catcher's interference and batter's interference with the catcher making a play. Formerly, catchers had tipped bats while hitters swung, and batters interfered regularly with catcher's throws on stolen base attempts.

# THE POSITIONS

## PITCHER

Bob Feller and Hal Newhouser — both Hall of Fame members — were undeniably the two top pitchers of the 1940s. The dream team quest then, became a search for back-up hurlers.

Qualified right-handed pitchers were Spud Chandler of the Yankees, Dizzy Trout of the Tigers, Bob Feller of the Indians, and Morton Cooper of the Cardinals.

While producing the decade's top won-lost percentage, .685, Spud Chandler won only 83 games in a career shortened by arm trouble. He was the Yankee ace in 1942, 1943 and 1946, winning 56 games and losing only 17 for those seasons.

Dizzy Trout won more than 20 games in 1943 and 1944 as he teamed with Hal Newhouser to give the Tigers the hottest one-two punch of the forties. In 1943 Trout led the league in games won with 20, and shutouts with 5. He hit his stride in 1944 as he surpassed all loop hurlers in complete games (33), shutouts (7), innings pitched (352) and ERA (2.12). Trout and Newhouser dominated the league during the war years, but the Tigers took only one pennant all that time.

**Bob Feller** is, of course, the shoo-in for dream team right-hander. Feller and his blazing fastball set standards against which all of his successors have been judged. He fanned 17 in a game as a Cleveland rookie, then hiked the whiff mark to 18. Feller's 348 strikeouts filled the stands in 1946.

Feller won 20 or more games four times in the 1940s, capturing 137 victories in six years. He led the league in wins six times in his career, four of those in the forties. Feller's four-year stint in the Navy prevented him from reaching the coveted 300-win mark for pitchers, but he put together three no-hitters, including one on opening day of 1946, and a record 12 one-hitters.

Morton Cooper was selected as dream team alternate. He was the ace of the St. Louis Cardinals' staff who pitched in three straight World Series, winning two of them. Cooper won 114 games during the decade, climaxing with a 65-22 record in the Cards' pennant-winning years from 1942 to 1944.

Morton and his brother Walker formed one of baseball's best known and best liked batteries. From a close-knit family, Mort courageously pitched and won the most difficult game of his career in the 1943 World Series, the day after his father died.

Left-handed candidates for the 1940s dream team featured number one choice **Hal Newhouser** of the Tigers, and alternate Harry Breechen of the Cardinals. Close scrutiny of the literature revealed no additional portsider who won as many as 90 games during the decade.

Hal Newhouser was wrongly stigmatized as a wartime phenomenon; he was actually the best AL left-hander in the 1940s. Other stars played some or all of the war years without having their records denigrated. But Newhouser was so dominant in 1944-1945 that it was forgotten he had two other 20-game seasons and that he won 170 games during the decade.

In 1944 he overcame the wildness that had plagued him in his first seasons with the Tigers. Newhouser was AL MVP for

*Bob Feller warms up. The no-contest choice for dream team right-hander of the forties, "Rapid Robert" pitched his magic for Cleveland his entire 18-year career. Though he lost four years of his prime to military service, Feller's decade statistics are still extraordinary — he led his league in strikeouts five of the seven years he pitched in the forties.*

Left: *Bob Feller whiffs Joe DiMaggio on his way to attaining a no-hitter against the Yankees on April 30, 1946.*

Above: *Hal Newhouser warms up. Dream team southpaw for the decade, Prince Hal led his league four times in wins, twice in ERA, twice in strikeouts and once in shutouts. Newhouser's .735 winning percentage and 1.81 ERA in 1945 helped him take his second consecutive MVP Award.*

Above right: *Alternate dream team right-hander Mort Cooper. The Cardinals' ace for the first half of the decade, Cooper won the National League MVP in 1942 for his league-leading 22 wins and 1.78 ERA.*

his 29-9 record and 2.22 ERA. The next year he was 25-9 and led the AL in shutouts with eight, and in ERA with 1.81. The Tigers won the pennant in 1945, and Newhouser won two more games in the World Series against the Cubs. In both 1944 and 1945 he led the AL in strikeouts.

All the top players returned in 1946, but Newhouser sailed on. He had the most wins of any pitcher at 26-9 and again led the league in ERA with 1.94. He had his greatest strikeout year with 275, but finished second to Bob Feller's 348. Newhouser was the top AL winner in 1948 with 21.

Harry "the Cat" Brecheen was the Cardinal pitcher of record when Enos Slaughter raced home from first to beat the Red Sox in the seventh game of the 1946 World Series. It gave Brecheen his third win of the Series, making him the first man to notch three since Stan Coveleski had accomplished the feat 26 years earlier. Brecheen remained the only left-hander to hold that record for 22 years.

In 1948 Brecheen posted a 20-7 mark and the NL's lowest ERA. He won 14 games or more six years in a row for the Cardinals, and pitched in three World Series, winning four games and losing one. After 11 seasons with the proud Cardinals, Brecheen migrated to the humble Browns and discovered the basis for their humility. His record was 5-13 despite a decent 3.07 ERA. The next year the Browns organization moved to Baltimore, and Brecheen became their pitching coach.

Nicknamed "the Cat" for the way he would pounce off the mound to field his position, Harry's World Series ERA of 0.83 is the second-best ever.

87

## CATCHER

Selection of the 1940s dream team catcher was made from Buddy Rosar of the Yankees, Indians and Athletics; Walker Cooper of the Cardinals, Giants and Reds; and Negro League great and Hall of Fame member Josh Gibson. Bill Dickey and Ernie Lombardi, who played less than half of the decade, were not considered.

Buddy Rosar played in two World Series as a back-up catcher to the Yankees' Bill Dickey. A bit-player who blossomed to start for six years, Rosar was not an outstanding hitter, but got the job done, as his .261 decade average indicates.

Lon Warneke, who pitched to Walker Cooper, pitched against him and umpired behind him, judged him to be a better catcher than Bill Dickey or Gabby Hartnett. Warneke's opinion aside, the six-foot-three Cooper did give the Cardinals, Giants, Braves and nearly every other team in the NL solid catching for years. He hit .300 four times and ended the decade with a .287 average. In three World Series, Cooper averaged .300, and his team won two of them. When he got too old

to do the job behind the plate, he remained as an effective pinch hitter.

The Giants wanted Cooper so badly in 1946 that they paid the Cardinals $175,000 for him while he was still in the Navy. In 1947 he hit a career-high 35 home runs for New York. Not as good as Dickey or Hartnett, but better than most, **Walker Cooper** was chosen for the 1940s dream team.

Josh Gibson, alternate choice for catcher, was a tremendous gate attraction for the Homestead Grays during the forties. He was known for his home run power, once hitting as many as 72 in a season.

In the beginning, the six-foot-one, 215-pound Gibson was a crude catcher, and did not learn the finer points of the position until he played winter ball.

Homestead teammates referred to him as "Boxer" because they said he caught foul pops as though he were wearing boxing gloves. Gibson mastered his craft eventually, handling every type of pitch from the spitter to the shineball.

At Pittsburgh with the Crawfords, Gibson's battery mate was Satchel Paige. The Crawfords regularly advertised that in the next game, Satch would strike out the first nine batters,

Left: *A gifted catcher and solid at the plate, Walker Cooper batted .287 for the decade. Dream team catcher of the forties, Cooper helped the Cardinals to the World Series three times.*

and Josh would clout a home run.

By 1946 Josh's career was on the decline, although he still batted .331 and led the Negro National League in homers. His weight had ballooned to 230 pounds, and he had started to drink heavily. Friends detected a personality change.

One morning in January 1947, Gibson complained of a headache. A doctor was summoned, but Gibson fell into a sleep from which he never awakened. A brain tumor was listed as cause of death. He was 35.

Opposite: *Cardinal pitcher Harry Brecheen (second from left) poses with other heroes of game seven of the 1946 World Series (left to right): Enos Slaughter, Eddie Dyer (manager) and Harry Walker. In the close series, dream team alternate lefty Brecheen pitched his way to three victories.*

Top and above: *Alternate dream team catcher Josh Gibson, pictured in the forties when he played for the Homestead Grays, was known as the black Babe Ruth. Gibson was elected to the Hall of Fame in 1972.*

# FIRST BASE

The best first basemen of the 1940s included Mickey Vernon of the Senators and Indians, Phil Cavaretta of the Cubs, Johnny Mize of the Cardinals and Giants, and Rudy York of the Tigers.

Mickey Vernon was a standard .283 hitter with little power. He led the AL in batting and doubles in 1946. He had only 61 home runs for the decade, but lack of power was not his only problem. He led the league in errors on four occasions. Vernon, though he won another batting title in 1953 with a .337 average, was not a fielder or hitter in the class of Johnny Mize or Rudy York.

Phil Cavaretta was a long-time Cub favorite. His .301 decade average included the 1945 NL batting crown. In the previous year he had led the league in hits. Cavaretta's 53 home runs during the 1940s indicate that he had even less power than did Mickey Vernon.

**Johnny Mize**, dream team first choice, and Rudy York, the alternate selection, had power and plenty of it. Johnny "Big Cat" Mize, who out-hit Rudy York by 35 points and out-slugged him by 104 points, finished among the top three in various offensive categories a total of 54 times during his career.

The burly slugger who swung a left-handed stick led the NL in home runs four times, and hit three in a single game on six occasions. During the decade he belted 217 round-trippers, and had a .303 batting average with a .560 slugging percentage. At the conclusion of his career with the Yankees, he played in five straight World Series. "The Big Cat" displayed feline dexterity around first base.

Rudy York, a rookie catcher in 1937, smashed 18 home runs for Detroit in August alone, the record for one month. For the season he slugged 35 homers in only 375 at-bats.

In 1940 the Tigers were well-stocked with catchers and needed York's big bat in the lineup. They moved slugger Hank Greenberg to left field and installed York at first base. The change did nothing for the Tiger defense, but it gave them a pennant-winning offensive attack. Greenberg was named MVP; York hit 33 homers and drove in 134 runs, batting .316.

York led the AL in homers and RBIs in 1943, and helped the Tigers win another flag in 1945. Traded to the Red Sox in 1946, he found himself on yet another pennant-winner. In the forties, York hit 189 home runs and had 854 RBI.

Above: *Giant first baseman Johnny "The Big Cat" Mize takes a hard cut during a 1946 pre-season practice game against the Braves. Known for his quick reflexes on the field and his power at the plate, this dream team first sacker was elected to the Hall of Fame in 1981.*

Right: *Rudy York, alternate dream team catcher for the decade, played for Detroit for most of his career, then finished his last four years with the Red Sox, White Sox and A's. One of York's best seasons at the plate was 1943, when he slugged .527 with 118 RBI and 34 home runs.*

# SECOND BASE

The top second base performers included future Hall of Famer Billy Herman of the Cubs, Dodgers, Braves and Pirates; Eddie Stanky with the Cubs, Dodgers and Braves; future Hall of Famer Bobby Doerr of the Red Sox; and Joe Gordon of the Yankees and Indians.

Early in the 1941 season, Billy Herman was sent off to Brooklyn. "I just bought a pennant," Dodgers owner Larry MacPhail crowed. He was right. Herman and his new double

Below: *In 1946 World Series action, Red Sox second baseman Bobby Doerr avoids the hard-sliding Cardinal Enos Slaughter as he completes a double play in game three. Doerr went on to bat .409 for the Series. Dream team second baseman of the decade, Bobby Doerr's quiet leadership on the field and consistent bat at the plate were assets to the Red Sox.*

Right: *Heavy-hitting Yankees and Red Sox pose after a 1942 game. From left to right: Joe Gordon, Ted Williams, Bobby Doerr and Bill Dickey. Doerr is the decade's dream team second baseman, while Gordon, his Yankee counterpart, is the alternate. "Flash Gordon" won the American League MVP Award in 1942.*

play partner, young Pee Wee Reese, coordinated beautifully, and the Dodgers won their first flag in 21 years. Herman, an ageing veteran by the 1940s, still had enough pop in his bat to average .290 in 724 games for the decade.

Eddie "the Brat" Stanky coaxed and wheedled a NL record 148 bases on balls from fed-up hurlers. At five-feet-eight, 170 pounds, his patented crouch made his strike zone seem like he was even smaller. Stanky led the league three times in bases on balls, and twice in on-base percentage. In a short career, Stanky played on two NL pennant-winners – Boston in 1948 and New York in 1951. His high on-base percentage made him an ideal lead-off man.

The dream team second baseman for the 1940s is **Bobby Doerr**, who combined sharp fielding with solid hitting. The alternate was Doerr's greatest competitor during the decade, Joe Gordon.

Bobby Doerr was a consistent fielder, a top double play man, and a fine clutch hitter whom Ted Williams called "the silent captain of the Red Sox." Doerr hit .285 for the decade with 887 RBI and 164 home runs. He once held the AL record by handling 414 chances without an error. He led AL second basemen in double plays, putouts, assists and fielding average in 1943 and 1946.

An outstanding run producer, Doerr drove in 100 runs five times in the 1940s. His .528 slugging percentage led all 1944 American Leaguers. He consistently out-hit his number one rival, Joe Gordon, though Gordon played on more pennant-winning teams.

Joe Gordon or Bobby Doerr – who was best? The question raged during the forties. Gordon played in New York where he acquired the predictable nickname "Flash," but he lived up to the label with his acrobatic defensive style. He ranged over the Yankee infield, making plays that other second basemen only dream about. In one game he made 11 assists. He was at the head of AL second sackers in assists four times. The flip side of that record was that in getting to balls others could not reach, Gordon sometimes fumbled. He led or tied in errors four times, too. It was worth the price. In the first six years he cavorted at second base for the Yankees, they went to five World Series.

Gordon seldom hit for average, but he had home run power. During the 1940s he batted .270 with a .459 slugging percentage. The one year he topped .300, hitting .322 in 1942, he was named AL MVP.

After he returned from military service, Gordon struggled through a .210 season, and the Yankees, figuring he was washed up, dealt him to Cleveland. There he combined with Lou Boudreau to form a deadly double-play combination.

In 1948 Gordon had his greatest season, batting .280, with 32 homers and 124 RBI, as the Indians won the world championship. At the completion of his career, he had 181 home runs and 710 RBI.

# THIRD BASE

Hot corner candidates for the 1940s dream team were Ken Keltner from the Indians, Hall of Famer George Kell of the Athletics and Tigers, Bob Elliott with the Pirates and Braves, and Stan Hack of the Cubs.

Ken Keltner is best remembered for two scintillating stops of Joe DiMaggio's line drives down the third base line to end his famous hitting streak at 56 games. In addition to being a good fielder, Keltner could hit the long ball when needed. He hit 31 homers and drove in 119 runs in 1948, Cleveland's World Championship season. Though a decent hitter at .269 for the decade, his batting average and on-base percentage were substantially lower than those of Bob Elliott and Stan Hack.

George Kell was a solid hitter and a sure-handed fielder with a strong, accurate arm. Many considered him to be the AL's premier third baseman in the 1940s and 1950s. He batted over .300 nine times and led the league with a .343 average in 1949, while playing for the Detroit Tigers. He topped AL third basemen in fielding percentage seven times, in assists four times, and in putouts and double plays twice.

Despite Kell's outstanding defensive statistics spread over two decades, and his .300-range batting, Elliott and Hack were even more productive, and played in more games during the 1940s. **Bob Elliott**, the first choice for hot corner guardian, had twice as many runs scored and nearly three times the RBI of Kell in just under twice as many games. Hack's batting average was one point higher, and his slugging average was one point lower, but he had a 50-point bulge in on-base percentage. What Kell did well, Hack did better in the forties. Hack was the alternate selection at third base.

Left: *The Boston Braves' Bob Elliott scores in game six of the 1948 World Series against the Indians, although Cleveland went on to take the game, 4-3, and the Series. Dream team third baseman, Elliott played for NL Pittsburgh and Boston clubs during the forties.*

Above: *Stan Hack, alternate dream team third baseman, played for the Cubs his entire 16-year career. Smiling Stan led his league in hits in 1940 and 1941, batting .305 for the decade.*

Bob Elliott was a powerful right-handed slugger who knocked in more than 900 runs and 109 homers during the decade. He participated in the 1941, 1942, 1944 and 1948 All-Star Games. An outstanding clutch hitter who once popped three home runs in a single game, he drove in over 100 runs from 1943 through 1945. He moved from the outfield to third base to help his team, and developed into a wide-ranging fielder. From 1942 through 1944, he led NL third basemen in assists and in errors.

After being traded to the Boston Braves in 1947, Elliott batted .317, slugged 22 homers, had 113 RBI and led the NL in fielding. He was chosen NL MVP, being the first third baseman so honored.

In 1948 Elliott helped lead the Braves' drive to the pennant. Nicknamed "Mr. Team," he paced the Braves in RBI with 100, runs scored with 99, home runs with 23, and walks with 131, and he struck out only 57 times. Although the Braves lost the Series, Elliott batted .333 and hit home runs in two consecutive at-bats against Bob Feller of the Indians in the fifth game.

"Smiling Stan" Hack played on four Cub pennant-winners and averaged .348 in World Series games, but the Cubs lost all four. *The Sporting News* chose him as its All-Star third baseman three years in a row, 1940-1942.

A lifetime .301 hitter, Hack hit .305 for the decade with a .403 OBA. He scored 639 runs in only seven years during the forties. He led the league twice in hits and twice in stolen bases.

As a veteran clutch hitter, Hack led the 1945 Cubs to the pennant on the strength of his 110 runs scored and .323 batting average. In the World Series, he made four hits, including the game-winner in the twelfth inning of game six to knot the Series at three games apiece. Though the Cubs lost in seven games, Hack belted a lusty .367 for the Series.

Hack's most famous hit came in the sixth game of the 1935 Series against the Tigers. Down three games to two, the score tied 3-3, he led off the ninth inning and smote one of Tommy Bridges' curveballs over the center fielder's head for a triple. A sacrifice fly would have given the Cubs the lead. But Billy Jurges struck out, Larry French bounced out and when Augie Galan finally got the long fly, it was too late. A half inning later the Tigers won the game and the Championship.

# SHORTSTOP

This position was one of the few really loaded with talent during the 1940s. Hall of Fame selectors have already tabbed Pee Wee Reese of the Brooklyn Dodgers, Luke Appling of the Chicago White Sox, and Lou Boudreau of the Cleveland Indians for baseball's Valhalla. Outstanding performers who are waiting in the wings for selection include Phil Rizzuto of the Yankees, Marty Marion of the Cardinals, Johnny Pesky of the Red Sox, and Vern Stephens of the Browns and Red Sox.

Pee Wee Reese was the captain of the great Dodger teams of the 1940s and 1950s, and it was these related intangibles as much as his outstanding fielding that brought Reese Hall of Fame recognition. His subtle leadership, competitive fire and professional pride complemented his dependable glove, reliable baserunning, and clutch hitting as significant factors in seven Dodger pennants.

As much as anyone, he was instrumental in easing the acceptance of Jackie Robinson as baseball's first twentieth-century black performer. Reese hit .269 with 108 steals for the decade; his main contribution was leadership, not offense.

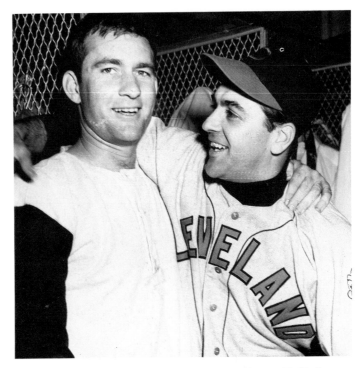

Above: *Player-manager Lou Boudreau (right) congratulates pitcher Bob Lemon after his game two win in the 1948 World Series. In his 1948 MVP year, dream team shortstop Boudreau led Cleveland to a World Championship, after batting a season .355 with 106 RBI, and going four-for-four in the pennant playoff.*

Opposite: *Future Hall of Famer Ted Williams loosens up. Dream team left fielder for the forties, "The Thumper" swung his magical bat for the Red Sox his entire 19-year career. During the decade his extraordinary hitting earned two Triple Crowns, four AL batting championships, and two MVP Awards. Six of the seven seasons he played of the forties, he led the league in walks, runs and slugging average.*

Luke Appling was a steady, durable shortstop who spent his entire 20-year career with the White Sox. Averaging .311 in the 1930s, and .311 in the 1940s, Appling won a batting title in 1936, and another in 1943. His average dipped below .300 for only two seasons during the forties.

Phil Rizzuto, the Yankee Scooter, was the Italian spark-plug of the formidable pennant-winners during the forties. An outstanding bunter, Rizzuto was the darling of the press, who may have misled the New York public about the shortstop's all-around ability. He was an average fielder with no power at the plate.

Marty Marion was considered the top fielding shortstop in the NL. Teams he played for won four pennants and three World Championships during the 1940s. In addition to fielding and leadership, he could occasionally supply two-base hits. Marion led the league in doubles with 38 in 1942. Other than that, Marion had almost no extra base power. He batted low in the lineup and his run production suffered.

Johnny Pesky was remembered for the play he did not make – the relay from shallow left as Enos Slaughter raced around the bases in the seventh game of the 1946 World Series. What fans forgot was that he was quite an offensive player. In only five seasons during the 1940s, Pesky scored 561 runs on 964 hits and 378 walks for a batting average of .316.

Few players lost as much to the war as Pesky. He led the league in hits three consecutive years – 1942, 1946 and 1947 – and scored more than 100 runs six times – 1942 and 1946 to

1950. Those missing three years would have been prime production time for the Boston shortstop. As the record stood, Pesky played only 746 games during the forties; not enough to be considered for the decade dream team.

The dream team choices among these talented men are Cleveland's playing manager **Lou Boudreau**, and Boston slugger Vern Stephens as alternate. Reese, Rizzuto and Marion did not hit as well as Boudreau or Stephens, and Appling was all average, no power.

Lou Boudreau combined fielding prowess, solid hitting, and managerial acumen to attain Hall of Fame recognition. He took the helm at Cleveland in 1942 at the age of 24. Six years later Boudreau hit .355 with 106 RBI, capped by a four-for-four day in the pennant playoff game. He led the Tribe to a World Championship and captured an MVP Award for himself.

An exceptional fielder, Boudreau led league shortstops in fielding average eight times, in double plays five times, and in putouts four times. His 134 double plays in 1943 set a record, as did his .982 fielding average in 1947. His arm was only so-so, and other shortstops had more range, but Boudreau's knowledge of hitters allowed him to compensate by positioning himself where the action was. A bold innovator and strategist, Boudreau devised the "Ted Williams' shift."

Vern Stephens, the dream team alternate, was Boston's hard-hitting shortstop. In 1949 he scored 113 runs, pounded 39 homers, drove in 159 runs and walked 101 times, as the Red Sox battled the fabled Yankees to the last day of the season before losing the pennant. To show that his season was no fluke, Stephens continued his assault on AL pitching the following year with 30 home runs, 125 runs scored and 144 RBI.

Stephens had joined the St. Louis Browns in 1942 and quickly became a star, racking up a .294 batting average and 92 RBI. Brown manager Luke Sewell claimed that he never saw a player develop as rapidly as Stephens. During the next five years with St. Louis, he batted around .290 with impressive RBI statistics, showed a formidable throwing arm, and was named to the AL All-Star teams in 1943, 1944, 1946 and 1948.

An early knee injury exempted him from military service. In 1944 he helped the Browns capture their first AL pennant by leading the league with 109 RBIs. Traded in November of 1947 to the Boston Red Sox, Stephens starred in a potent lineup that included Ted Williams, Bobby Doerr, Johnny Pesky and Dom DiMaggio. In that setting, he added to his reputation as a clutch hitter and frequently flashy fielder.

# LEFT FIELD

No other candidates for the dream team left-field position came close to Ted Williams of the Red Sox and Stan Musial of the Cardinals. The duo were vastly superior to anyone else at any other position during the decade. It was agony choosing one of these superstars over the other, but **Ted Williams** was selected as dream team left fielder. He had a higher batting average and superior power, hitting almost 100 more home runs in fewer games than Musial. The alternate, then, is Stan Musial.

The Red Sox' Ted Williams was one of baseball's greatest hitters, and the last player to reach the elusive .400 mark in batting. Combining keen vision with quick wrists and a scientific approach to hitting, he set numerous records despite missing nearly three full seasons to military service. The Splendid Splinter, so-called for his slender build, achieved a .406 batting average in 1941, Triple Crowns in 1942 and 1947, MVP

Awards in 1946 and 1949, and AL batting championships in 1941, 1942, 1947 and 1948.

Williams scored 951 runs, batted in 893, smacked 270 doubles and ripped 234 home runs – with a batting average of .356 – in just seven years during the 1940s. He led the AL in on-base percentage seven of the years between 1940 and 1949 minus the three years off for World War II.

Terrible Ted, as he was named by Boston area sportswriters, was a consummate professional in the batters' box and on the playing field. He routinely arrived at the ballpark two hours ahead of other players so that he could take batting practice alone; just him, the pitching machine and a bat. Williams could hit like no one else.

Stan "the Man" Musial was a dead-armed Class C pitcher who became a slugging major league outfielder. He topped the .300 mark 18 times and won seven NL batting titles with his famed corkscrew stance and his ringing line drives. The three-time MVP played in 24 All-Star games. He was nicknamed "The Man" by Dodger fans for the havoc he wrought at Ebbets Field.

Spreading alarm and despondency among NL pitchers in the 1940s, Musial hit .346, and won three batting titles. In 1948 he had the greatest year of any National Leaguer as he led the circuit in runs, hits, doubles, triples, RBI, batting average, on-base percentage and slugging average, and lacked only one homer to lead in that category as well. Incredibly, he was not the unanimous pick for MVP that year.

Left: *Stan "the Man" Musial batted .331 over his 22-year career with the St. Louis Cardinals, accompanying them to the World Series four times during the forties. Alternate dream team left fielder, Musial won the National League MVP Award in 1943, 1946 and 1948.*

Below left: *Future Hall of Famer Joe DiMaggio smacks a hard liner in a 1941 game against the Senators. The Yankee Clipper, an easy choice for dream team center fielder, batted .324 for the decade, with a batting title and two MVP Awards.*

Right: *Enos Slaughter scores the run that won the 1946 World Series for the Cardinals, in a famous dash home from first in game seven. Dream team right fielder, Slaughter was known for his hustle and his clutch hitting.*

## CENTER FIELD

Candidates for the center-field dream team position were George Case of the Senators and Indians, Hall of Famer Joe DiMaggio of the Yankees, and Augie Galan of the Cubs, Dodgers, Reds, Giants and Athletics.

George Case was a speed merchant who could not hit. He led the league in stolen bases in five consecutive seasons, six times altogether. Case scored more than 100 runs in four seasons, leading the league in 1943. Using his speed to shepherd the center-field pastures, he was a good fielder who scored high in Bill James' range factors. But he could not hit well enough, nor could he consistently get on base. His .332 decade on-base percentage was the lowest among non-catchers, excluding pitchers, of any player surveyed for the dream team.

The inescapable first team choice for the dream team was **"Jolting Joe" DiMaggio.** He was one of the game's most graceful athletes – a "picture player" both at bat and in center field. Many rate his 56 consecutive-game hitting streak in 1941 as the top baseball feat of all time.

DiMaggio, with his wide stance, was the 1939 and 1940 batting champion. He was MVP in 1939, 1941 and 1947. DiMaggio amassed 180 homers, averaged 112 RBI per season, and had a .324 batting mark during the 1940s. Twice he led the league in RBI and home runs. He was best remembered as "The Yankee Clipper," a proud ship leading the Yankees to safety in pennant harbor, year after year after year.

Augie Galan, the dream team alternate, was a pint-sized infielder who made a successful switch to center field. His best year of the decade was 1945 when he hit .307, scored 114 runs, knocked in 92, walked 114 times and stole 13 bases. Some of his best offensive years occurred during the 1930s, when he played on two pennant-winning Cub teams. Chicago traded him to Brooklyn in 1941, just in time for the first Dodger pennant in 21 years.

Galan, whose parents were born in France, was always a favorite among fans. Ballplayers liked him as well; he was a valuable man on the team during the unsettled forties.

## RIGHT FIELD

Candidates vying for right field on the dream team of the 1940s were Tommy Holmes of the Braves, and Hall of Fame members Enos Slaughter of the Cardinals, and Mel Ott of the Giants.

Tommy Holmes had a hitting streak of 37 games in 1945, his best season, when he also stroked a league-leading 224 hits including 47 doubles and 28 home runs. That year he scored 125 runs while knocking in 117. Holmes had five consecutive seasons hitting more than .300. He began as a promising hitter, but when he started to fade, he went fast, and retired after two straight seasons of batting under .200.

**Enos Slaughter** and Mel Ott were chosen as the 1940s dream team right fielder and alternate. Holmes was too erratic to make the team. Ott, who was dream team right fielder for the 1930s, still had enough pop in his bat in the 1940s to be runner-up to Slaughter.

At Columbus, Georgia, in 1936 Enos Slaughter was rebuked by manager Eddie Dyer for failing to hustle. He vowed never to loaf on a ball field again. Thus was born one of the game's greatest hustlers and fiercest competitors. His nickname was "Country," but his middle name was "Consistency." His flat, level swing made him a .300 hitter, and an outstanding contact hitter in clutch situations. He was famous for his mad dash home from first base on Harry Walker's double to win the 1946 World Series for the Cardinals. Slaughter hit .312 with a .483 slugging average for the decade.

Mel Ott said, "Every time I sign a baseball, and there must have been thousands, I thank my luck that I wasn't born Coveleski or Wambsganss or Peckinpaugh." Ott had to have a sense of humor to manage the Giant teams that he had. He tried to lead by example, which was finally followed in 1947 as the Giants set a major league record with 221 homers.

Ott was a New York Giant hero for 22 seasons and their manager for seven seasons. In the 1940s he hit 142 home runs in 866 games in which he drew 573 bases on balls. Master Melvin was a batter to be feared in the Giants' Polo Grounds, even in the waning years of his Hall of Fame career.

LEFT FIELD

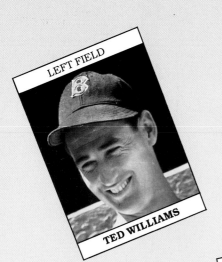

**TED WILLIAMS**

CENTER FIELD

**DUKE SNIDER**

SHORTSTOP

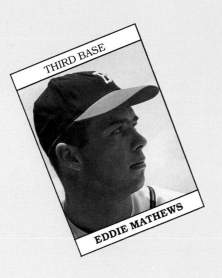

**ERNIE BANKS**

SECOND BASE

**NELLIE FOX**

THIRD BASE

**EDDIE MATHEWS**

PITCHER (LH)

**WARREN SPAHN**

PITCHER (RH)

**ROBIN ROBERTS**

CATCHER

**YOGI BERRA**

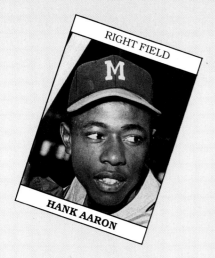

RIGHT FIELD

HANK AARON

FIRST BASE

STAN MUSIAL

# THE GREATEST PLAYERS OF THE
# FIFTIES

## ALTERNATE DREAM TEAM

| | | | |
|---|---|---|---|
| **Pitcher** | Early Wynn (rh) Whitey Ford (lh) | **Third Baseman** | Al Rosen |
| | | **Shortstop** | Pee Wee Reese |
| **Catcher** | Roy Campanella | **Left Fielder** | Minnie Minoso |
| **First Baseman** | Gil Hodges | **Center Fielder** | Mickey Mantle |
| **Second Baseman** | Red Schoendienst | **Right Fielder** | Al Kaline |

## HONORABLE MENTION

| | | | |
|---|---|---|---|
| **Pitcher** | Bob Lemon Hoyt Wilhelm Curt Simmons Billy Pierce | **Third Baseman** | George Kell |
| | | **Shortstop** | Phil Rizzuto Al Dark |
| **Catcher** | Del Crandall | **Left Fielder** | Frank Robinson |
| **First Baseman** | Ted Kluszewski Joe Adcock | **Center Fielder** | Willie Mays Richie Ashburn Larry Doby |
| **Second Baseman** | Bobby Avila Johnny Temple | **Right Fielder** | Carl Furillo |

# THE SETTING

While the postwar U.S. economy and birthrate boomed, so did baseball. In the first part of the decade, team owners grew wealthy. Players, while glad to be home and back at the ballpark, were growing discontented. They wanted a share of the silk purse. They pursued a pension plan with thinly veiled threats of unionization. The United States Congress investigated the possibility of monopoly in organized baseball.

Television rapidly replaced an evening at the ballpark as family entertainment in small-town America. The minor leagues dried up. By 1958 even economic stalwarts like the venerable Texas League were experiencing severe monetary problems.

One new element in the game was the proliferation of black players following their introduction to the major leagues by Brooklyn in 1947. The Dodgers, led by former Negro League players Jackie Robinson, Don Newcombe and Roy Campanella, quickly became the most powerful NL team of the 1950s.

# GAME STRATEGY

Batting strategy – waiting for the right pitch and uppercutting it – was the same as in the 1940s, but without the corollary of drawing walks. The 1950s tactic was to get men on base, then wait for a power hitter to blast a pitch out of the park. The number of home runs burgeoned as teams tailored their players to fit their ballparks, instead of the other way around, like the Tigers and Pirates had tried to do in the past.

Master strategist Casey Stengel managed the Yankees from 1949 to 1960. He revived the concept of platooning, and introduced the concept of the relief pitcher as a principle of the staff.

Joe Page, and later Ryne Duren, often entered the contest with the victory on the line and saved it. Other clubs followed the Yankee lead. By the end of the decade, the Pittsburgh Pirates had the premier relief pitcher in the major leagues. Every team that did not have an Elroy Face was looking for one.

Stengel, who had had trouble hitting left-handed pitching, had his best years as a player platooning for the New York Giants in the 1920s. He tried the system with the Yankees, and won five pennants and five World Championships in a row by platooning first base, third base and an outfield position. The Yankees' roster regularly included 11 or 12 players who appeared in more than 90 games during those seasons.

# FACTORS INFLUENCING PLAYER PERFORMANCE

There was a general overhaul of the baseball rules in 1950. Archaic interpretations were removed, and modern practices were codified and added to the official regulations.

Successful teams had a couple of players or coaches designated to watch the opponents and steal their signs. Old-time experts like Chuck Dressen of the Dodgers, Leo Durocher of the Giants, and Frank Crosetti of the Yankees, provided instruction to the new generation of sign stealers.

Bob Turley was one of the best – so his Brown, Oriole and Yankee teammates claim. The Yankees' irascible Billy Martin stole a squeeze sign from Dressen in the seventh game of the 1952 World Series. The resulting last-moment pitchout thwarted the Dodgers, and the Yankees went on to win the game and the Series.

The New York area teams dominated baseball in the 1950s. Appreciative fans flocked to the ballparks. In other parts of the country, game attendance dwindled because teams were not competitive. The old city stadiums began to decay; fans moved out to the suburbs, and did not care to drive downtown anymore.

Franchises began to relocate. Milwaukee, Baltimore, Kansas City, Los Angeles and San Francisco made lucrative offers to lure major league teams.

With West Coast cities on the senior circuit, travel began to be a bigger factor in player performance. Long-distance travel and major league game schedules can tire a team in the dog-days of August and September.

# THE POSITIONS

## PITCHER

Pitchers in the 1950s were reluctant to give up the reins to relievers. They pitched an astounding number of complete games by today's standards. The number of complete games for the pitching staff of the league-leading team declined from 88 to 59 as the decade progressed. The last staff to complete 100 games in a season pitched for the White Sox in 1941.

The decade was actually a pitcher's nightmare. It was a time of home run slugging in ballparks with short foul lines. The hurlers who excelled did so by keeping the ball low, changing speeds and throwing strikes.

All of the dream team candidates for right-handed pitcher became members of the Baseball Hall of Fame. They were Bob Lemon of the Indians; Hoyt Wilhelm of the Giants, Cardinals, Indians and Orioles; Robin Roberts of the Phillies; and Early Wynn of the Indians and White Sox.

Bob Lemon was transformed from a weak-hitting infielder to a Hall of Fame pitcher. He won 152 games during the fifties. Lemon's seven 20-game seasons included five in the decade. He led the AL once in strikeouts, four times in innings pitched, five times in complete games, and three times in games won. He was a tough hurler who finished his career with a 3.23 ERA, 31 shutouts, and a 207-128 record.

Hoyt Wilhelm's career was much like his knuckle ball, darting from here to there. It began with a home run in his first big-league at-bat. He pitched for a quartet of teams in the fifties, winning 62 games, saving 58 more, and leading the NL in ERA once.

Traded from Cleveland to Baltimore in 1958, Wilhelm was greeted by Oriole manager Paul Richards, an old-time catcher who realized the difficulty of handling Wilhelm's elusive pitch. During the sixties, Richards would introduce "the Big Bertha glove." It was an oversized model designed specifically to catch the knuckle ball. The reason the pitch was so hard to catch was the same reason that it was so hard to hit. Nobody, including the guy throwing it, knew where it would go.

One of the game's premier relief pitchers, Wilhelm got a rare start in Baltimore against the Yankees in 1959. He pitched a no-hitter. Mickey Mantle, the star slugger of the Yankees, joked that his fastball and curve were lousy.

The dream team right-handed pitcher, **Robin Roberts**, and the alternate, Early Wynn, were selected for their outstanding pitching and leadership abilities.

Burly Early Wynn would probably bristle at being chosen as alternate. For him, every ball game was a war. He set the AL record for seasons pitched by hurling for 23 years. He won 300 games for Washington, Cleveland and the Chicago White Sox. During the fifties, he was a 20-game winner on five occasions, and started 31 or more games for 10 straight seasons. Wynn won the Cy Young Award in 1959 at the age of 39, when his 22-10 record was an essential element in the White Sox's pennant-winning season.

Wynn was a leader on and off the field. On the field he cursed batters and made statements like, "My grandmother

*Dream team right-hander Robin Roberts winds up for the pitch. The durable finesse and fastball pitcher hurled for the Phillies most of his 19-year career. During the decade the future Hall of Famer pitched his way to six consecutive 20-win seasons, leading the league in wins four of those years. Roberts appeared in five All-Star Games of the fifties.*

knows better than to take a toehold on me," when asked if he would dust off his own grandmother. Off the field, Wynn worked with Robin Roberts to secure retirement pay for major league baseball players. Wynn is still fighting today for his age group to be accepted into the current pension plan.

Robin Roberts was the ace of the Phillies' staff for most of his brilliant 19-year career. Despite pitching for what was usually a second division team, the durable workhorse with the great fastball and pinpoint control won 286 games. Almost 200 of the victories came during the 1950s, with six consecutive 20-win seasons.

In 1950 Roberts paced the Phillies to their first flag in 35-years, with a 20-11 record. During the decade he led the NL in games started six straight years, complete games for five straight, and innings pitched five straight.

Batters took advantage of Roberts' pinpoint control. He was reluctant to move the hitter off the plate, so he surrendered a record number of home runs. His nice-guy approach and businesslike demeanor led Roberts to become a leader in the baseball pension struggle. Pampered athletes of today have Roberts to thank for their substantial pension plans, but they do not realize it.

The 1950s dream team candidates for left-handed pitcher were notable portsiders Curt Simmons of the Phillies, and Billy Pierce of the White Sox, plus Hall of Fame left-handers Warren Spahn of the Braves and Whitey Ford of the Yankees.

Curt Simmons, whose late-season recall for active military duty almost cost Philadelphia's Whiz Kids the 1950 pennant, was a top NL pitcher when he was not bothered by arm trouble. Simmons won 110 games during the decade, leading the league with six shutouts in 1952. He unfortunately also had three seasons with an ERA over 4.00.

Billy Pierce was a stylish southpaw who has drawn votes for the Hall of Fame in five separate elections. He won 155 games during the 1950s, and had two consecutive 20-game seasons. Pierce was the ERA champion in 1955 with a 1.97 mark. He led the AL in complete games for three straight years and was the loop's strikeout king in 1953. As good as Pierce was, Spahn, one of the all-time greats, and Whitey Ford, the money pitcher on baseball's most powerful team, were much better.

**Warren Spahn**, dream team lefty, was the winningest left-hander in the game's history with 363 victories. He was a 20-game winner 13 times, including eight of ten seasons during the fifties. He led the NL in wins eight times and in complete games nine times. He was the ERA champ in 1947, 1953 and 1961, making him the only pitcher ever to lead the league in ERA during three different decades.

Spahn set the NL lifetime mark for innings pitched over his 21-year career, during which he hurled two no-hitters and was the 1957 Cy Young Award winner. Bill James rated him

Above left: *Early Wynn, alternate dream team right-hander, was a fierce competitor who divided his 23-year career between the Senators, Indians and White Sox. Wynn's 22-10 1959 season won him the Cy Young Award.*

Above: *The Braves' ace southpaw, Warren Spahn, pictured at spring training. The future Hall of Famer and dream team lefty won 20 games or more eight times in the fifties, pitching for the*

Boston and Milwaukee Braves for most of his distinguished 21-year career.

Above right: *The Yankees' Whitey Ford winds up for a pitch in game four of the 1950 World Series. Ford allowed just seven Philly hits in this final game win. Dream team alternate southpaw for the decade, "The Chairman of the Board" pitched in 11 World Series during his 16-year career. He holds all-time firsts for World Series wins (10) and strikeouts (94).*

second only to Lefty Grove as most valuable career left-handed starter in baseball history.

Spahn, the master of control and of getting the batter to hit his pitch, was not always that way. Having fought three years in Europe during the World War II, he came to the big league scene as a 25-year-old fireballer. After leading the league in strikeouts four straight years, his fastball faded. Spahn developed a wicked screwball and tantalizing change-up, plus he got smarter and smarter. His ability to place his pitches and vary the speeds kept batters always off-stride.

Dream team alternate choice for southpaw pitcher, Edward "Whitey" Ford was known to his teammates as the "Chairman of the Board" because he controlled the destiny of the 1950s Yankees with his good left arm and wily brain. As

the main pitcher of a staff that won eight pennants in ten years during the fifties, Ford pitched many big games for the Bronx Bombers. The shrewd southpaw molded a lifetime record of 236-106 that gave him the best won-lost percentage (.690) of any twentieth-century pitcher who has more than 200 wins. He paced the AL in victories three times.

Due to manager Casey Stengel's irregular pitching staff rotation, Ford started fewer games than most of his contemporaries. His record of 121 wins balanced against only 50 losses makes his decade percentage .707. Ford was the most winning pitcher on baseball's most winning team.

The 1961 Cy Young Award winner, Ford set many World Series records. His Fall Classic triumphs include 10 victories, 33 and two-thirds consecutive scoreless innings, and 94 strikeouts.

Left: *Yogi Berra tries to catch a foul fly during the September 28, 1951 no-hitter pitched by teammate Allie Reynolds. Dream team catcher Yogi Berra played for the Yankees from 1946 through 1963, appearing in 14 World Series along the way. The future Hall of Famer batted .286 and won three MVP Awards during the decade.*

Above: *Alternate dream team catcher Roy Campanella makes the out at home during 1949 World Series action against the Yankees. Brooklyn Dodger kingpin from 1948 through 1957, Campanella hit more than .300 and drove in more than 100 runs in each of his three MVP years. This alternate dream team catcher was elected to the Hall of Fame in 1969.*

# CATCHER

Catchers were cast in the mold of Yogi Berra during the fifties. Several years ago Bill James did a comparison piece on Bill Dickey and Yogi Berra. The point of the article was that Berra was a better catcher than Dickey, whom his peers considered to be the greatest catcher in the history of the game. James wondered where that left Berra, then decided that it left him with a legitimate claim to be the greatest catcher of all time. Berra's impact on the position was such that during the 1950s and 1960s most of the catchers looked and acted like Yogi.

The talent pool for the 1950s dream team catcher was formed by Del Crandall of the Braves and two Hall of Famers, Yogi Berra of the Yankees, and Roy Campanella of the Dodgers.

Crandall, who tallied a distant third to Berra and Campanella, had 30 games less than Campy, and 300 fewer RBI. He was a solid performer at the plate, but his offensive output was much lower than that of the two Hall of Fame receivers. Crandall was a top catcher: he won three Gold Glove Awards.

**Yogi Berra**, the 1950s dream team catcher, out-performed other catchers in every measurable statistical category. The great backstop played on more pennant-winning teams, 14, than any other player, and he wore Yankee pinstripes on 10 World Championship teams.

Tutored by Bill Dickey, Berra became a polished receiver as well as an accomplished hitter. He set the career home run record for AL catchers. During the decade, Berra topped the 100-RBI mark five times. He was MVP three times and lost a fourth award when teammate Phil Rizzuto was selected. The year he lost the MVP Award to Rizzuto, Berra scored 116 runs, pounded 28 homers, knocked in 124, batted .322, slugged .533, and struck out only 12 times.

Berra was selected for 15 successive All-Star games. His successful career continued after he retired as a player; as manager of the Yankees and the Mets, he won pennants in 1964 and 1973, respectively.

Roy Campanella, dream team alternate, is one of baseball's most beloved players. An automobile accident left him in a wheelchair, but he became a symbol of baseball's greatness, touring the country and providing inspiration for fans of all ages. As a player Campy was a superb catcher, and a batter who hit both for average and with power. The roly-poly receiver was quick and agile behind the plate and possessed a rifle arm which he used to gun down potential base stealers.

In addition Campanella was an expert handler of pitchers and a natural leader of the Brooklyn Dodgers from 1948 to 1957. The three-time MVP hit more than .300 in each of the award-winning years 1951, 1953 and 1955, the same years that he drove home more than 100 runs. Campy hit 211 home runs in eight years of competition during the decade. He pushed and pulled the Dodgers to four pennants in five years, from 1952 to 1956.

# FIRST BASE

Managerial craving to put more home run hitters into the lineup coincided with the decade's platoon craze to move heavy hitters from other positions into the first base slot. Fielding was not nearly as important as hitting at this position during the 1950s decade.

Ted Kluszewski of the Reds, Pirates and White Sox; Joe Adcock of the Reds and Braves; Hall of Famer Stan "the Man" Musial of the Cardinals; and Gil Hodges of the Dodgers, make up the group of qualified dream team candidates.

Kluszewski, who became famous for his cut-off sleeves, produced five consecutive seasons in which he had more home runs than strikeouts. He hit .302 and slugged 239 home runs with 891 RBI and a .517 slugging percentage for the decade. Big Klu led the league with 49 home runs and 141 RBI as he hit 40 or more homers in three straight seasons. He had four straight 100-RBI years, and better than a .300 batting average five consecutive seasons.

Left: *Dream team first baseman Stan Musial belts a home run at the Polo Grounds. The perennial All-Star and future Hall of Famer won four batting crowns in the fifties.*

Below: *Stan Musial is congratulated by teammates as he crosses the plate after belting a two-run homer in game four of the 1944 World Series.*

Above: *Brooklyn Dodger Gil Hodges mugs for the camera at spring training in 1955. This alternate dream team first sacker played for the Dodgers — first in Brooklyn and then in Los Angeles — for most of his 18-year career, appearing in seven World Series along the way. A Gold Glove fielder and power hitter, Hodges was an all-round player.*

Joe Adcock was a power hitter for the highly competitive Milwaukee Braves team that was loaded with home run sluggers during the 1950s. On July 31, 1954, he hit four home runs and a double to set a major league record for total bases that has yet to be matched.

**Stan Musial**, the 1940 dream team left field alternate, was the 1950 dream team first choice for first base. He out-hit his closest competitor by almost 30 points and out-slugged the second place hitter by 70 points. Continuing his famed corkscrew batting stance, "Stan The Man" was a pure hitter averaging .330 with 95 runs scored, 97 RBI, 35 doubles, 26 home runs and 84 walks for the decade.

Musial won four batting crowns in the fifties as he batted over .300 for 16 consecutive seasons. He was a perennial All-Star, and held most of the NL career records until Hank Aaron broke them.

Gil Hodges, the dream team alternate at first, was one of the top guns in the Dodgers' Murderers' Row of 1948 to 1959. He slugged 310 home runs and drove in 1001 during the fifties. Hodges played on seven Dodger teams who won pennants, six in Brooklyn and the last in 1959 for Los Angeles. He was considered one of the best fielders among NL first basemen, and was voted the first three Gold Glove Awards for the position.

Hodges was an even-tempered gentleman of immense strength, both in physique and character. His inner strength helped him persevere during the extended batting slumps that he was prone to have. Most Dodger fans recall with sympathy Hodges's frustrating 1952 World Series when he went 0-for-21. Followers sent him batting tips, and lit candles for him in church. Fewer remember that he hit a glorious .364 the next year in the Series or that he drove in both runs of the final game in 1955, as the Dodgers won their first World title.

*White Sox second baseman Nelson Fox avoids Ray Coleman's high spikes and turns the double play in a July 1951 game against the St. Louis Browns. Nellie Fox, who led AL second basemen five times in turning double plays, and batted .300 for the decade, is the dream team choice for the fifties.*

# SECOND BASE

The accent was on putouts and assists at the keystone sack during the fifties. Covering ground to prevent hits was a priority for second basemen.

The four top candidates of the decade were Bobby Avila with the Indians, Johnny Temple of the Reds, Nellie Fox of the White Sox, and Hall of Fame member Red Schoendienst of the Cardinals, Giants and Braves.

Bobby Avila came from the Mexican Leagues to start for the Indians for eight years. He led the AL in hitting in 1954 with a .341 average. Avila's hitting was solid; he had a .280 average for the decade.

Johnny Temple hit over .300 three times, and scored more than 82 runs for five consecutive years. Fielding was his strength; he led the league in putouts three times, and in assists once. In 1955 Temple teamed with shortstop Roy McMillan to lead other second basemen with 119 double plays. Hitting .291 for the decade, Temple still did not quite measure up to Nellie Fox or Red Schoendienst.

**Nelson Fox**, the dream team second baseman of the fifties, was known for his choke-up batting grip and huge wad of tobacco. Fox was the heart of the Go-Go White Sox of the 1950s, teaming first with Chico Carrasquel and then with Luis Aparicio to form the AL's premier keystone combination.

He led the league's second basemen five times in turning double plays.

Considered a poor hitter when he first arrived in the majors, Fox learned to punch out short drives and led the AL seven straight years (1954-1960) in singles and four years in total hits. He batted .300 or better six times, and had a .300 decade average. He struck out about as often as Chicago has an honest election, and ranks as the third most difficult batter to whiff in history.

Nellie's playing style was characterized by pluck and all-out hustle. He also had an infectious spirit. When the White Sox won their first pennant in 40 years in 1959, Fox was named Most Valuable Player, though several other players had better statistics.

Albert "Red" Schoendienst, dream team runner-up, was credited by his roommate, Stan Musial, as having "the greatest pair of hands I've ever seen." Schoendienst was a sleek, far-ranging second baseman for 18 seasons with the Cardinals, Giants, and Milwaukee Braves. He led the NL in fielding percentage and hit .300 or better in seven seasons during the fifties. He led the NL in doubles with 43 in 1950, and in base hits with 200 in 1957.

When elected to the Hall of Fame in 1989, Schoendienst had worn a Major League uniform for 45 consecutive seasons as player, coach, and manager. Twice he managed the Cardinals to the World Series.

# THIRD BASE

Fundamental abilities required to play third base during the fifties included handling hot shots, guarding the line, making strong accurate throws, and coming in for bunts. Third basemen were also expected to hit and hit with power.

The choice for hot corner guardian was among Hall of Famers Eddie Mathews of the Braves and George Kell of the Tigers, Red Sox, White Sox and Orioles; and Al Rosen of the Indians.

George Kell was a solid hitter and a sure-handed fielder with a strong, accurate arm. Some fans considered him to be the premier third baseman of the AL in the 1940s and 1950s. He batted over .300 six times and led the loop in hits and doubles in 1950 and 1951. While leading AL third basemen in fielding percentage five times, his range appeared to be limited. Kell never led the league in total chances. He was the

Left: *Leading National League hitters pose before the 1949 All-Star Game at Ebbets Field. From left to right: Jackie Robinson, Ralph Kiner, Al Schoendienst and Willard Marshall. Alternate dream team second baseman, Red Schoendienst patrolled the infield for 19 years, with three teams. This superb player was elected to the Hall of Fame in 1989.*

Above: *Eddie Mathews demonstrates his fielding style. Dream team third baseman of the fifties, Mathews belted 299 home runs for the decade. He was elected to the Hall of Fame in 1978.*

league leader only once in assists, and once in double plays during the fifties. Both Mathews and Rosen were in the prime of their lives and possessed considerably more power than Kell.

**Eddie Mathews**, dream team third baseman for the 1950s, became the seventh player in major league history to hit 500 home runs. He finished his career with 512. Mathews walloped 30 or more home runs seven straight seasons, reaching the 40 mark on four occasions during the fifties. In 1953 his 47 homers for the Milwaukee Braves established a season record for third basemen (since broken by Mike Schmidt), and he won the NL home run title. Mathews led the league again with 46 home runs in 1959. His 299 round-trippers for the decade was surpassed only by Gil Hodges and Duke Snider.

Al Rosen, the dream team alternate was, for a few years, one of the most feared hitters in the AL. He played 35 games for the Indians from 1947 to 1949, but couldn't move Ken Keltner off third base until 1950. That year, Rosen's 37 homers set an AL rookie record not broken until 1987. In 1953 Rosen was AL MVP, narrowly missing the Triple Crown with a .336 batting average, while leading the league with 43 homers (still a record for AL third basemen) and 145 RBI.

In 1954 Rosen was on his way to an equally impressive season when he suffered a broken finger. The injury permanently affected his grip on the bat. He returned to the lineup and helped the Indians set the AL record with 111 victories, but his batting statistics fell off badly. Rosen retired two years later. In the five years from 1950 to 1954 he averaged .298, with 31 home runs and 114 RBI.

# SHORTSTOP

Two holdovers from the previous decade, Phil Rizzuto of the Yankees and Pee Wee Reese of the Dodgers, were also candidates for the shortstop position on the 1950s dream team. Newcomers for the dream team contenders were Al Dark of the Giants, Cards and Cubs; and Ernie Banks of the Cubs.

Al Dark was a college football player at Louisiana State University, and a no-holds-barred hustler. His batting average, .289, and slugging average, .418, were second highest among shortstops of the era. Dark's hard-nosed, aggressive style earned the respect of his teammates.

Phil Rizzuto was the Yankee Scooter, and a deadly bunter. Voted AL MVP in 1950, Rizzuto batted .324 with 200 hits, 125 runs scored, and an on-base percentage of .439. Those statistics were only part of his contribution. Rizzuto also led the league in putouts and assists. In 1950 a panel of distinguished, old-time players and writers declared that there was only one active player who could have been successful in the dead-ball era. That player was Phil Rizzuto. Nonetheless, the Scooter could not hit well enough to make the dream team, even as an alternate.

For 19 years, **Ernie Banks**, 1950s dream team shortstop, delighted Wrigley Field fans with his long and frequent home runs, his steady fielding and his cheerful disposition. During the fifties, Banks hit more than 40 home runs four times. He smashed five grand slams in 1955. In 1958 his 47 round-trippers were the most ever hit by a shortstop.

Opposite top: *Ernie Banks knocks out his 500th homer in a game against the Braves on May 12, 1970. The dream team shortstop of the fifties, Banks played for the Cubs his entire 19-year career. A steady fielder and a power hitter, Banks led his league with a .614 slugging percentage, 47 homers and 129 RBI in 1958. He was elected to the Hall of Fame in 1977.*

Left: *Ernie Banks receives his second consecutive MVP*

*Award in May of 1960, for his 1959 season performance. National League President Warren Giles presents the award at Wrigley Field.*

Above: *Shortstop Pee Wee Reese tries to turn a double play while leaping over Billy Martin in 1955 World Series action. Alternate dream team shortstop, "The Little Colonel" played for the Dodgers his entire 16-year career, playing in seven World Series along the way. He was elected to the Hall of Fame in 1984.*

Banks led the Senior Circuit in home runs with 47, RBI with 129, and slugging average with .614, in 1958. He followed that MVP year with another year almost as good, when he belted 45 homers, drove in 143 and hit .304 to win a second MVP.

Banks came to the Cubs from the Kansas City Monarchs in 1953. Most baseball historians consider the sale of Banks' contract to the white major league to represent the end of top competitive play in the Negro Leagues.

Harold "Pee Wee" Reese, alternate pick, continued his heady play and inspired leadership of the previous decade. His Dodgers won four pennants in five years during the fifties. In the seventh game of the 1955 World Series, Reese fielded a grounder off the bat of the Yankees' Elston Howard and threw him out at first base to capture the first World Championship in Brooklyn Dodger history.

Reese did not fare well in Los Angeles after the Dodgers moved away from beloved Brooklyn in 1958. He retired in 1959 at the age of 41. He immediately became Dizzy Dean's sidekick on baseball's televised Game of the Week.

# LEFT FIELD

The best players of the decade in left field were Frank Robinson of the Reds, Ted Williams of the Red Sox, and Minnie Minoso of the Indians and White Sox.

Frank Robinson, who was Rookie of the Year in 1956, did not play enough games to qualify for the dream team of the fifties, although he hit .298 and slugged 134 homers in just 596 games.

Since Stan Musial moved to first base, **Ted Williams** was chosen without much competition for dream team left fielder. "The Thumper" hit AL pitching to the tune of .336, the decade's highest average. In addition to batting average, he led all other players of the 1950s in on-base percentage, slugging average, and bases on balls.

Williams added two more batting crowns to the four he won in the 1940s. His .388 batting average in 1957 was the highest average since his own .406 in 1941. Williams left the active role of a ballplayer in classic form, bowing out with a home run in his last major league at-bat.

Minne Minoso, alternate dream team left fielder, did not have a full season in the majors until he was 28 years old.

Left: *Ted Williams follows the flight of the home run ball he hit in the last at-bat of his illustrious career, on September 27, 1959. Dream team left fielder for the second consecutive decade, Williams led all major leaguers in the fifties in batting, slugging, walks and on-base percentage.*

Opposite below: *Minnie Minoso is congratulated at the plate after belting a home run in his first at-bat for the White Sox, on May 2, 1951. This alternate dream team left fielder combined speed on the basepaths with power at the plate, and hit for average as well.*

Right: *Dodger favorite Duke Snider smiles as he is congratulated by manager Charlie Dressen while rounding third on his two-run homer that won game one of the 1952 World Series against the Yankees. "The Silver Fox" played all but the last two seasons of his 18-year career with the Brooklyn and L.A. Dodgers, his slick fielding and power hitting helping them to six World Series. This dream team center fielder was elected to the Hall of Fame in 1980.*

When he burst on the scene with the White Sox in 1951, Minoso immediately became one of the most exciting players in the AL. During the fifties, he led the league in stolen bases three times, in triples three times, and in doubles once. Minoso compiled a decade batting average of .306. Among all decade players, he was fourth in the decade in triples, and second in stolen bases.

## CENTER FIELD

In the 1950s the center fielder was often the best all-around player on the team. The position was stocked with good fielders who could really tear the cover off the ball.

Besides the Hall of Famers Duke Snider of the Dodgers, Mickey Mantle of the Yankees, and Willie Mays of the Giants, candidates for the dream team were stars Richie Ashburn of the Phillies, and Larry Doby of the Indians, White Sox and Tigers.

Richie Ashburn won two batting crowns as he led the NL in hits three times and captured the triples title twice. Ashburn was a lead-off man with discipline and a good eye. He re-ceived 828 bases on balls to lead the league in on-base percentage three times during the decade. Ashburn was a great ballplayer whose power was limited. He would have been the alternate center field pick in most other decades, but not this one.

Larry Doby was the first black player in the AL. Before he came to Cleveland to help the Indians capture the 1948 World Championship, his Newark Eagles' team won the Negro League Championship. Doby continued his long-distance hitting with 32 homers and 126 RBI, leading the league as he powered the Indians to the 1954 pennant. The formidable outfielder had several inconsistent years. He was a slugger, but not in the class of Snider, Mays or Mantle.

Willie Mays, the New York Giants "Say Hey Kid," played the game with unlimited enthusiasm. He excelled in all phases — hitting for average, hitting with power, fielding, running and throwing. May's staggering career statistics include 3283 hits, 660 home runs, and a .302 batting average.

The electrifying center fielder compiled a ton of records in the 1950s alone. He was the NL Rookie of the Year in 1951; batting champ and MVP in 1954. Mays led the league in 1955 with 51 home runs. Three times he led the league in triples and in slugging percentage, four times in stolen bases, once in runs

Left: *A young Duke Snider demonstrates his batting stance. With 389 homers as a Dodger, Snider leads the club in round-trippers.*

Above left and right: *The switch-hitting Mickey Mantle, as a Yankee prospect at 1951 spring training. Alternate dream team center fielder, "The Commerce Comet" helped the Yanks win 12 pennants in his first 14 years. In the fifties the future Hall of Famer won two MVP Awards, a Triple Crown, and led his league in many offensive categories.*

scored, and once in hits. Some fans preferred to watch him in the field, where he won three Gold Gloves during the decade – including the first ever given, in 1957. As good as he was in the fifties, he was even better in the sixties.

For the fifties, **Duke Snider** is the dream team number one pick on the basis of better collective statistics. Mantle was selected as alternate over Ashburn and Doby because of more production and more power. Mantle was chosen over Mays because he hit more home runs, scored more runs, and drove in more runs than Mays.

Duke Snider was the smooth-fielding, power hitting center fielder for the Brooklyn and Los Angeles Dodgers. The strong, intense, left-handed hitter with the majestic swing batted .307, smashed 326 home runs, and drove in 1031 runs during the decade. He hit 40 or more homers five consecutive years, from 1953 to 1957. His 11 World Series round-trippers and 26 RBI were the most ever by a National Leaguer. He hit four home runs in both the 1952 Series and the 1955 Series. He is still the Dodgers' all-time home run leader.

The courageous Mickey Mantle achieved greatness despite an arrested case of osteomyelitis, numerous injuries and frequent surgery. Every swing was an adventure. During the 1950s the powerful Yankee switch hitter belted 280 homers, including 52 in 1956. Many fans consider his 565-foot tape-measure blast off the Senators' Chuck Stobbs the longest home run ever hit. Mantle scored 994 runs, leading the league four times as he tallied 100 runs seven straight times in nine years. He won a Triple Crown in 1956, slugged .705, and, as frosting on the cake, led the league with 132 runs.

The clutch home run was the Mickey Mantle trademark. He helped the Yankees win 12 pennants in his first 14 years in the majors. A three-time MVP, 1956, 1957 and 1962, he holds a number of World Series records.

# RIGHT FIELD

The concentration on offense during the decade placed a premium on getting outs. The rocket arm in right field began to be treasured once again. The ability to turn baserunners into outs was the difference between an average team and a winning team.

Dream team candidates for the fifties right field position include Brooklyn favorite Carl Furillo of the Dodgers, and two Hall of Famers: Hank Aaron of the Braves, and Al Kaline of the Tigers.

Carl Furillo, the Reading Rifle, was the working-class hero of the Dodgers in Brooklyn. He gunned down enough runners

Above: *The Milwaukee Braves' one and only Hank Aaron follows through on his power stroke. Dream team right fielder of the decade, Aaron played most of his distinguished 23-year career with the Braves, both in Milwaukee and Atlanta. The future Hall of Famer topped off an extraordinary decade* *performance at the plate with an MVP season in 1957, when his league-leading 44 homers, 118 runs scored and 132 RBI helped his team to the Series, and his .393 Series batting average helped his team take the championship from the Yankees.*

to lead the league in assists in 1950 and 1951, before they grew too wary to run on him. Not only a fielder, he topped NL hitters with a .344 batting average in 1953. Even with his decade average of .298, his power and consistency were not as good as Aaron's or Kaline's.

**Hank Aaron**, the dream team right fielder, had not yet become synonymous with home runs in the 1950s. Despite Aaron's heroics, Eddie Mathews was the star in Milwaukee. Aaron won two batting titles, led the league twice in hits, twice in doubles, once in runs scored and once in RBI during the fifties. He scored 612 runs and knocked in 617 in just six seasons. As NL MVP in 1957, Aaron pounded Senior Circuit pitching for 44 home runs, scored 118 times and knocked in 132, all league-leading marks. During the 1950s he averaged 102 runs, 103 RBI, 34 doubles, 30 home runs and had a .322 batting average and a .559 slugging percentage.

Aaron went on to hit 755 round-trippers. He also set all-time records for the most games, at-bats, total bases and RBI. His lifetime batting average was .305.

Al Kaline, the decade alternate, was a model of consistency, who got the job done with a minimum amount of fanfare. The quiet, durable Tiger outfielder accumulated 125 home runs, compiled a batting average of .311, and a slugging average of .488 during the decade. He won the AL batting title in 1955 at the age of 20. His reputation as a clutch performer was enhanced by his .379 average against St. Louis in the 1968 World Series.

LEFT FIELD

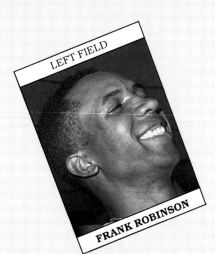

**FRANK ROBINSON**

CENTER FIELD

**WILLIE MAYS**

SHORTSTOP

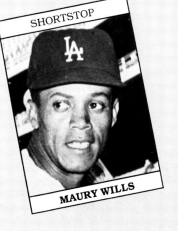

**MAURY WILLS**

SECOND BASE

**PETE ROSE**

THIRD BASE

**RON SANTO**

PITCHER (LH)

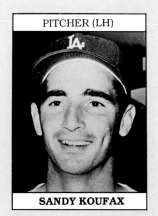

**SANDY KOUFAX**

PITCHER (RH)

**BOB GIBSON**

CATCHER

**ELSTON HOWARD**

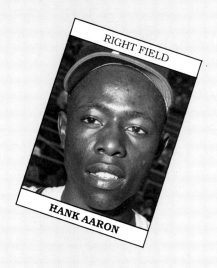

RIGHT FIELD

HANK AARON

FIRST BASE

HARMON KILLEBREW

# THE GREATEST PLAYERS OF THE
# SIXTIES

## ALTERNATE DREAM TEAM

| | | | |
|---|---|---|---|
| **Pitcher** | Juan Marichal (rh) <br> Jim Kaat (lh) | **Third Baseman** | Brooks Robinson |
| | | **Shortstop** | Luis Aparicio |
| **Catcher** | Bill Freehan | **Left Fielder** | Carl Yastrzemski |
| **First Baseman** | Willie McCovey | **Center Fielder** | Mickey Mantle |
| **Second Baseman** | Bill Mazeroski | **Right Fielder** | Roberto Clemente |

## HONORABLE MENTION

| | | | |
|---|---|---|---|
| **Pitcher** | Jim Bunning <br> Don Drysdale <br> Steve Barber <br> Whitey Ford | **Shortstop** | Chico Cardenas <br> Zoilo Versalles |
| | | **Left Fielder** | Billy Williams <br> Lou Brock |
| **Catcher** | John Romano | **Center Fielder** | Curt Flood <br> Vada Pinson |
| **First Baseman** | Orlando Cepeda <br> Norman Cash | | |
| **Second Baseman** | Cookie Rojas <br> Julian Javier | **Right Fielder** | Al Kaline <br> Roger Maris |
| **Third Baseman** | Jim Ray Hart <br> Eddie Mathews | | |

# THE SETTING

The decade opened to the shock of Bill Mazeroski's home run, hit in the bottom of the ninth inning of the seventh game of the World Series. The titanic clout lifted the ecstatic Pittsburgh Pirates over the stunned New York Yankees, who had set Series records for runs scored and base hits, yet lost. The upsetting home run was only the first in a chain of events that would shake baseball to its very foundations.

The American and National Leagues expanded from eight teams each, to ten near the beginning of the decade. One hundred marginal players were thrown into the fray, and expected to perform at big league levels. Talent was so thinly diluted that long-time pundits predicted record-setting years for the 1961 AL and 1962 NL players. The scribes were not disappointed. The most sacred record of all fell to Roger Maris of the New York Yankees when he hit 61 home runs in 1961, breaking Babe Ruth's record of 60 set in 1927.

Several cities gained major league experience during the sixties when franchise shifts and repeated expansions occurred. America's national game became a truly international sport with the advent of the Montreal Expos. Other cities new to big league baseball included Atlanta, Minnesota, Oakland, San Diego and Seattle. These additional sites for major league games boosted total attendance slightly over that of the previous decade. Attendance per game actually went down, from 16,162 in 1960 to 14,005 in 1969.

# GAME STRATEGY

The stolen base returned as an offensive weapon in the 1960s. Maury Wills of the Dodgers electrified the country as he surpassed Ty Cobb's 1915 mark of 96 pilfered sacks. Wills ended the 1962 season with 104 steals and the NL MVP Award. The role of the stolen base and the expanding strike zone caused a return to the good old days of playing for one run. In fact, the debate over whether it is better to use a sacrifice bunt or the hit-and-run began in earnest during this decade. The debate led to the publishing of new statistics known as "Sabremetrics" – developed by members of SABR, the Society for American Baseball Research – during the next decade.

The home run continued to be the main offensive threat, but more and more of them came with the bases empty. The enlarged strike zone lulled pitchers and managers to sleep, since no problem was so bad that three strikeouts in a row would not cure it. The Los Angeles Dodgers were the dominant team. They had two Hall of Fame pitchers – Sandy Koufax and Don Drysdale – plus a raft of other outstanding twirlers, but no offense. A journeyman pitcher with the Cardinals, Larry Jaster, tossed five shutouts against the Dodgers in 1966 to set an all-time record. He simply threw the ball down the middle of the plate and Los Angeles could not do anything with it.

The low run totals during the 1960s led to the best quote of the decade. Don Drysdale, upon being told that Sandy Koufax had just tossed another no-hitter, asked, "did he win?"

# FACTORS INFLUENCING PLAYER PERFORMANCE

Strategy took a back seat to rule changes as the principal modifying factor of the 1960s. On January 26, 1963, the Baseball Rules Committee voted to expand the strike zone. Previously it had been defined as extending from the batter's armpits to the top of his knees, but the 1963 ruling described the strike zone as the area from the shoulders to the bottom of the knees. The latter zone was in effect until 1969, when the moguls of baseball decided to reinstate the former definition.

The Baseball Rules Committee had no idea what effect the new zone would have on offense. There must have been some feeling that home runs had become too cheap. Whatever the reasoning for lengthening the strike zone, two statistics show that it certainly had an effect on the game. Batting averages plummeted during the decade, and strikeout totals soared upward.

New equipment was designed to help the hitter in his uphill battle with overpowering pitching. Elston Howard of the Yankees invented the weighted donut that is placed on the bat while warming up. In addition to the donut, batting gloves appeared on the scene. At first the gloves were similar to golf gloves with the fingers cut out. In time, hitters started wearing fully enclosed gloves.

Batting averages during the "high strike" 1960s are lower than for any other decade. The new strike zone made life miserable for hitters. Good offensive statistics in 1961, 1962 and 1969 saved the sixties' batters from embarrassment.

Baseball's popularity suffered during the decade. National polls ranked professional football, instead of baseball, as the number one sport for the first time. The shapers of America's game had forgotten that the main attraction of baseball was that it is consistent. Inconsistency of players' performances and of the players themselves – caused by the fluctuating strike zone – turned traditional fans away from baseball. It would take the extraordinary performances of the seventies to regain their allegiance.

## PITCHER

Rule changes profoundly affected pitchers during the decade. The enlarged strike zone, in effect from 1963 to 1968, led to a period of unparalleled numbers of strikeouts, and ERAs under 2.00. Reducing the strike zone and lowering the mound in 1969 gave the hitter more control over the plate.

Right-handed pitchers flourished during the decade. The pool of dream team talent yielded Jim Bunning of the Tigers, Phillies, Pirates and Dodgers, and three Hall of Famers: Don Drysdale of the Dodgers, Bob Gibson of the Cardinals, and Juan Marichal of the Giants.

*Future Hall of Famer Bob Gibson pitches in game two of the 1964 World Series. This dream team right-hander pitched for the Cardinals his entire 17-year career.*

*Gibson's 1968 performance — which won him both the MVP and Cy Young Awards — included a 22-9 won-lost record and a league-leading 268 strikeouts.*

Jim Bunning fashioned a 150-104 won-lost record during the decade. He had 2019 strikeouts. The father of nine children, Bunning pitched a perfect game on Father's Day, 1964, at Shea Stadium. The gem gave him no-hitters in both leagues. Bunning was a successful player and later, a U.S. Congressman, but Gibson and Marichal made the dream team by winning more games.

Drysdale was a hard-throwing, competitive, side-arm hurler. He won 158 games and lost 126 during the decade, compiling a 2.81 ERA with 1910 strikeouts. Drysdale held one of baseball's most remarkable records — pitching 58 consecutive scoreless innings (six straight shutouts) in 1968. Orel Hershiser of the Dodgers topped the mark in his last start of the 1988 season. The Cy Young Award winner in 1962, Drysdale teamed with Sandy Koufax to form one of the most intimidating pitching duos in modern times.

**"Bullet" Bob Gibson**, the dream team first choice, exemplified competitiveness and consistency as he skillfully dominated the 1960s hitters with his fastball and slider. A

superb athlete, he attended Creighton University on a basketball scholarship, and once played basketball with the Harlem Globetrotters. Gibson's athletic ability made him one of the best hitting pitchers in the last 50 years. With 24 lifetime home runs and a .206 batting average, Gibson was allowed to stay in games when hurlers who were not so good with the bat would have been yanked for a pinch hitter.

Gibson was 251-174 lifetime, with a 2.91 ERA over 17 seasons. He was rewarded with two Cy Young Awards and was the 1968 NL MVP. During the 1960s the scowling Gibson won 164 games in regular season play, and seven consecutive games in the World Series. The talented right-hander struck out 2071 batters while compiling a decade ERA of 2.70.

Gibson's 1968 season was vintage Cooperstown — 22-9 won-lost record, 1.12 ERA, 13 shutouts and 268 strikeouts. He was at his best when in a clutch situation.

Juan Marichal, the alternate dream team right-hander, was the Dominican dandy who influenced a whole generation of younger pitchers with his high leg kick and straight overhand fastball. He won 191 and lost 88 during the decade, enjoying six 20-game seasons. Marichal pitched a no-hitter against Houston in 1963. Twice he led the NL in complete games and shutouts, finishing 197 contests during the decade, fanning 1840 batters, and compiling a 2.64 ERA. Marichal was named to 10 All-Star teams.

Above: *The hard-throwing Giant pitcher Juan Marichal prepares to unleash some heat on his way to a four-hit shutout against the Mets in May of 1967. Alternate dream team right-hander for the decade, "The Dominican Dandy" was San Francisco's ace for 14 seasons.*

Right: *The great Sandy Koufax on his way to blanking the Twins in game five of the 1965 World Series. Runaway choice for dream team lefty of the decade, Koufax had his best years in the sixties, when he threw four no-hitters and won three Cy Young Awards.*

Forced into relative obscurity by the awesome Sandy Koufax, who plied his wares in the media capital of Los Angeles, Marichal was every bit as valuable. He won 25 games twice and 26 once. He started 37 or more games seven times, completing 30 of his 38 starts in 1968. He was one tough Dominican before the phrase was made popular by Joaquin Andujar in the 1980s.

The left-handed pitchers for the dream team were chosen from among Steve Barber of the Orioles, Yankees and Pilots; Jim Kaat of the Senators and Twins; and two Hall of Famers: Whitey Ford of the Yankees and Sandy Koufax of the Dodgers.

Steve Barber, beset by arm trouble most of his career, was a difficult pitcher to hit when he was healthy. He won 20 games in 1963, and 18 in 1961, and led the AL that year with eight shutouts. Barber won 111 games during the decade.

Whitey Ford, who was on the downhill side of a great career, was to have his best statistical years under new Yankee manager Ralph Houk. Ford won 115 games during the decade. He won the Cy Young Award in 1961, with a 25-4 record. It is interesting to note that Ford's 24-7 record two years later failed to draw a single vote for the Cy Young Award.

**Sandy Koufax**, the runaway number one choice, was the best pitcher in baseball from 1961 until his retirement in 1966. It took him several years to gain control of his blazing fastball and sweeping curve, but then he dominated the game like no pitcher before or since. In that period, every game he threw bordered on a no-hitter or shutout. From 1963 to 1966 he averaged 24 victories and 7 defeats for a percentage of .774, with 307 strikeouts and an ERA of 1.85. He won the Cy Young Award three times in four years, and pitched four no-hitters. Twice he fanned 18 batters in a single game, and his 382 whiffs in 1965 is still a NL record. After his retirement at age 30, due to circulatory problems, he became the second youngest Hall of Fame inductee.

Jim Kaat, the alternate left-hander for the sixties, played parts of 25 seasons as a major league pitcher – an all-time record until Tommy John caught on with the Yankees in 1989

*Above: Alternate dream team southpaw of the decade, Jim Kaat demonstrates his pitching style. The durable pitcher, whose major league career extended from 1959 through 1983, hurled for Minnesota for most of the sixties, when he recorded 142 wins.*

*Right: Elston Howard tries to block the plate, but the throw is late. Dream team catcher for the decade, Howard went to the World Series 10 of his 14 seasons in the majors. The Gold Glove catcher won his league's MVP Award in 1963.*

for his twenty-sixth season. Kaat won 142 games during the decade, with a high of 25 in 1966. The previous year he pitched the Twins into the World Series. Kaat won game two and the underdog Twins stretched the Series to seven games before Koufax, on two days rest, dashed the Twins' hopes with a three-hit shutout.

Kaat was a real workhorse. He started more than 40 games twice during the 1960s, three times in his career. He led the league in innings pitched once and in complete games once. Twice Kaat topped the loop's hurlers in games started. He topped 200 innings pitched 14 times in his lengthy career, eight times during the sixties. Kaat was also a skillful fielder. He won 16 consecutive Gold Gloves.

# CATCHER

Receivers of the 1960s wore the "Tools of Ignorance," as catcher's gear was once called. A best-selling baseball book by Joe Garagiola, published in 1960, regales the reader with jokes about ballplayers, specifically catchers. It has always taken a special kind of man to willingly bear the brunt of play behind the plate.

Catcher in the 1960s was one of the few positions of any time period that had no representative in the Hall of Fame. The best of the lot were Elston Howard of the Yankees and Red Sox; John Romano of the Indians, White Sox and Cardinals; and Bill Freehan of the Tigers.

**Elston Howard** is the dream team catcher for the sixties. The alternate is Bill Freehan rather than John Romano. Though out-hit by Romano, Freehan fielded so well that he received five Gold Gloves during the decade.

Elston Howard was the Yankees' first black starter; he played left field while waiting to replace Yogi Berra behind the plate. When Howard finally got the catching job in 1961, he wasted no time proving that he knew what he was doing. Whitey Ford, Ralph Terry and Jim Bouton became 20-game winners with Howard calling the shots behind the plate.

Howard won the MVP Award in a year that was not his best. Although he hit 28 home runs, he drove in only 85 runs. His batting average was .287. The next year Howard hit .313, and led the league in putouts and fielding, winning his second

straight Gold Glove Award. He played on nine pennant-winners with the Yankees, and one with the Red Sox in 1967.

John Romano was the top power-hitting catcher in the AL during the sixties. Though out-hit by Elston Howard, Romano out-slugged the Yankee catcher, hitting 124 homers for the decade. Romano was a good hitter, but not a fielder in the class of Howard or Freehan.

Bill Freehan, dream team alternate at catcher, had a .262 decade average with 110 home runs and a slugging average of .410. He had his best year in 1968 when the Tigers won the World Series in seven games against the Cardinals. Freehan hit .263 with 25 homers, 84 RBI, 73 runs, 24 doubles, and a slugging average of .454.

An outstanding defensive catcher, Freehan won five consecutive Gold Gloves. He led the league in putouts five straight years. He was best remembered for blocking the plate so effectively in the fifth inning of the fifth game of the 1968 World Series that Cardinal speedster Lou Brock was unable to reach the plate to score.

# FIRST BASE

Five first basemen hit more than 250 home runs each during the sixties. It was a hitter's position that was easy enough to play that Harmon Killebrew of the Senators and Twins, Ernie Banks of the Cubs, and Mickey Mantle with the Yankees made successful career-prolonging moves to first base during the decade.

The dream team selection list includes a Most Valuable Player, a batting champion and two Hall of Famers: Orlando Cepeda of the Giants and Cardinals, Norman Cash of the Tigers, Harmon Killebrew of the Old Senators and Twins, and Willie McCovey of the Giants.

Orlando Cepeda, called "Cha-Cha" by his teammates, was an inspirational force on three pennant-winning teams during the decade. For his efforts in propelling the 1967 Cardinals to the pennant, he received the MVP Award. Cepeda hit .295 with 254 home runs and 896 RBI in the 1960s.

*Left: Minnesota's first baseman Harmon Killebrew waits for the throw in 1965 World Series action with the Dodgers. The power-hitting dream team first sacker played for the Twins most of his 22-year career. During the sixties he led the league in homers and home run percentage five times, in RBI once, in walks twice and in slugging average twice.*

*Right: Harmon Killebrew pauses for a photo. Killebrew was elected to the Hall of Fame in 1984.*

*Below: Willie McCovey lets a ball go by during game three of the 1962 World Series against the Yankees. Alternate dream team first baseman, "Stretch" played for San Francisco for most of his 22-year career, leading the league four times in home run percentage. In his 1969 MVP year, McCovey led in homers, RBI and slugging average.*

"Stormin'" Norman Cash was a typical hard-living, hard-hitting player of the late 1950s and early 1960s. He won a batting title using a corked bat, and he used it to pop 278 home runs during the decade. Cash had an impressive 830 RBI and a .498 slugging percentage.

**Harmon Killebrew** was chosen dream team first baseman by virtue of his superior offensive statistics. He was a muscular, all-around fielder with monumental home run numbers. Killebrew hit 573 career round-trippers (393 of them in the 1960s) ranking fifth on the all-time list, second only to Ruth in the AL.

During the sixties, Killebrew tied or led the AL in home runs five times, belted over 40 in six seasons, and knocked in over 1000 runs. He is third among the game's power hitters in home run frequency.

Killebrew's best year was 1969, when he hit 49 home runs with 140 RBI, 145 walks, 106 runs, an on-base average of .430 and a slugging average of .584. His team, the Twins, won the Western Division, but lost the pennant to Baltimore in three straight games.

Dream team alternate first baseman Willie "Stretch" McCovey swung a big bat. His booming home runs forced the Giants to choose between him and Orlando Cepeda. The Giants traded Cepeda and kept McCovey for the balance of his Hall of Fame career. Although playing hurt throughout much of his 22-year career, the first baseman with the sweeping swing belted 521 career homers, tops among NL left-handed hitters, and tenth on the all-time list. McCovey's 18 lifetime grand slam home runs are second only to Lou Gehrig's 23. McCovey led the NL in homers three times, and in RBI twice during the 1960s.

McCovey was the NL's Rookie of the Year in 1959, its MVP in 1969, and the "Comeback Player of the Year" in 1977.

# SECOND BASE

With an emphasis on pitching and defense that grew out of the strike zone change, a premium was placed on second basemen who could turn the double play. Of course, that emphasis only lasted as long as the high strike. By 1969 every manager wanted the second baseman who could both turn the double play and hit 20 home runs.

Second base dream team candidates are Cookie Rojas of the Reds and Phillies, Julian Javier of the Cardinals, Pete Rose of the Reds, and Bill Mazeroski of the Pirates.

Cookie Rojas was an All-Star second baseman who swung a solid .260 stick, and fielded his position like a magician. His best year was 1965 when he hit .303 with the Phillies.

Julian Javier was the slick fielder who melded the Cardinal infield into a championship unit. A clutch player, he had a .333 batting average for 19 games in four World Series.

Dream Team selection **Pete Rose** was the most exciting player of his era; "Charlie Hustle" monopolized baseball's center stage throughout his entire career. Red manager Sparky Anderson declared that he has never been associated with a more competitive player.

In an exhibition game during his rookie year, Rose ran out a walk. The opposition sneered, "Charlie Hustle." Rose turned the put-down into a compliment. He played hard every day, wherever he was needed, and he loved every inning. Long after those who jeered at him had hung up their spikes, Rose was still winning games with headfirst slides and key hits.

Above all, Rose was a winner. He was Rookie of the Year in 1963. During the 1960s, he won two batting titles, had four 200-hit seasons, and ended the decade with five .300 seasons.

Bill Mazeroski, the dream team alternate, was possibly the greatest-fielding second baseman ever. His 1706 double plays constitute the all-time record for second basemen. Around Pittsburgh they called him "No-Hands" because the ball seemed to go from the shortstop's shovel pass to second base and then to first with Mazeroski barely touching it. He led the league in assists nine times, double plays eight times, putouts five times, and fielding average three times.

Maz also hit the most dramatic World Series home run; a game-ending blow against the Yankees in the bottom of the ninth to win the seventh game and make the Pirates World Champions for 1960.

Generally he was a fair hitter, and in a friendlier park, would have been better. Mazeroski had a respectable .262 decade batting average with some power. The game-ending homer in 1960 was his second round-tripper of the Series, his two-run blast having provided the margin of victory in Game One.

# THIRD BASE

Dream team candidates for third baseman include slugger Jim Ray Hart of the Giants, Hall of Famer Eddie Mathews of the Braves and Tigers, slugger Ron Santo of the Cubs, and Hall of Famer Brooks Robinson of the Orioles.

In his brief career, Jim Ray Hart showed a great deal of power; he slugged .478 with 142 homers in only 865 games. From 1964 to 1968 he averaged 83 runs, 28 home runs, 89 walks, and a .284 batting average. Injuries cut short Hart's promising career.

Eddie Mathews, dream team third baseman in the fifties, became the seventh player in major league history to hit 500

home runs, finishing his career with 512. Though on the down side of his Hall of Fame career in the sixties, he still packed some wallop. Mathews' 213 homers and 718 bases on balls during the decade gave him strong slugging and on-base percentages, .469 and .369 respectively.

**Ron Santo**, dream team third baseman for the 1960s, was the Brooks Robinson of the NL who could hit. If he was not quite the fielder Robinson was, he out-hit and out-homered Robinson, and drove in more runs than the AL third baseman. With Ernie Banks and Billy Williams, Santo provided tremendous power for the Chicago Cubs.

Santo had the fourth highest total of home runs among third basemen, with 342. Only Mike Schmidt, Eddie Mathews and Craig Nettles hit more. Santo had seven consecutive seasons of 94 or more RBI, and 25 or more home runs. In 1969 he drove in 129 runs as the Cubs made their strongest bid for a pennant in the sixties. Santo aggravated pitchers; he led the league in walks four times.

In the field, Santo was double-play champ five times, putout king six straight times, and assist leader seven years straight. Among NL third basemen, only Schmidt rivals him in total chances.

Brooks Robinson, dream team alternate for the 1960s, established a standard of excellence in fielding for modern-day third basemen. He played 23 seasons for the Baltimore Orioles, setting major league records for games, putouts, assists, chances, double plays and fielding percentage.

A clutchhitter as well, Robinson batted .277 with 186 homers and 836 RBI during the 1960s. He was the AL MVP in 1964, and World Series MVP in 1970.

## SHORTSTOP

Players who held infield positions, especially shortstop, in the 1960s, were very different from their counterparts who played at the turn of the century. Earlier infielders were the leading power hitters and best all-around players on the team. In the 1960s the position was tended by small, speedy, slick-fielding glovemen who could get on base, then steal second. Major league scouts discovered Latin America as a source for lean, quick, powerful athletes. It became a leading supplier of big league shortstops.

Candidates for the 1960s' dream team shortstop are Chico Cardenas of the Reds and Twins; Zoilo Versalles of the old Senators, Twins and Dodgers; Maury Wills of the Dodgers; and Hall of Famer Luis Aparicio of the White Sox and Orioles.

Chico Cardenas, the Cuban-born shortstop, was a good, solid fielder who hit .263 for the decade, and won a Gold Glove in 1965. He played for the pennant-winning Cincinnati Reds in 1961, and for the division champion Twins in 1969.

Left: *Pete Rose, pictured as a rookie for Cincinnati in 1963, played with the Reds for most of his 24-year career. Dream team second baseman for the decade, "Charlie Hustle" started his career with Rookie of the Year honors.*

Below: *The Pirates' Bill Mazeroski is accompanied, on the last leg of his home run trot, by third base coach Frank Oceak (44) and excited fans after belting one of the most* *famous home runs of all time: a World-Series-winning blast against the Yankees in 1960. Alternate dream team second baseman, "Maz" ended up with the all-time second baseman's record for double plays.*

Below right: *Brooks Robinson, alternate dream team third baseman for the sixties, takes a cut at the plate. This excellent fielder and clutch hitter played for the Orioles for 23 seasons.*

Zoilo Versalles won an MVP Award in 1965. He led the AL with 126 runs scored, 45 doubles and 12 triples that year, and the Twins captured the pennant. A Cuban right-handed hitter, Versalles struck out frequently, but he paced the AL in triples three consecutive seasons. Known primarily for his glove, Versalles led the league in putouts, assists, double plays and fielding average in 1962, and won Gold Glove Awards in 1963 and 1965. After leading the league three straight years in errors, he was traded by the Twins to the Dodgers.

**Maury Wills**, the 1960s dream team shortstop, brought the stolen base as an offensive weapon back into baseball. No NL player had stolen 50 bases since Max Carey had in 1923, but Wills grabbed that many in 1960. Two years later he shattered Ty Cobb's 1915 record of 96 and became the first man to break 100 in this century. Wills' 104 steals lit the way for the Brocks, Hendersons and Colemans, and changed the nature of the game. The steals also won him an MVP Award.

Opposite: *Ray Santo at the plate. This dream team third baseman played for the Cubs for 14 years. During the sixties the wide-ranging fielder led his league in double plays five times, and in putouts and assists seven times. Santo also led the league in walks four times and batted .280 for the decade.*

Left: *Future Hall of Fame third baseman Brooks Robinson. In his MVP season of 1964, Robinson batted .317* *with 118 RBI and 28 home runs.*

Below: *Maury Wills slides into third base. This dream team shortstop played most of his career with the Los Angeles Dodgers, going to the World Series with them four times along the way. When Wills stole 104 bases in his MVP year of 1962, he broke the single-season record set by Ty Cobb in 1915. His speed and reflexes were a defensive asset as well; he won two Gold Gloves.*

Wills was the shortstop for the Los Angeles Dodgers, a team long on pitching and short on power. His steals were of more value to the Dodgers than they might have been to a team of greater batting proficiency. Wills led the NL in stolen bases six straight years, from 1960 to 1965, and he finished his 14-year career with 586. In addition to the 104 in 1962, he stole 94 in 1965.

Although he had no home run power, Wills was more than a one-dimensional player. He had a career batting average of .281, and he twice won Gold Gloves as a shortstop. With Wills at short, the Dodgers won four pennants.

Luis Aparicio, dream team alternate, was one of the best shortstops of his time. A graceful fielder with exceptional range and hands, he still holds major league shortstop records for most games, assists, chances and double plays. Aparicio also played a part in the resurrection of the stolen base, stealing over 50 bases three straight seasons, and leading the AL in steals a record nine consecutive times. He was a starter for 18 seasons with the White Sox, Orioles and Red Sox.

During the sixties, Aparicio hit .259 with an on-base percentage of .363, tops among sixties shortstops. His 342 stolen bases ranked him third behind Maury Wills and Lou Brock. He played in two World Series, in 1959 with the Go-Go White Sox, and in 1966 with the powerful Baltimore Orioles.

Left: *Maury Wills slides safely into second with his 47th steal of the 1962 season, on his way to smashing Ty Cobb's stolen base record. Wills led the National League in stolen bases six consecutive seasons during the sixties.*

Above: *The Orioles' Frank Robinson is out at second as Maury Wills flips the ball to Jim Lefebvre in game three of the 1966 World Series.*

*Baltimore went on to win game four and sweep the Series when Robinson homered for the game's only tally. Dream team left fielder for the decade, Robinson began his career as NL Rookie of the Year. This Hall of Famer is the only player to be named MVP in both leagues: he was named NL MVP in 1961, and AL MVP in 1966, the year he also won the Triple Crown.*

# LEFT FIELD

Star hitters were put in left field where they could save their energy for batting. Teams with outstanding players in left field won pennants during the decade.

Left field dream team candidates for the sixties are all members of the Baseball Hall of Fame. They are Billy Williams of the Cubs, Lou Brock of the Cubs and Cardinals, Frank Robinson of the Reds and Orioles, and Carl Yastrzemski of the Red Sox.

Billy Williams was "just a ballplayer, trying to win every day." He was not colorful, but the soft-spoken Cub with the sweet swing hit .291 for the decade, with 249 homers and 853 RBI. Williams was the NL Rookie of the Year in 1961. He won a batting title in 1971 and held the NL mark for consecutive games (1117) until it was surpassed by Steve Garvey in 1983.

Lou Brock was an excellent ballplayer whose best years fell half in one decade and half in another. In the sixties, Brock was the catalyst of the 1964, 1967 and 1968 Cardinal pennant-

winners. He was an exciting player who saved his best performances for the national spotlight of the World Series. He starred in the Fall Classics with a .391 batting average, 14 stolen bases, and a slugging percentage of .655 in 21 World Series games.

**Frank Robinson**, the dream team left fielder for the 1960s, ripped 316 homers, scored 1013 runs, and drove in 1011 runs during the decade – more than any other left fielder. His .560 slugging average was second only to Hank Aaron's for all players during the decade. Robinson was Rookie of the Year in 1956, and the only man ever to be named MVP in both leagues (Cincinnati in 1961 and Baltimore in 1966). He developed into an aggressive and intelligent leader, and went on to manage the Indians, Giants and Orioles.

A devastating hitter, Robinson led the league in slugging percentage four times during the sixties. Traded to Baltimore because he was an "old 30," he wreaked havoc on AL pitching, capturing the Triple Crown with 49 homers, 122 RBI and a batting average of .316. The Orioles hung on to him long enough to win pennants in 1966, 1969, 1970 and 1971 – four flags in six years. Robinson finished his active baseball career as a playing manager for Cleveland. He once put himself in the game to pinch hit, and responded with a game-winning home run. His 586 career home runs rank him fourth on the all-time list.

Carl Yastrzemski is the alternate dream team left fielder. A three-time batting champion (1963, 1967 and 1968), he was the AL MVP in 1967 when he won the Triple Crown.

During that year Yastrzemski led the league with 44 home runs, 112 runs scored, 121 RBI, 189 hits, a .326 batting average, a .421 on-base average, and a .622 slugging percentage. He was one of the decade's premier batters, leading in doubles three times, in on-base percentage four times, and in hits, walks and slugging average two times during the sixties.

When Yastrzemski retired in 1983, after 23 seasons in the Boston outfield, he was the all-time Red Sox leader in eight categories: games played, at-bats, runs, hits, doubles, total bases, RBI and extra-base hits. Yaz played with graceful intensity in more games than any other American Leaguer and was the only AL player with over 3000 hits and 400 home runs.

# CENTER FIELD

The transition of the center fielder from the slugger to the far-ranging gloveman is exemplified by the four dream team candidates. Two of them, Curt Flood of the Cardinals and Vada Pinson of the Reds and Cardinals, were fleet-footed base-stealers. The other two, Willie Mays of the Giants and Mickey Mantle of the Yankees, came from the previous era of home run sluggers.

Curt Flood became well known for his refusal to report to his new team when traded in late 1970. Before his monumental challenge to baseball's reserve clause, Flood put together a respectable career. He hit over .300 six times during the sixties, and led the league in putouts four times, and in chances per game three times. Flood had the highest single-season fielding average ever in 1966 with a perfect 1,000.

When Vada Pinson's career was over, he had more hits than anyone else who has not been inducted into the Hall of Fame. He hit .292 for the decade with 310 doubles and a slugging average of .495.

**Willie Mays** was chosen as dream team center fielder for the sixties. The Say Hey Kid matured into one of the game's greatest sluggers during the decade. Mays rode the winds in

Opposite: *Carl Yastrzemski at the plate. Yaz, who inherited Boston's left-field position from Ted Williams, had a tough act to follow, but he pulled it off. This alternate dream team choice played for the Red Sox his entire 23-year career. A three-time batting champ with a Triple Crown and MVP Award under his belt, Yastrzemski was a durable and talented player.*

*He was elected to the Hall of Fame in 1989.*

Above: *The Yankee phenomenon Mickey Mantle ended his Hall of Fame career in 1968, but not before winning a third MVP Award in 1962, and clouting 256 homers with a .282 batting average for the decade. Mantle is the alternate dream team center fielder.*

San Francisco's Candlestick Park for 350 homers, 1050 runs scored, 1003 RBI and 259 doubles, leading the NL in homers three times during the sixties. In the same period he drove in 100 or more runs for seven consecutive years.

In 1965 Mays hit 52 home runs exactly 10 years after his first 50-homer season. The home runs gave the former NL Rookie of the Year his second MVP Award. His trophy case includes nine Gold Gloves won in 10 seasons. Mays' staggering career statistics include 3283 hits, 660 home runs and a .302 average.

Mickey Mantle, the dream team alternate, trailed Roger Maris in two straight MVP elections by a combined total of seven votes. Mantle then won his third MVP Award in 1962. As a testament to the influence of Mantle, Roger Maris, who batted in front of Mantle, was never walked intentionally in 1961, the season he hit 61 home runs.

During the sixties Mantle batted .282 and slugged .541, with 256 homers. He had the highest on-base percentage, .415, for the decade. Mantle was near the end of an injury-filled career in which the Yankees won 12 pennants and seven World Championships in his first 14 years.

Left: *The Giants' Willie Mays prepares to make contact for the 2000th hit of his career, in a game against the Dodgers on September 1, 1963. The 22-year career of this dream team center fielder is studded with awards, from Rookie of the Year and two MVP Awards to nine Gold Gloves.*

Below: *The Pirates' Roberto Clemente blasts a homer against Baltimore in game six of the 1971 World Series. Though Pittsburgh lost this game, Clemente's round-tripper the next day made the difference as his team gained the World Championship. Alternate dream team right fielder, for the decade Clemente batted .328 and led the league in assists five times.*

Right: *Hank Aaron belts a home run to deep left field in game four of the 1957 World Series. Dream team right fielder for consecutive decades, Aaron batted .308 during the sixties.*

# RIGHT FIELD

The tactic of putting the big bopper in right field where he could do the least amount of damage was not always necessary. Sometimes the slugger could field and throw, as well as launch home runs.

Dream team candidates for right fielder include three Hall of Famers and the Home Run Champ: Al Kaline of the Detroit Tigers, Roger Maris of the New York Yankees and St. Louis Cardinals, Hank Aaron of the Milwaukee and Atlanta Braves, and Roberto Clemente of the Pittsburgh Pirates.

Al Kaline, the 1950s' alternate right fielder, could still hit, and hit with power; he accumulated 247 doubles and 210 home runs on his way to a .295 decade batting average. His reputation as a clutch performer was enhanced by his .379 average against St. Louis in the 1968 World Series. Kaline's bases-loaded single in the seventh inning of game five won the game and began the historic Tiger comeback. As well as Kaline performed during the decade, the 1960s belonged to Aaron and Clemente in right field — both had super decades.

Roger Maris pursued the ghost of Babe Ruth in 1961 — one of the most nerve-wracking, intense baseball seasons ever. All eyes were focused on the home run duel between Mantle and Maris in 1961. That was the season New Yorkers stopped booing Mickey Mantle and started hating Roger Maris.

Maris was a very good ballplayer; his fielding won him a Gold Glove the previous season. His severe uppercut swing was tailor-made for the right-field stands in Yankee Stadium. Even before the season opened, sportswriters predicted that Mantle and Maris would make a run at Babe Ruth's elusive 60 home run mark. In nationally televised, pressure-packed games, Maris pursued the Bambino, and passed him in the 162nd game of the season.

After his record-breaking season, Maris suffered a wrist injury that severely limited his ability to swing the bat. After a couple of mediocre seasons, the Yankees peddled him to the Cardinals. There he caught fire again and fueled the Red Birds to two more pennants in 1967 and 1968.

**Hank Aaron**, the right fielder for the sixties' dream team, literally owned the decade. Though he never had one exceptional season, he led all other decade players in runs, RBI and slugging percentage. He was second to all other players in hits and home runs. So little appreciated was Aaron that he finished no higher than third place in the MVP voting at any time in the decade. Yet, during those 10 years, he slapped 1819 hits, scored 1091 runs, and drove in 1107 runs with 309 doubles and 375 home runs. Aaron even stole 204 bases.

In the next decade, Aaron would assault, surpass and extend Babe Ruth's all-time home run record to an amazing level — 755. He also set all-time records for the most games, at-bats, total bases and RBI. His lifetime batting average was .305.

The Pirates' Roberto Clemente played with an intensity that won him universal admiration and secured his dream team selection as alternate in right field. "The Great One" pounded Senior Circuit pitching for a .328 decade mark that encompassed four batting crowns. Clemente was equally brilliant in right field; he paced outfielders in assists five times with his rifle arm.

Despite an unorthodox batting style, Clemente topped the .300 mark nine of ten seasons, twice exceeding .350 during the 1960s. He amassed 3000 hits in his career, and he was the NL MVP in 1966. The star of the 1971 World Series, Clemente batted .414. In fact, he hit successfully in all 14 World Series games that he played. Clemente died in a plane crash in December 1972, on his way to Nicaraguan earthquake victims with relief supplies. The Baseball Writers Association of America voted Clemente into the Hall of Fame at the next available opportunity, foregoing the requisite five years of retirement before election. Pittsburgh fans mourned their hero. On a hillside overlooking Three Rivers Stadium, a special arrangement of lights spelled "Adios Amigo."

LEFT FIELD

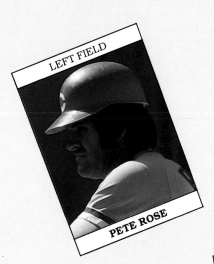

**PETE ROSE**

CENTER FIELD

**AMOS OTIS**

SHORTSTOP

**DAVE CONCEPCION**

SECOND BASE

**JOE MORGAN**

THIRD BASE

**MIKE SCHMIDT**

PITCHER (LH)

**STEVE CARLTON**

PITCHER (RH)

**TOM SEAVER**

DESIGNATED HITTER

**HAL McRAE**

CATCHER

**JOHNNY BENCH**

RIGHT FIELD

REGGIE JACKSON

FIRST BASE

WILLIE STARGELL

# THE GREATEST PLAYERS
## OF THE
# SEVENTIES

## ALTERNATE DREAM TEAM

| | | | |
|---|---|---|---|
| **Pitcher** | Jim Palmer (rh) | **Shortstop** | Bert Campaneris |
| | Vida Blue (lh) | **Left Fielder** | Jim Rice |
| **Catcher** | Ted Simmons | **Center Fielder** | Cesar Cedeno |
| **First Baseman** | Tony Perez | **Right Fielder** | Bobby Bonds |
| **Second Baseman** | Rod Carew | **Designated Hitter** | Willie Horton |
| **Third Baseman** | George Brett | | |

## HONORABLE MENTION

| | | | |
|---|---|---|---|
| **Pitcher** | Catfish Hunter | **Second Baseman** | Bobby Grich |
| | Nolan Ryan | | Dave Cash |
| | Bert Blyleven | | |
| | Ferguson Jenkins | **Third Baseman** | Bill Madlock |
| | Bob Forsch | | Brooks Robinson |
| | Phil Niekro | **Shortstop** | Larry Bowa |
| | Gaylord Perry | | Mark Belanger |
| | Luis Tiant | | |
| | Don Sutton | **Left Fielder** | Lou Brock |
| | Mike Torrez | | George Foster |
| | Ron Guidry | **Center Fielder** | Fred Lynn |
| **Catcher** | Carlton Fisk | **Right Fielder** | Dave Parker |
| | Thurman Munson | | Dave Winfield |
| **First Baseman** | Steve Garvey | | |
| | Willie McCovey | | |

# THE SETTING

Rioters, strikers, free thinkers, free lovers, and men with long hair found their way to the ballparks of America in the 1970s. And not all of them were in the stands. Trends of society, even radical trends, have always been reflected in baseball. The national game showed us once again that it was a microcosm of the world around it, that it could act as a vehicle for societal change.

Conflict was the tone of the day. Protesters cried out against U.S. involvement in Vietnam. Riots and general unrest were the responses to racism and bigotry. One observed turmoil in baseball as well: player versus management, management versus fans, press versus player, and Yankee owner George Steinbrenner versus the world. Free agency set owner against owner in fervent bidding wars.

An indication that the 1970s would be full of surprises came early in 1969, when Baseball Commissioner William "Spike" Eckart called a conference at the winter meetings. He wanted to discuss baseball problems and develop some solutions. Imagine Eckart's chagrin when baseball owners decided the solution was to replace him. They planned to break the two leagues into four divisions, and expand major league baseball into four additional cities. Baseball made this bold attempt to rebuild dwindling fan support. One result: the Miracle Mets, whose exuberant fans tore up Shea Stadium, not once but twice, during the team's amazing drive to the top of the baseball world. After the Mets, anything could happen, and it did.

# GAME STRATEGY

Strategy took a giant step – but historians have not decided whether it was forward or backward – when the AL voted to accept the Designated Hitter (DH). It was an old idea, first brought to the AL by Connie Mack in 1905, and defeated in NL vote in 1930. The DH led to a decrease in pinch hitters, and to increases in complete games by pitchers, and in home runs.

The free thinking of the 1970s created a variety of conflicting game strategies. The diamond became a classroom for baseball minds. Mike Marshall of the Expos pitched in 106 games. The Baltimore Orioles won a pennant with four 20-game winners on its pitching staff; the Cincinnati Reds won four pennants with only one 20-game winner. Lou Brock stole 118 bases. Reggie Jackson hit three home runs in the last game of the 1977 World Series, and the once proud Baltimore Orioles hired a witch to remove a curse from them. Baseball, in its own divergent way, represented the diverse American culture.

Relief pitching reached its zenith. Managers Dick Williams of the Oakland A's, and Sparky Anderson of the Cincinnati Reds skillfully employed one-pitch specialists to produce record-setting results. Williams won three consecutive World Series Championships. He was a pioneering manager who alternated relievers, left-handed Darold Knowles with right-handed Rollie Fingers. Williams' successor traded Knowles, as the conventional wisdom of the day was to bring in "the stopper," not a set of stoppers.

Sparky Anderson won four pennants on the strength of prime time regulars and a 10-man pitching staff. Among his 1975-1976 juggernauts there were no pitchers with more than 15 victories, but nine different hurlers with 10 or more wins.

# FACTORS INFLUENCING PLAYER PERFORMANCE

Unionization, free agency, new stadiums and rule changes influenced the performance of baseball players in the 1970s. Salaries began to increase exponentially.

Two opposing forces, the players' union movement under the direction of Marvin Miller, and baseball team owners with the support of new Commissioner Bowie Kuhn, pushed and pulled the players until they were forced to put up a united front. As they united players became more and more isolated from the public generally, and from sportswriters specifically.

Free agency made millionaires of certain players. Talent, however, had little to do with who got the million-dollar contracts. Timing and negotiating were the primary ingredients in the recipe for a fat, free-agent contract. This quirk of fate caused owners, players and fans to adjust their thinking about player performance. One additional home run or pitching victory might mean an extra $150,000 to the player at contract time. As the decade progressed, the emphasis was placed on accumulating statistics.

The new ballparks with astroturf, large foul territories and symmetrical boundaries were not advantageous for hitters. Actually, they were not parks, they were giant donuts with seats, called stadiums. The contour of the stadium and the accompanying effect on batting averages has been fully discussed in *The Bill James Baseball Abstracts*.

The most important rule change affecting player performance was the institution of the DH. AL teams acquired an additional hitter in the batting order. Initially there was experimentation to find the type of DH that would best help the team. Clubs quickly decided on the home run bat. Several baseball stars were able to prolong their careers and paydays because of the DH rule.

# THE POSITIONS

## PITCHER

Some of the best right-handed pitchers of all time played ball in the 1970s. The era is likely to produce more Hall of Fame pitchers than any previous decade since the early 1900s. Twelve men were considered for dream team right-handed pitcher. They are: Catfish Hunter of the Athletics and Yankees; Nolan Ryan of the Mets and Angels; Bert Blyleven of the Twins, Rangers and Pirates; Ferguson Jenkins of the Cubs, Rangers and Red Sox; Bob Forsch of the Cardinals; Phil Niekro of the Braves; Gaylord Perry of the Giants, Indians, Rangers and Padres; Luis Tiant of the Twins, Red Sox and Yankees; Don Sutton with the Dodgers; Mike Torrez of the Cardinals, Expos, Orioles, Athletics, Yankees and Red Sox; Tom Seaver of the Reds; and Jim Palmer of the Orioles.

Catfish Hunter was the first of the great 1970s pitchers to retire and consequently, the first to be enshrined in the Hall of Fame. He became the first modern free agent when Athletic owner Charles Finley voided his contract by failing to fulfill a clause of it. Hunter, in an unprecedented bidding war, signed a multimillion dollar contract with the Yankees. He repaid the Yanks by pitching them to three straight pennants and two World Championships, from 1976 to 1978. He won 169 games during the decade before arm trouble ended his career.

Nolan Ryan produced the greatest strikeout season in baseball history when he struck out 383 hitters during 1973. The feat is even more amazing when viewed in light of the fact that he did not face puny-hitting pitchers, but designated hitters. Ryan's longevity as a fastball ace continued to astound veteran baseball watchers. He won 155 games in the seventies.

Bert Blyleven won 148 games during the decade, pitching on two division winners and one World Championship team. He was known for the best curveball of the decade. In his greatest season Blyleven won 20, threw nine shutouts and struck out 258, fashioning a 2.52 ERA in 1973.

Ferguson Jenkins was a 20-game winner four times during the 1970s, compiling a 178-130 record. A control pitcher, he led the league five times in fewest bases on balls per nine innings. Working for second-division teams, Jenkins never pitched in post-season play.

Bob Forsch did not break into the majors until 1974. He was a consistent winner for 16 years. He tossed two no-hitters, one in 1978 and another in 1983. Also an excellent hitter for a pitcher (.213 lifetime average), Forsch pitched the Red Birds into three World Series during the eighties.

Phil Niekro won 164 games during the seventies on his way to 318 lifetime victories. He was another superb pitcher who never played in the World Series. A knuckleball pitcher who helped himself with fine fielding, Niekro was voted five Gold Gloves Awards, two of them in the 1970s.

Gaylord Perry, who was called the Ancient Mariner late in his career while with Seattle, used shoe polish, saliva, Vaseline, Brylcreme and anything else to get an edge on the batter. He picked up 314 victories in his long career. During the 1970s he won 189 games and two Cy Young Awards. Perry was a 20-

*Hall of Famer Tom Seaver in action. Dream team right-hander of the seventies, "Tom Terrific" was a clever pitcher with excellent control and heat. He pitched a no-hitter and won two Cy Young Awards during the decade, with a 178-111 won-lost record.*

game winner four times. His best season was 1972; he won 24 games, completed 29, struck out 234 batters, and had an ERA of 1.92.

Luis Tiant, the son of all-time Cuban baseball great Luis Tiant, Senior, used a snake-like windup before firing the ball toward the plate. By the end of 1979, Tiant had suffered only one losing season. He won 142 regular-season games during the seventies, and two more in the 1975 World Series.

Don Sutton was a player who was not particularly impressive to fans or sportswriters, yet he won 324 games. Sutton pitched 200 or more innings every season from 1966 through 1986, except for the 1981 strike season. Such consistency should put him in the Hall of Fame. During the seventies, Sutton won 166 games and pitched in three World Series for the Dodgers.

Mike Torrez was a pitcher who flirted with greatness. He won two complete-game victories in the 1977 World Series, then started the 1978 playoff match for the Red Sox against the Yankees. Torrez's chance for immortality went flying over the fence with Yankee Bucky Dent's three-run homer. Still, Torrez won 142 games during the seventies.

In one of the closest dream team contests, **Tom "Terrific" Seaver** won the right-handed pitching spot by virtue of three Cy Young Awards, a dominating fastball and slider, and elegant style. Jim Palmer, with eight 20-game seasons during 1970s, is the alternate.

Left: *Jim Palmer winds up for the pitch. This alternate dream team right-hander pitched his entire 19-year career with the Orioles. During the seventies he turned in eight 20-win seasons, won three Cy Young Awards, and pitched in five All-Star Games. He was elected to the Hall of Fame in 1990.*

Right: *Steve Carlton pitched for the Phillies for 14 seasons of his 23-year career. A dominating pitcher, this dream team lefty led the league in 1972 in wins (27), ERA (1.97) and strikeouts (310) to win his first of two Cy Young Awards during the decade.*

Below right: *Oakland's ace Vida Blue throws a strikeout pitch to the Twins' Harmon Killebrew on his way to a no-hitter on September 22, 1970. Alternate dream team southpaw, Vida Blue pitched for the A's, Giants and Royals during his 17-year career. With his league-leading 1.82 ERA and eight shutouts, Blue won the Cy Young Award in 1971.*

Tom Seaver may have been the best of all the great pitchers since World War II. He won 311 games, struck out 3640 batters, and compiled a career ERA of 2.86. But most importantly he was able to win with both good and bad teams. As Rookie of the Year in 1967, he was 16-13 with the seventh-place Mets. In 20 years of pitching, his personal winning percentage exceeded his team's winning percentage in 16 seasons.

During the 1970s, Seaver won his second and third Cy Young Awards, one in 1973 with a 19-10 record for the pennant-winning Mets, and the other two years later with a 22-9 record and an ERA of 2.38. For the decade he had 178 victories and 111 losses.

Although Seaver led the NL in strikeouts five times, had 10 seasons with over 200 strikeouts, and set the NL record with 19 whiffs in a nine-inning game, he was never just a "thrower." He exhibited excellent control and pitch selection from the beginning of his career. Seaver just happened to throw a 98 mile-per-hour fastball.

Jim Palmer, dream team alternate, won 186 games in the 1970s for the Orioles, who were League Champions five times. The handsome right-hander won 268 games in his career, despite suffering a sore arm after shutting out the Dodgers as a 20-year-old in the 1966 World Series. The injury kept him out of the majors for virtually two years. When he got back, Palmer won 20 or more games in four straight seasons, from 1970 to 1973. After an off year, he put together four more years of winning more than 20 games, from 1975 to 1978. Palmer won three Cy Young Awards, in 1973, 1975 and 1976. He led the AL in ERA in 1973 and 1975.

The top left-handers of the decade were Ron Guidry of the Yankees, Steve Carlton of the Cardinals and Phillies, and Vida Blue of the A's and Giants.

Ron Guidry burst onto the scene at Yankee Stadium, with

69 wins in three seasons, including an incredible 25-3 year with a 1.74 ERA. Guidry did not pitch enough seasons to qualify as a dream team candidate, though he was great at the close of the decade.

**Steve Carlton**, dream team left-hander for the 1970s, refused to grant interviews for most of his career. He let his pitching do his talking, and it came through loud and clear. Along with Warren Spahn and Sandy Koufax, Carlton was one of the three best NL left-handers of all time. He won 329 games, second only to Spahn among lefties. He had 4131 strikeouts, including 19 in one game. Carlton won four Cy Young Awards, two during the seventies.

Carlton is the only man to win the Cy Young Award while playing for a last place team. That was in 1972, after he was traded by the Cardinals to the Phillies. He had an amazing 27-10 season with Philadelphia, who won only 32 that Carlton did not pitch. He led the NL in wins, ERA and strikeouts that year, and earned a record salary from the Phillies the following year — $167,000. Carlton took special delight during 1972 in whipping his former team, the Cardinals, who had refused to give him a raise after his 20-9 season in 1971. He beat the Red Birds four times, allowing a total of only two runs. One of those wins was his 100th. Carlton's 300th victory was also over St. Louis.

Carlton had four 20-win seasons during the decade, as the Phillies moved from the basement to being contenders, and finally becoming World Champions in 1980. He won two games in the 1980 World Series, including the game six clincher.

Using a fastball, curve and legendary slider, the six-foot-

Left: *Johnny Bench bangs one the opposite way. This dream team catcher played for the Cincinnati Reds his entire 17-year career. Starting off with NL Rookie of the Year honors in 1968, Bench became a perpetual Gold Glove winner and a threat at the plate. He led his league in homers twice and in RBI once during the seventies.*

Above: *Ted Simmons, alternate dream team catcher for the decade, played for St. Louis from 1968 through 1980, then was traded to the Braves. Solid at the plate, Simmons smacked 20 or more homers four times during the seventies, slugging .454.*

four lefty was a workhorse, leading the NL in innings pitched five times. When Carlton suffered a strained shoulder in 1985, he went on the disabled list for the first time in his career.

Vida Blue, dream team alternate left-hander for the 1970s, had a career like a rollercoaster ride. He was aided in his 1972 contract holdout by President Richard Nixon, who boldly announced that Vida Blue was the best pitcher in baseball. The tall, slender southpaw became involved in drugs, which greatly affected his performance. In his first full year of pitching at the major league level, Blue won 24 games and the Cy Young Award as the frisky A's won the first of their five straight division titles. He never fared well in World Series play, with an 0-3 record for eight appearances. For all of his troubles, Blue still won 155 during the decade and finished his career in 1986, with 209 wins.

# CATCHER

During the 1970s catching was once again the shortest path to the majors. Gone were the thick, heavy-thighed, ponderously slow runners of bygone eras. In their places came a crop of tall, medium-built young men whose bodies adapted well to the physical stress of the position.

Dream team candidates for catcher were Carlton Fisk of the Red Sox, Thurman Munson of the Yankees, future Hall of Fame member Johnny Bench of the Reds, and Ted Simmons of the Cardinals.

Carlton Fisk was the protagonist in one of the most memorable scenes in modern baseball. In the twelfth inning of game six of the 1975 World Series, he hit a home run that took forever to get over the wall. The image of Fisk, galloping sideways toward first base, waving the ball fair with his arms, is etched in the memories of millions of baseball fans who watched on television. But Fisk has been much more than a one-hit hero. He was Rookie of the Year in 1972, when he hit .293 with 22 homers. Considered a long ball threat for two decades, in the seventies Fisk hit 144 round-trippers.

Thurman Munson began his career as a Rookie of the Year. The heart of the three-time Yankee pennant-winning team of the seventies, Munson won the MVP Award for his 1976 season, when he batted .302, hit 17 homers and drove in 105 runs. He was an All-Star pick in 1971 and from 1973 to 1978. Munson's career was tragically cut short in August of 1979, when he was killed in a plane crash.

**Johnny Bench**, dream team catcher for the 1970s, was possibly the best all-around catcher of all time. He set the standards against which other catchers are compared.

Rookie of the Year in 1968, the Oklahoma Indian controlled the game on both sides of the plate. He could hit with power as his .267 batting average, 290 home runs and 1013 RBI during the seventies attest. Throwing out opposing baserunners, calling pitches and blocking home plate were his greatest skills in the field. Bench won two MVP Awards, in 1970 and 1972, and 10 Gold Gloves during his 17 seasons as the receiver for the Big Red Machine.

Dream team alternate selection Ted Simmons was an outstanding hitter as catchers go. At bat he was one of the best, hitting over .300 seven times in his 16 seasons as a regular. Five times he had 20 or more homers, and he had eight seasons of 90 or more RBI. He hit .297 and slugged .454 for the decade.

Simmons was sometimes ridiculed for his defense, but in 1973 he led NL catchers in assists. That may reflect the liberties baserunners were taking.

**Willie Stargell 8**

# FIRST BASE

The nature of first base as a position for home run hitters remained unchanged from the 1930s. Managers became accustomed to having 25 to 40 home runs a season from their first sackers.

The dream team selection list includes Steve Garvey of the Dodgers, Tony Perez of the Reds and Expos, and Hall of Famers Willie McCovey of the Giants and Padres, and Willie Stargell of the Pirates.

Steve Garvey passed Billy Williams' NL mark of consecutive games played, then extended the new record to 1207. The streak was indicative of Garvey's Iron Man nature. He hit and fielded in streaks, batting .300 or more six of seven years and winning four straight Gold Gloves in the 1970s. His decade batting average was over .300, but he lacked power. His 159 homers would have been good for a catcher, but it was an unsatisfactory total for a dream team first baseman.

Willie McCovey was the 1960s dream team alternate first baseman. Though his home run statistics had fallen off, McCovey still inspired fear in opposing pitchers; he walked once in every six at-bats during the decade. McCovey's on-base percentage, .370, trailed decade leader Willie Stargell's by a single point, though the Pirate slugger had him by 77 points on slugging average.

**Willie Stargell**, the dream team choice for first baseman of the seventies, combined charisma and power in his play. He crushed 475 career homers, 296 of them in the 1970s. He led the NL with 48 in 1971 and 44 in 1973. Stargell drove in 906 runs and slugged .554 for the decade. His influence extended beyond the chalk lines and into the clubhouse, where his inspirational leadership contributed to Pirate World Championships in 1971 and 1979. He tied with the Cardinals' Keith Hernandez for MVP in 1979.

Tony "Doggie" Perez, the dream team alternate first baseman, was one of the biggest gears in the Big Red Machine of the 1970s. The congenial first baseman helped put the Reds in four World Series. He knocked in 90 or more runs 11 straight seasons, from 1967 to 1977.

Perez's career totals included 1652 RBI and 1272 runs scored. His decade totals included 954 RBI, 303 doubles, 226 home runs and a .283 batting average. Perez hit 40 home runs in 1970. He hit .300 a couple of times and finished with a respectable .279 average for 23 seasons. Yet, amazingly, he never led the league in a single important offensive statistic.

Perez was a solid, consistent player. He was also a good enough glove man to play third base for five seasons for Cincinnati so that slugger Lee May could play first base.

Perez hit .435 in the 1972 World Series. In the 1975 Series, he went 0-for-15, then exploded with two homers and four RBI to win the fifth game.

# SECOND BASE

Three factors enter into the selection process for second basemen: hitting, fielding and turning the double play. Managers were still not sure in the 1970s which aspect of the position was more important; the decade featured a variety of each type of player.

Second base dream team candidates are Bobby Grich of Baltimore; Dave Cash of Pittsburgh, Philadelphia, Montreal and California; Joe Morgan of Cincinnati; and Rod Carew of Minnesota and California.

Opposite: *Willie Stargell at bat. Though he started with Pittsburgh as an outfielder, by the early seventies Stargell was the regular at first base. This dream team player contributed to his team's appearance in six NLCS and two World Series during the seventies. He topped off his co-MVP season of 1979 by batting .400, with four doubles and three homers, in the Series, helping the Pirates win it all.*

Above: *The Reds' Joe Morgan pops one foul. The dream team second baseman played most of his illustrious 22-year career with Houston and Cincinnati, retiring in 1984. During the seventies Morgan exhibited his many talents: speed (488 stolen bases), power (173 homers), discretion (1181 bases on balls), and defensive excellence (five Gold Gloves).*

149

Left: *Rod Carew demonstrates his hitting style. Alternate dream team second sacker, Carew played with the Twins from 1967 until 1979, when he was traded to California, where he played until his retirement in 1985. Carew switched from second to first base in the mid-seventies. A masterful hitter, Carew's six batting titles during the decade include his 1977 MVP season, when he also led the league in runs scored, triples and hits.*

Opposite left: *Dream team third baseman of the seventies, Mike Schmidt played for the Phillies from 1972 until his retirement early in 1989. Schmidt won eight consecutive Gold Gloves, but his talent at the plate was even more evident. During the decade he led his league in homers three times, walks once, and slugging average once, helping his team to three consecutive trips to the NLCS.*

Opposite right: *Mike Schmidt on deck. During the seventies Schmidt averaged 95 RBI, 33 home runs, 98 walks and 96 runs a season.*

Bobby Grich began his career with promise, winning four Gold Glove Awards from 1973 to 1976, twice scoring 90 runs, and walking more than a hundred times. Then he was traded to the Angels, who thought they were getting a Rod Carew with power. Grich tried to live up to their expectations; he hit 30 home runs one year.

Dave Cash appeared to be the rising star of the NL as he put together back-to-back 200-hit seasons and scored 111 runs in 1975. Then a career-stifling injury slowed him so much that he was out of baseball by age 32. Cash hit .287 for the decade.

**Joe Morgan** was selected dream team second baseman for the 1970s. He was one of the best-hitting second basemen of all time. Little Joe Morgan stood only five-foot-seven, but he played more games at second base than did any man except Eddie Collins, and won back-to-back MVP Awards in 1975 and 1976.

Morgan began his career with Houston, where twice he scored more than 100 runs in a season, and developed the ability to draw walks. Traded to Cincinnati in 1972, he came into his own as a star with the Big Red Machine. In 1975, his first MVP year, Morgan batted .327 with 17 homers, 107 runs

scored, 94 RBI and 67 stolen bases. The next year he hit .320 with 27 homers, 113 runs scored, 111 RBI and 60 stolen bases.

For the decade, Morgan batted .282 with 1005 runs scored, 720 RBI, 275 doubles, 173 home runs, 1071 bases on balls, 488 stolen bases, and a .406 on-base percentage.

In the field Morgan won five Gold Gloves, and in 1977-1978 put together a string of 91 straight games without an error. Above all, he was a winner. He led the Reds to five division titles and three World Series.

Rod Carew, alternate second baseman for the decade, won more batting championships than did any other major league player except Ty Cobb. Carew, the moody Panamanian, sprayed 3053 hits to win seven AL titles for Minnesota, including four in a row from 1972 through 1975. In 1969, when Carew won his first batting crown with .332, he stole home seven times, tying a mark set by Brooklyn's Pete Reiser. In 1972 Carew hit a league-leading .318 without a single homer, the only batting champ ever to do that. Fifteen of his hits that year were bunts. Carew's highest batting mark was .388 in 1977, tying Ted Williams' mark of 1957 for the second highest batting average in the majors since 1941. That year Carew also led in runs scored (128), and triples (16). He was named MVP.

# THIRD BASE

Third base was a hitter's position, and managers placed a high average batter or a home run slugger there. The installation of astroturf on many fields effectively cancelled the bunt as an offensive weapon. Therefore, those playing third base were seldom called on to make the bare-handed snap throw to first while charging forward at full speed.

The list of prospective dream team third basemen for the seventies includes a four-time batting champion, one Hall of Fame member, and two who are sure to be Hall of Famers. They are Bill Madlock of the Rangers, Cubs, Giants and Pirates; Brooks Robinson of the Orioles; Mike Schmidt of the Phillies; and George Brett of the Royals.

Bill "Mad Dog" Madlock won two batting titles with the Cubs, then played in the World Series with the 1979 Pirates. He batted .320 for the decade and led all third basemen with a .378 on-base percentage. Madlock added two more batting titles with the Pirates in 1981 and 1983.

Brooks Robinson, dream team alternate in the 1960s, established a standard of excellence for modern-day third basemen. He played 23 seasons for the Baltimore Orioles, setting major league records for games, putouts, assists, chances, double plays and fielding percentage. He won 16 consecutive Gold Gloves.

A clutch hitter who by the 1970s was losing his power, Robinson batted .254 with 72 homers and 449 RBI during the decade. He was the World Series MVP in 1970, when he hit .429 and stopped the Reds with several spectacular plays at third.

**Mike Schmidt**, the 1970s dream team third baseman, was not only the greatest hitter ever to play third base, but was arguably the greatest fielder. His home runs were famous; less well known were his 404 assists in 1974, the most ever by a NL third baseman. Three years later his 396 assists were the second highest total in NL history. He won Gold Gloves eight years in a row.

Schmidt also won eight home run crowns (he hit 235 homers during the seventies) four RBI titles and three MVP Awards. His home run-to-at-bat ratio ranks in the top 10 of all time, and he was one of only 14 major leaguers to hit more than 500 home runs. Schmidt's slugging put the Phillies into the playoffs six times.

George Brett is the dream team alternate. A vivacious heartthrob, Brett was the jewel in batting coach Charlie Lau's crown. He never hit .300 in the minor leagues, yet hitting off his front foot with the distinctive one-hand follow-through that Lau taught, the left-handed slugger went on to win three AL batting titles, in 1976, 1980 and 1990.

Three times, in 1975, 1976 and 1979, Brett led the AL in both hits and triples during the same season, a feat matched only by Ty Cobb. In 1979 Brett became one of only five players to have 20 doubles, triples and home runs in the same season.

151

Left: *George Brett prepares to tag out an Indian baserunner at third. Alternate dream team third baseman for the decade, Brett was as solid in the field as he was at the plate – he led the league in putouts (140) in 1976, and in assists (373) in 1979.*

Above: *George Brett takes signals from the third base coach. Brett's offensive performance helped the Royals to six league championship series and two World Series, where his clutch hitting (.341 batting average in post-season play) shone.*

Left: *The Athletics' Bert Campaneris poses with his bat. This alternate dream team shortstop was a perpetual All-Star selection, a speedy baserunner and a solid hitter.*

Right: *Dave Concepcion bangs a hard liner. Although his decade batting was respectable but not brilliant, Concepcion came through at the plate during post-season play, batting .351 over five NLCS.*

Above: *The Reds' shortstop Dave Concepcion – dream team choice for the decade – on the field.*

# SHORTSTOP

Baseball managers have always mimicked success. The Baltimore Orioles became successful with slick-fielding shortstops who did not always hit well. Managers of other teams followed suit. During the decade of the seventies a shortstop who hit .250 was considered an asset as long as he could make the routine play, and was able to go into the hole to nab the runner at first.

Dream team candidates for shortstop of the 1970s include Larry Bowa of the Phillies, Mark Belanger of the Orioles, Dave Concepcion of the Reds, and Bert Campaneris of the Athletics, Rangers and Angels.

Larry Bowa was a throwback to the old blood-and-guts type of player who flourished around the turn of the century. A decent performer both in the field and at the plate, he captured two Gold Gloves and scored 725 runs, though saddled with a .262 decade batting average.

Mark Belanger, the glue that held the Orioles together, earned eight Gold Gloves. His lack of hitting certainly was not a concern for his teammates, since they won five division championships during the seventies.

Bowa, Belanger and Concepcion were all excellent fielders with awards to prove it. **Dave Concepcion** was a considerably better hitter with more power than any of the candidates, therefore is picked the dream team shortstop. Bert Campaneris was a strong hitter, and he was a good enough glove man to

anchor an infield that appeared in six League Championship Series and three World Series. "Campy" is the dream team alternate.

Dave Concepcion wore number 13 on the Big Red Machine. One of its top fielders, Concepcion popularized the technique of bouncing long throws from the hole to first to get runners who would have beaten high-arc tosses. His revolutionary technique helped him garner five Gold Gloves.

With a decade batting average in the .260s, Concepcion did not set any hitting records, but he had more power than any of the decade's other shortstops. Although his batting average topped .300 only twice, he got hot in post-season play. He averaged over .400 in the 1975 and 1979 playoffs, and over .300 in the 1970, 1972 and 1976 World Series. In the 1975 Fall Classic, Concepcion came up in the ninth inning of game two, with the Reds losing 1-2, two out, and Johnny Bench on second base. He slapped a single to tie the score, stole second, and scored on Ken Griffey's double to win the game.

Bert Campaneris, nicknamed "Campy," was a great athlete. He could pitch with either hand, and did so at Daytona Beach in the Florida State League in 1962. The major leagues quickly passed a rule prohibiting "switch pitching," which really should be called the Campaneris Rule.

Settled at the shortstop position, Campaneris sparked the Athletics to five division titles and three World Championships with his stolen bases, 336 in the 1970s, and occasional home runs. Campy hit .254 with 700 runs scored for the decade. He was selected for six All-Star teams.

# LEFT FIELD

One left fielder who is in the Hall of Fame, a home run champion, another who is a sure bet for the Hall, and an MVP top the dream team candidates for the 1970s. They are Lou Brock of the Cardinals, George Foster of the Reds, Pete Rose of the Reds, and Jim Rice of the Red Sox.

Lou Brock earned his nickname "Mr. Excitement" as the Cardinal lead-off man during the seventies. He stole 551 bases, including a NL record 118 in 1974. Despite his stolen bases, .298 batting average and 843 runs scored, Brock was unable to propel the Red Birds into another World Series, where he had excelled during the sixties.

George Foster became the first baseball player to make $2 million per year when he signed with the New York Mets in 1982. His tremendous salary was based on the potential he showed in the 1970s. In 1977 Foster became the first major leaguer for more than 10 years to hit 50 home runs in a season. He just missed 150 RBI. Foster hit .287 with 201 homers during the 1970s, but had a low RBI total (690) for so many home runs.

**Pete Rose**, the decade leader in hits with 2045, was the top choice for left field on the 1970s dream team. He was the most exciting player of his era. Charlie Hustle monopolized center stage with his unsuccessful pursuit of Joe DiMaggio's

hitting streak in 1978. He pursued and surpassed Ty Cobb's lifetime hit record in 1985.

Rose played more games than did any other ballplayer, batted more times, made more hits, had the second most doubles, and had fourth most runs scored. He had 2045 hits during the 1970s. Rose won three batting titles and made the NL All-Star team at five different positions. He was Rookie of the Year in 1963, MVP in 1973, and played in his last World Series in 1983.

Rose played on four pennant-winning teams in Cincinnati during the 1970s, then he signed a lucrative contract with the Phillies in 1979 and helped them win two more pennants in the 1980s. *The Sporting News* voted him Player of the 1970s, then its Man of the Year in 1985.

Jim Rice, dream team alternate left fielder for the seventies, was made for Fenway Park, and he took complete advantage of it. He and Fred Lynn enjoyed splendid rookie seasons in 1975 to lift the Red Sox from third place to first, then to take the pennant. An injury kept Rice out of the World Series, which Boston lost to the Reds in seven games.

His best season was 1978, capped by the thrilling pennant race with New York, which the Yankees won in a playoff game. Rice led the league in homers with 46, in RBI with 139, in triples with 15, and in hits with 213, with a .315 batting average. He was voted MVP over New York's Ron Guidry in a hotly debated election.

Left: *Pete Rose looks the ball into the catcher's mitt, ready to argue the call. This dream team second baseman of the sixties made the switch to outfield and excelled there as well; he is dream team left fielder of the seventies. Rose won the NL MVP Award in 1973, leading the league that year in hits (230) and batting average (.338). His .313 decade batting average helped the Reds to five NLCS contests and four World Series.*

Right: *Jim Rice at the plate. "The Boston Strongman" took over left field from Carl Yastrzemski in 1975, to continue a tradition of excellence in that position. Alternate dream team left fielder, Rice capped off a decade in which he hit for power while batting .310, with a 1978 MVP performance.*

# CENTER FIELD

The previous decade's aging superstars, who had lost much of their ground-covering ability, were replaced in the outfield by speedy fly catchers reminiscent of earlier eras. While the new stadiums did not feature the vast center-field territories of earlier twentieth-century ballparks, they shortened power alleys and speeded up the roll of the ball with astroturf. The center fielder of the 1970s had to move fast.

The decade's top players in center were Fred Lynn of the Red Sox, Amos Otis of the Royals, and Cesar Cedeno of the Astros.

Fred Lynn started his major league career as had no player ever before. He won Rookie of the Year and the American League MVP Award. Lynn and fellow rookie Jim Rice powered the Red Sox to the pennant and into a memorable World Series showdown with the Big Red Machine in 1975. Lynn, who suffered from frequent injuries, was never able to live up to the great promise of his first year. He did not play enough games during the seventies to qualify for the dream team.

**Amos Otis**, with slightly more collective offensive statistics and three Gold Gloves, won the dream team center-field spot over Cesar Cedeno. Otis was an underrated player. He helped Kansas City win four division titles and one pennant between 1976 and 1980. During the 1970s he hit a strong .284, with 159 homers, 861 runs scored and 753 RBI. His .429 batting average in the 1978 League Championship Series fueled a valiant but futile effort to upset the Yankees.

Two years later Otis hit .333, as the Royals won the League Championship Series. He then hit .478 in the World Series against Philadelphia, including a home run in game five to bring Kansas City to within one run of victory.

Otis was one of the best baserunners of the seventies. When he led the AL in stolen bases in 1971 with 52, he was caught only eight times. The year before that he had done even better with 33 out of 34 — the only time he was caught was when he attempted to steal home.

A fine fielder, Otis went 165 straight games without an error in 1970-1971. He led the league's outfielders in putouts, assists, double plays and total chances both years.

Dream team alternate center fielder Cesar Cedeno made the mistake of compiling back-to-back .320 years. He staggered through the remainder of his career under that back-breaking baggage of "Potential." For one brief period, he was the player everyone predicted he would be. In 1985 the Cardinals picked him up late in the season. In 28 games, Cedeno hit .434 to help St. Louis to the division title. Again he slumped in post-season play, hitting only .167 in the League Championship Series and .133 in the Fall Classic.

Cedeno's decade totals, including a .288 batting average, 777 runs scored, 292 doubles, 148 home runs and 427 stolen bases, would look a lot better if so much had not been expected of him.

Left: *The Royals' Amos Otis at bat. A clutch hitter, clever base stealer and excellent fielder, Otis wins the dream team center field spot for the seventies. Twice during the decade he led the league in doubles, and once in stolen bases, helping the Royals to four league championship contests. Otis ended his 17-year career in 1984, with Pittsburgh.*

Right: *Cesar Cedeno in the on-deck circle. Close runner-up for dream team center fielder, Cedeno batted .288 for the decade, with 292 doubles, 148 round-trippers and 427 stolen bases. Cedeno played for the Astros from 1970 through 1981, then went to Cincinnati, St. Louis and Los Angeles, where he finished his career in 1986.*

# RIGHT FIELD

Right field continued to be the home run hitter's position during the 1970s. Hank Aaron launched his assault on Babe Ruth's lifetime home run record from his traditional spot in right field. Managers came to expect power and RBI from the position.

Dream team candidates for right field are Dave Parker of the Pirates; Dave Winfield of the Padres; Reggie Jackson of the Athletes, Orioles and Yankees; and Bobby Bonds of the Giants, Yankees, Angels, White Sox, Rangers and Indians.

Dave Parker was a star, winning back-to-back NL batting titles, hitting more than .300 five straight years, and smashing 122 home runs in five years. He deserved to be baseball's first million dollar man. Involvement with drugs would turn Parker's career into a nightmare in the eighties; he lost his once powerful batting stroke. But Parker would re-emerge to play at his previous levels with Cincinnati and Oakland.

Dave Winfield was probably the best all-around athlete in the majors during the seventies. The six-foot-six, 220-pound Winfield was drafted to play three professional sports, including football and basketball. Luckily for baseball fans, he opted to step directly from the University of Minnesota campus into a regular job in the San Diego outfield in 1973. During the 1970s Winfield established himself as one of the NL's premier players, hitting over .300 twice, leading the league in RBI, and earning a Gold Glove.

**Reggie Jackson**, on the strength of over 292 home runs and 922 runs driven in, was selected right fielder for the 1970s dream team. "Mr. October" was perhaps the most electrifying hitter of the 1970s. "I'd like to be able to light the fire a little bit," he said. And he did.

Jackson was at his best in the World Series, hitting .357, the ninth highest Series average ever. His Series slugging average of .755 was the best of all time. Jackson was most famous for driving three home runs on three pitches in the final game of the 1977 Fall Classic to sink the Dodgers.

Jackson was a winner. In 12 years, 1971 to 1982, his teams – the A's, Yankees and Angels – won 10 division titles and five World Championships. Jackson won the MVP Award in 1973, when he led the league with 32 homers and 117 RBI for Oakland's champs. Perhaps his longest wallop was his home run in the 1971 All-Star Game. It hit a light tower above the roof of Tiger Stadium.

Jackson finished sixth on the all-time home run list with 563. During the seventies he won two home run crowns and drove in 922 runs. He also struck out more than any other man in history, 2597 times – once in every four at-bats. But Jackson considered the strikeouts a bargain price for the homers.

Dream team alternate right fielder Bobby Bonds, who should have been nicknamed "the Traveling Man," was never able to live up to his vast potential, which most baseball people believed to be on a level between Willie Mays and Mickey Mantle. Bonds combined power and speed like no player had done before him. In 1969 he became only the fourth player to hit 30 home runs and steal 30 bases in a season. Bonds repeated that feat four times during the seventies. In that decade, he stole 380 bases and hit 280 home runs. He led the league in runs scored and in total bases in 1973.

After seven seasons with the Giants, Bonds became a nomad, spending the next seven years with seven teams, all of them waiting for his instant offense. In 1979, at age 33, he hit 25 home runs and stole 34 bases for Cleveland, barely missing a sixth 30-30 season.

# DESIGNATED HITTER

As the DH position evolved, managers experimented with the type of player who could help the club win games. Baltimore Oriole manager Earl Weaver attempted to manipulate the position by listing his pitcher as the DH and pinch-hitting for the pitcher who stayed in the game. This strategy was outlawed by the AL office.

The designated hitter selection list was short for the decade of the 1970s, since career DHs had not yet developed. Candidates for the dream team are Hal McRae with the Royals, and Willie Horton of the Tigers, Rangers, Indians, A's, Blue Jays and Mariners.

Willie Horton, dream team alternate by default, capped a productive career as an outfielder by becoming a full time DH in 1975. His season of 29 home runs and 106 RBI for Seattle in 1979 drew three votes for the annual MVP Award.

**Hal McRae**, dream team DH for the seventies, became a star with the Kansas City Royals, whose scoreboard would proclaim "Big Mac Attack" after the slugger got a hit. He was named the top DH in the AL five times.

McRae, a disciple of the Charlie Lau school of hitting, managed to combine good home run power (106 for the decade) with a good batting average (.289 for the decade). He hit a career-high .332 in 1976, but on the last at-bat of the season, was nosed out of the running for the batting crown by teammate George Brett.

Left: *Reggie Jackson, whose brilliant post-season hitting earned him the moniker "Mr. October," played for five American League teams during his 21-year career. Dream team right fielder of the seventies, Jackson averaged 29 homers, 83 runs and 92 RBI a season during the decade, helping the A's and Yankees to seven ALCS contests and four World Series. Jackson's .755 World Series slugging average remains the all-time record. He was elected to the Hall of Fame in 1993.*

Right: *The Kansas City Royals' Hal McRae, dream team DH of the seventies, hit for both power (106 decade homers) and average (.289 decade batting average).*

Overleaf: *Fireworks explode over Cincinnati's Riverfront Stadium and Pete Rose is surrounded at first base by teammates after his 4192nd hit broke Ty Cobb's long-standing record. Pete Rose is dream team choice for consecutive decades, at second base and in left field.*

LEFT FIELD

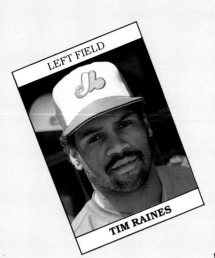

**TIM RAINES**

CENTER FIELD

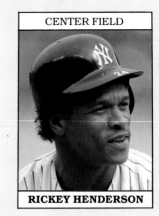

**RICKEY HENDERSON**

SHORTSTOP

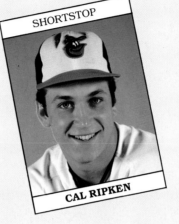

**CAL RIPKEN**

SECOND BASE

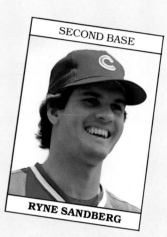

**RYNE SANDBERG**

THIRD BASE

**MIKE SCHMIDT**

PITCHER (LH)

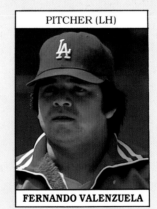

**FERNANDO VALENZUELA**

PITCHER (RH)

**DWIGHT GOODEN**

DESIGNATED HITTER

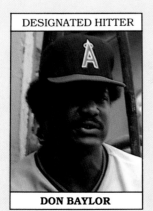

**DON BAYLOR**

CATCHER

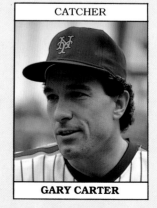

**GARY CARTER**

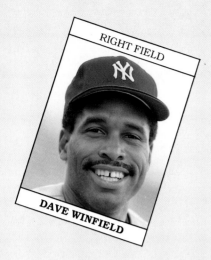

RIGHT FIELD

DAVE WINFIELD

# THE GREATEST PLAYERS
# OF THE
# EIGHTIES

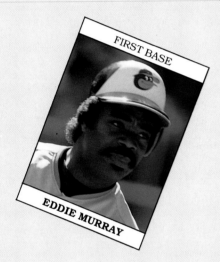

FIRST BASE

EDDIE MURRAY

## ALTERNATE DREAM TEAM

| | | | |
|---|---|---|---|
| **Pitcher** | Roger Clemens (rh) Frank Viola (lh) | **Shortstop** | Ozzie Smith |
| | | **Left Fielder** | Jim Rice |
| **Catcher** | Lance Parrish | **Center Fielder** | Dale Murphy |
| **First Baseman** | Don Mattingly | **Right Fielder** | Darryl Strawberry |
| **Second Baseman** | Lou Whitaker | **Designated Hitter** | Hal McRae |
| **Third Baseman** | Wade Boggs | | |

## HONORABLE MENTION

| | | | |
|---|---|---|---|
| **Pitcher** | Charlie Hough Dave Stieb Jack Morris Steve Carlton | **Shortstop** | Robin Yount Alan Trammell |
| | | **Left Fielder** | Vince Coleman George Bell |
| **Catcher** | Carlton Fisk Tony Pena | **Center Fielder** | Willie Wilson Andre Dawson Tony Gwynn Kirby Puckett |
| **First Baseman** | Kent Hrbek Keith Hernandez | | |
| **Second Baseman** | Frank White Willie Randolph | **Right Fielder** | Harold Baines Dave Parker |
| **Third Baseman** | George Brett Carney Lansford Graig Nettles Howard Johnson Bill Madlock Buddy Bell Tim Wallach Gary Gaetti Ken Oberkfell | | |

## THE SETTING

Baseball was better than ever in the 1980s. Players in the 1980s were highly motivated and more sensitive to pressure than in any previous decade. The term "salary drive" translated into a barrage of doubles, home runs, and RBI which were used to convince the general manager to raise the amount of annual compensation for the player. In 1986 the New York Mets used a series of television commercials depicting the Mets as the 1986 World Champions, in a not-so-subtle attempt to pressure their players into winning the pennant and World Series. The dutiful Mets responded by winning it all.

Baseball was solid at the major league level. Cities continued to set attendance records. Clubs had lucrative national and cable television contracts. Extensive radio networks served thousands of fans who lived far from major league ballparks.

The minor leagues expanded after three decades of shrinking. Franchises in Albany, St. Petersburg and Utica were sold during the eighties for record prices. Some day the 1980s will be called the "Golden Age of Baseball." More people were making a living from baseball and its peripheral industries than one could imagine.

## GAME STRATEGY

The strategy of the 1980s was based upon relief pitching. Few starters were encouraged to pitch complete games; 10-man staffs were fully used by every manager. Whitey Herzog of the St. Louis Cardinals won a pennant in 1985, and taught managers a lesson. Herzog used left- and right-handed stoppers out of the bullpen, emulating Dick Williams of the Oakland A's in the 1970s.

Wily Sparky Anderson, manager of the Detroit Tigers, gave managers another lesson in 1984 when he shot off the starting block with a 35-5 record, then played .565 ball for the duration of the year, and coasted to the division title. The well-rested Tigers easily won both the pennant and World Series. Sparky showed everyone that games count just as much in April as in September.

Offensive strategy became varied during the eighties because of the emphasis on individualism. Since each at-bat had the capability to produce a statistic that could be used in salary negotiations, batters and pitchers showed an intensity of play that did not exist in the previous decades. Such focused attention resulted in a great variety of plays. Fans could see the squeeze play, the hidden-ball trick, the hit-and-run play and double steals, sometimes all in the same game.

## FACTORS INFLUENCING PLAYER PERFORMANCE

Rule changes in the eighties were mainly cosmetic; interpretations were cleaned up. In 1988 umpires began to enforce the balk rule in its strictest interpretation. The result was a new set of balk records.

The factor that had the most influence on ballplayers of the decade was the incredible amount of money they had the potential of earning. Along with the thrill of being paid millions of dollars came the agony of unexpected problems. Young men who were not accustomed to such stratospheric sums of money did not know what to do with it. Some squandered it away and retired from baseball as poor as when they began. Others became involved with illegal drugs and wasted their money, their careers, and their health.

Even those who used their incomes wisely faced the tremendous pressure of failure — failure to perform, failure to win and failure to get more money — and all televised live to millions of people.

# THE POSITIONS

## PITCHER

Due to good health and advances in medical technology, many of the same star pitchers of the seventies were still around in the eighties. Diet, conditioning and fewer innings pitched kept many high-salaried aces productive and competitive in their late thirties and early forties.

The top right-handed pitchers considered for the dream team are Charlie Hough of the Dodgers and Rangers, Dave Stieb of the Blue Jays, Jack Morris of the Tigers, Dwight Gooden of the Mets, and Roger Clemens of the Red Sox.

Charlie Hough, the 40-year-old knuckleball pitcher, got better as he grew older. Hough, with 128 wins during the eighties, came up with the Dodgers as a relief pitcher, and did not become starter until 1982 with the Rangers. After that he was one of baseball's best pitchers, baffling and consistent.

Dave Stieb is well known for taking three perfect games into the ninth inning, yet losing the no-hitter all three times. Stieb was originally signed as an outfielder, but a .192 batting average in the Florida State League convinced him that his future lay on the pitching mound. After his conversion, Stieb won 140 AL games, led the league in ERA in 1985, and pitched in seven All-Star games, where his ERA was 0.93.

*The Mets' Dwight Gooden on the mound. With a 17-9 won-lost record and a league-leading 276 strikeouts, "Dr. K" won Rookie of the Year honors in 1984. For an encore in 1985, he turned in a league-leading 24 wins and 1.53 ERA to win the Cy Young Award. Gooden is dream team right-hander of the eighties.*

Jack Morris is the decade leader in victories with 162, despite suffering a sore shoulder in 1989 that limited his performance. During the eighties Morris won 15 or more games for eight years, yet led the AL only once – in the strike year of 1981, with 14. A two-time 20-game winner, he pitched in four All-Star games and won two World Series games in the Tigers' 1984 blitz of the Padres.

Two relative newcomers, Dwight Gooden and Roger Clemens, were selected as the dream team right-handed pitcher and alternate. Both own Cy Young Awards and have been considered the dominate pitcher in their respective leagues.

**Dwight Gooden**, dream team right-hander, won the Cy Young Award in 1985 when he led the NL with a 24-4 record, 268 strikeouts and a 1.53 ERA. Gooden won the Rookie of the Year Award in 1984 when he had a 17-6 record and a rookie record 276 strikeouts. "Dr. K's" 100-39 won-lost record was tops among 1980s starting pitchers.

Gooden's leadership on the Mets was never more apparent than in 1987, when the team floundered while he underwent rehabilitation for drug abuse. When Gooden returned, the Mets caught fire and pursued the league-leading Cardinals in a vain effort to defend their 1986 World Championship. A good hitter for a pitcher, on September 21, 1985, he drove in four runs against the Pirates.

Roger Clemens, when healthy, was the most intimidating pitcher in the AL during the decade. The six-foot-four Texan won back-to-back Cy Young Awards in 1986 and 1987. The

Far left: *Dwight Gooden is the youngest 20-game winner in modern history and the first pitcher with 200 or more strikeouts in each of his first two years in the National League.*

Left and below: *Roger Clemens winds up for the pitch, and throws. Alternate dream team right-hander for the eighties, the intimidating Clemens won back-to-back Cy Young Awards in 1986 and 1987, leading the league those years in wins and winning percentage. For his 1986 performance, which helped the Red Sox to the World Series, he also won the MVP Award.*

latter achievement came despite holding out of spring training in a contract dispute. Clemens won 79 games in the last four years of the eighties. He fanned 10 or more in a game 38 times for a Red Sox all-time record. He set an all-time record with 20 strikeouts in a nine-inning game, versus Seattle on April 29, 1986.

Clemens' decade record, 95-45, and his won-lost percentage of .678, was second only to Dwight Gooden's. Clemens' domination of the AL pitching scene was not without travail. In 1985, following two straight injury-plagued seasons, his right shoulder was surgically rebuilt. He rebounded from the possible career-ending operation to win the Cy Young Award in 1986. His performance prompted Met announcer Tim McCarver to quip "If Clemens goes on to win the Cy Young (in 1986) there will be a lot of pitchers standing in line for the same operation."

Most 1980s managers spent the winters hunting for the elusive left-handed starter. The list of good ones was short. The best in the eighties were Steve Carlton of the Phillies,

Left: *The Twins' Frank Viola followed up a 17-10, 2.90 ERA 1987 season in which he pitched the winning game of the World Series, with a Cy Young Award in 1988. Late in the 1989 season, the alternate dream team southpaw joined the New York Mets.*

Right: *The Dodgers' hard-throwing Fernando Valenzuela is the decade's dream team left-hander. Beginning his promising career with a Rookie of the Year and Cy Young Award season in 1981, Valenzuela went on to win 128 games during the eighties, helping his team to four league championship series and two World Series.*

Giants, White Sox, Indians and Twins; Fernando Valenzuela of the Dodgers; and Frank Viola of the Twins and Mets.

Steve Carlton won four Cy Young Awards, including those in 1980 and in 1982. Of Carlton's 329 lifetime victories, 104 occurred in the eighties. He played with five clubs in his last three years in the majors. Carlton refused, like Warren Spahn before him, to believe that his great career was finished, but a 16-43 won-lost record over the last three seasons finally convinced him to retire.

**Fernando Valenzuela** is the dream team left-handed pitcher for the 1980s. Valenzuela was the NL Cy Young and Rookie of the Year winner in the 1981 strike-shortened season, when he was 13-7. Valenzuela led the league in complete games, shutouts, innings pitched and strikeouts.

As a climax to his initial major league season campaign, Valenzuela pitched one of the gutsiest performances in World Series history. With the Dodgers down two games to none, Valenzuela started in Los Angeles. Despite the fact that Valenzuela gave up six hits, four runs and four walks in the first three innings, Dodgers manager Tom Lasorda stuck with his

Mexican ace. Two hours later, that decision was validated; Valenzuela allowed only six more baserunners in the next six innings. The Dodgers rallied to win the game, 5-4.

Valenzuela was the epitome of competive spirit, as his 5-1 record in post-season play attests. He won 128 games during the 1980s.

Frank Viola is the 1980s dream team alternate left-handed pitcher. He was the 1988 Cy Young Award winner with a 24-7 record. Viola was the winningest left-hander, with 117 wins in the majors during the last seven seasons of the decade.

Viola had a 3-1 record in post-season play, with his biggest victory coming in game seven of the 1987 World Series. Acquired by the Mets in a trade in August 1989 to bolster their staff in the late season pennant drive, Viola was able to win only five games, and the Mets fell short of their goal.

While attending St. John's University, Viola had pitched his team to the College World Series. Along the way, he defeated Ron Darling in a 1-0, 12-inning NCAA regional game thriller that college baseball fans still talk about. Darling had a no-hitter through 11 innings.

Right and below: *The Mets'
Gary Carter in action. Carter
played for the Montreal Expos
from 1974 to 1985, when he
was traded to the Mets for
four players. In the eighties,
this dream team catcher led
the league in putouts four
times, assists twice, double
plays twice and fielding
average twice. To
complement his fielding
prowess, Carter usually hit
well in the clutch, and hit for
power.*

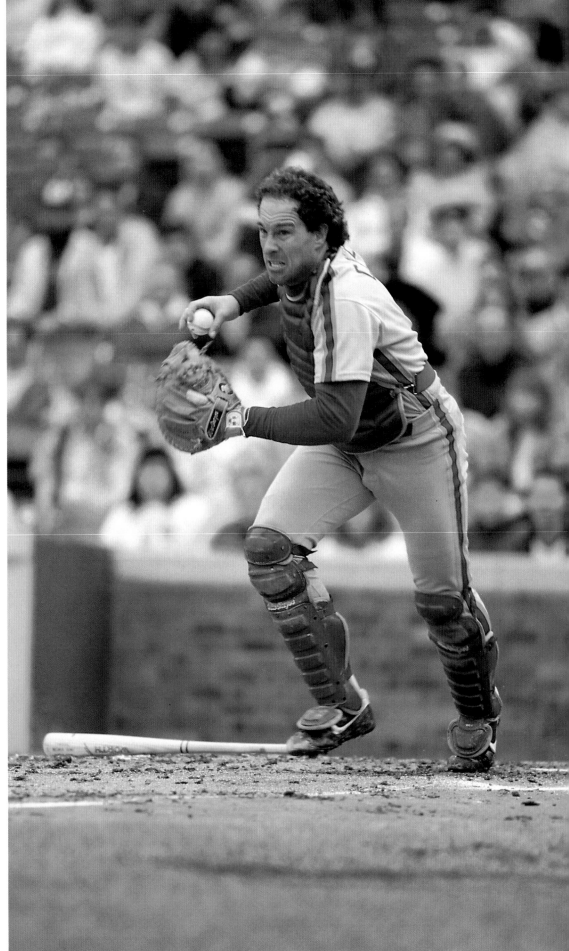

Opposite: *Detroit's Lance
Parrish warms up the pitcher.
Alternate dream team choice
of the decade, this big catcher
was a perpetual All-Star
selection and three-time Gold
Glove winner. Parrish played
his first 10 years with Detroit,
then signed with
Philadelphia in 1987. His 33
homers in 1984 helped the
Tigers to win it all.*

# CATCHER

A strange phenomenon occurred during the 1980s in major league baseball. Catchers born after 1957 forgot how to catch. In the post-Johnny Bench era, most receivers squatted and attempted to backhand the low-and-away pitch. Fans became accustomed to hearing: "wild pitch, it was in the dirt," but catching was not always like that. Once upon a time, receivers moved for outside pitches and blocked balls in the dirt.

During the 1980s, old-timers such as Ted Simmons, Bob Boone, Carlton Fisk, Gary Carter, Jim Sundberg, Rick Dempsey and Terry Kennedy reached the end of the decade still on active rosters. The only possible reason was that these fellows knew how to catch, and would remain in baseball until another generation learned the trade.

The best of 1980s' catchers were Carlton Fisk of the Red Sox and White Sox, Tony Pena of the Pirates and Cardinals, Gary Carter of the Expos and Mets, and Lance Parrish of the Tigers, Phillies and Angels.

Carlton Fisk was a hard-hitting and durable catcher. In 1985 at the age of 37, he hit 37 homers and batted in 107 runs. Two years later he surpassed the 300 mark for career home runs. As a catcher he established the major league mark for games caught, passing Bob Boone in 1993.

Tony Pena has, in some circles, long been considered the best catcher in the NL during the 1980s. A fine thrower, he twice led the league in assists and won two Gold Gloves, though not in the same years. Pena led 1980s catchers with a .274 batting average.

**Gary Carter** was chosen 1980s dream team catcher over Fisk and Pena. Carter was a better fielding catcher and produced more runs. He was also a team leader.

Gary Carter was frequently criticized by his teammates, sportswriters and fans for his sunshine personality. Friendly, cooperative, and enthusiastic, Carter has never been involved in a scandal.

Long regarded as the best-throwing backstop in the NL, Carter slipped a bit in the last few years of the decade. He made up for his aging arm in part with good footwork and a quick release. Widely admired as a handler of pitchers, Carter was credited for the development of Dwight Gooden into a star.

Carter's decade batting average was in the middling range, but his power statistics were excellent: 207 home runs, with a high of 32 in 1985, and 800 RBI, including a league-leading 106 in 1984.

Lance Parrish, dream team alternate catcher, was originally signed as a third baseman, but was switched to catcher in his second professional season. He has been selected to the AL All-Star team six times and won the Silver Slugger award for offensive excellence four times, 1980 and 1982, 1983 and 1984. The winner of three Gold Gloves in the early eighties, he set an All-Star Game record in 1982 by throwing out three of four runners. Parrish hit for power when the occasion demanded it. He hit a seventh-inning home run off Goose Gossage in game five of the 1984 World Series.

# FIRST BASE

First base was a power position during the eighties. When the great hitter Rod Carew moved to first base in an attempt to prolong his productive career, he was booed by the California Angels' fans, who clamored for a young power hitter.

The powerful first base candidates for the 1980s dream team included Kent Hrbek of the Twins, Keith Hernandez of the Cardinals and Mets, Eddie Murray of the Orioles and Dodgers, and Don Mattingly of the Yankees.

Kent Hrbek found out that when you hit 200 homers in eight years, the press learns how to pronounce your name no matter what the spelling. Hrbek, one of the finest young power

Below left: *The Yankees' Don Mattingly takes the throw in an attempt to pick off the Twins' Dan Gladden. In his first full season, this alternate dream team first baseman led the league with 207 hits, 44 doubles and a .343 batting average.*

Below right: *The Orioles' Eddie Murray belts a long ball. This dream team first baseman began his promising career as 1977 Rookie of the Year, and continued through the eighties as a top home run and RBI producer. He won consecutive Gold Gloves in 1982, 1983 and 1984.*

hitters in the game, held his own with the veteran sluggers. His grand slam in the sixth game of the 1987 World Series sunk the Cardinals and sent the Twins into the Series finale in an upbeat mood.

Keith Hernandez was the best fielding first baseman of the eighties, and possibly of all time. He won 10 Gold Gloves. Hernandez could cover bunts on the third base side of home plate and still make a play at first. A batting champ and MVP in 1979, Hernandez fashioned a .296 lifetime average (.300 in the 1980s) with 1124 runs and 1071 RBI.

**Eddie Murray**, the top RBI man of the decade, and one of its leading home run hitters, is the dream team first baseman. Don Mattingly, who holds the leading batting and slugging averages among eighties first basemen, is the alternate.

Eddie Murray averaged over 100 RBI per season for his first 11 seasons, yet led the AL only once – in strike-shortened 1981. He also tied for the lead in homers that season with 22. Probably the most powerful switch-hitter since Mickey Mantle, Murray was the model of consistency for Baltimore until injuries cut into his homer and RBI totals. Fans who had cheered him turned against him and booed. Murray demanded a trade, and generally handled the situation poorly. Though he played in only two World Series, 1979 and 1983, he and the Orioles were in the thick of six pennant races. Murray's batting average in September of those years was .318.

Murray, who commands a multimillion dollar salary, donates much of it to provide summer camps for city kids.

Don Mattingly won the AL batting title with a .343 average in 1984, his first full major league season. Since then, he has been one of the most consistent hitters in baseball. Perhaps no hitter in baseball today has combined high average with home run power to the same extent.

Mattingly topped 200 hits three times, 30 homers three times, and 100 RBI five times. His 145 RBI in 1985 led the AL. He led in doubles in 1984, 1985 and 1986. The 1985 MVP, Mattingly has been voted the top player in baseball in more than one poll.

## SECOND BASE

Top fielders at second base got little respect from the fans or management during the eighties. They both wanted hitters at second base. Dream team candidates for the keystone position were Frank White of the Royals, Willie Randolph of the Yankees and Dodgers, Ryne Sandberg of the Cubs, and Lou Whitaker of the Tigers.

Frank White was the most skilled fielder of the 1980s. He frequently picked up balls which most second basemen could never reach, and he made it look easy. With eight Gold Gloves, White would be headed for the Hall of Fame if he could hit. He had a .260 decade batting average with a .298 OBA.

Willie Randolph was the New York press candidate for the Hall of Fame when he played for the Yankees. After he moved to Los Angeles, the Hall of Fame accolades stopped. While not a bona fide candidate for Cooperstown, Randolph was a good offensive player with 754 runs scored and 777 walks during the decade, making an on-base percentage of .377.

**Ryne Sandberg** is a Hall of Fame candidate and the 1980s dream team choice for second base. Sandberg was the top NL second baseman of the 1980s, and may be rated one of the best ever by the time he is finished. He could probably play any of the infield positions. Sandberg has an above-average range and arm. If he lacks the flash of more acrobatic second-sackers, he is a lot steadier and has home run pop in his bat.

In 1984, when the Cubs won their division, Sandberg hit .314 with 19 homers and 19 triples. He led the league in three-baggers and in runs scored with 114. Sandberg was the runaway MVP Award choice.

Lou Whitaker, who began his career as a third baseman, was not as good as Frank White in the field, but was more of an offensive threat at the plate. Whitaker is the dream team second base alternate.

"Sweet Lou" was the AL Rookie of the Year in 1978. From his auspicious debut – three hits in his first major league game – Whitaker teamed with Alan Trammell for 10 solid years of excellent infield play. Whitaker led the AL in fielding with a .988 mark in 1982, and in 1985 he won his third Silver Slugger Award and third Gold Glove.

Left: *The Yankees' Don Mattingly at the plate. In 1987 Mattingly hit home runs in eight consecutive games, and belted a record six grand slams.*

Top: *Dream team second sacker Ryne Sandberg readies himself to make a play. Sandberg, also known as "Ryno," has anchored the Cubs' infield since 1982. In 1984 his MVP season* performance helped the Cubs win their division. The perpetual Gold Glove winner played in four All-Star Games during the decade.

Above: *The Tigers' Lou Whitaker makes a play. This alternate dream team second baseman was Rookie of the Year in 1978, and went on to win multiple Gold Gloves. "Sweet Lou" teamed with Alan Trammel to form a formidable defensive duo.*

Left: *Mike Schmidt blasts a long ball. Dream team selection for the second consecutive decade, Schmidt holds all-time records for home runs and RBI for third basemen. Multiple Gold Gloves attest to his defensive skill, and numerous league-leading offensive statistics demonstrate his power at the plate.*

Right and below: *Wade Boggs sharpened his defensive abilities to match his peerless hitting. This alternate dream team third baseman batted .349 as a rookie, and followed that with five batting titles in his next six seasons. In 1989 Boggs recorded his fourth consecutive season with 200-plus hits and 100-plus walks.*

# THIRD BASE

The hot corner was a position of outstanding players during the 1980s. Three surefire Hall of Famers — Mike Schmidt of the Phillies, George Brett of the Royals, and Wade Boggs with the Red Sox — are among the finest players ever to play third base.

During the 1980s several other very good players and possible Hall of Fame candidates played the position. They were Carney Lansford of the Red Sox, Angels and A's; Graig Nettles of the Yankees, Padres, Braves and Expos; Howard Johnson of the Tigers and Mets; Bill Madlock of the Pirates, Tigers and Dodgers; Buddy Bell of the Rangers, Reds and Astros; Tim Wallach of the Expos; Gary Gaetti of the Twins; and Ken Oberkfell of the Cardinals and Braves.

Carney Lansford won a batting title in 1981 while playing for the Red Sox. He averaged .295 for the decade and appeared in an All-Star Game.

Graig Nettles won the AL home run title in 1976 and remained a four-base threat his entire career. Nettles retired in 1989 with 390 home runs. He played in two World Series, batting .400 and .250.

Howard Johnson progressed from a .240 hitter with 12 homers, 10 stolen bases and 50 RBI in 1984, to a .265 batting average with 36 homers, 32 stolen bases and 99 RBI in 1987. In 1989 he batted .287, hit 36 homers, stole 41 bases and drove in 101 runs. Johnson has flourished as an offensive threat for the New York Mets.

Bill "Mad Dog" Madlock added the 1981 and 1983 NL batting crowns to the two that he won during the seventies. That made him a member of a select group of six National Leaguers who have won four or more batting championships. He hit .291 for the 1980s. When he was traded to the friendly, pennant-contending Los Angeles Dodgers in 1985, he became "Glad Dog."

Buddy Bell, the son of former Cincinnati great Gus Bell, had four seasons batting over .290 during the eighties, including a high mark of .329 in 1980. Bell showed good power, 201 lifetime homers, and won six Gold Glove Awards.

Tim Wallach, a fine all-around athlete, appeared in four All-Star Games in the eighties. Wallach hit a home run on his first major league at-bat, won a Gold Glove, and even pitched a scoreless inning in 1987. He had been named *The Sporting News* College Player of the Year as a first baseman in 1979.

Gary Gaetti hit two homers to power the Twins past the Tigers in the first game of the 1987 American League Championship Series. It was the first post-season play for the Twins in 18 years. After Gaetti's power initiated the Twins' surge, there was no stopping them as they rolled through the Detroit Tigers and St. Louis Cardinals to become World Champions. Always a power hitter, Gaetti had 185 homers in eight years of the decade.

Ken Oberkfell, a utility man who frequently played 150 games, was heartbroken to leave the Cardinals when they announced his trade in 1984. Recovering somewhat, Oberkfell continued to play the steady, run-producing baseball that he played for the Cardinals.

George Brett, a cinch to be inducted into the Baseball Hall of Fame, was the decade's third-best player at the hot corner. Brett's .311 decade batting average does not approach Boggs' .352, nor do Brett's 193 round-trippers fare well against Schmidt's 313 decade homers.

Brett's .390 batting average in 1980 came within a point of John McGraw's 1899 mark for highest batting average by a third baseman. It was the closest assault on .400 since Ted Williams' .406 in 1941. In 1980 Brett also knocked in 118 runs in 117 games to become the first player since Joe DiMaggio in 1948 to drive in more than one run per game played. His clutch hitting ability was never in doubt as his lifetime averages in Championship Series, World Series and All-Star play were .340, .373 and .292 respectively.

**Mike Schmidt**, the top power hitter of the 1980s, is the dream team third baseman. During the decade, Schmidt hit 313 homers, scored 832 times, drove in 929 runs and walked 819 times. He won five home run titles, three RBI championships, and was voted six Gold Gloves. All this in only half of his career; he was also the 1970s dream team third base pick.

Dream team alternate third baseman Wade Boggs will always be remembered as one of the best hitters of the 1980s — perhaps the best. Certainly his batting averages put him at the head of the class. As a rookie in 1982, Boggs batted a terrific .349. It turned out to be an "off" year. In subsequent years he topped .350 except for in 1984, when he "slumped" to .325. Three times Boggs batted over .360. All this added up to five AL batting crowns in his first seven seasons.

In the Red Sox scheme of play, Boggs' job was to get on base and be driven in. He did that so well that he compiled a streak of seven straight seasons of scoring 100 or more runs.

# SHORTSTOP

The 1980s dream team candidates for shortstop are Robin Yount of the Brewers, Alan Trammell of the Tigers, Cal Ripken of the Orioles, and Ozzie Smith of the Padres and Cardinals.

Robin Yount, who played shortstop before arm trouble sent him to center field, was the hit leader for the 1980s. He passed Willie Wilson early in 1989. A solid contender for the Hall of Fame as a shortstop, Yount was only an average center fielder during the eighties.

Alan Trammell was the Renaissance man of the eighties at shortstop — he could do it all. He hit with power — 130 homers, scored runs — 815, hit for average — .290, and could field and throw. He won four Gold Gloves and even hit in the clutch. Trammell's .450 average with two home runs and six RBI won the 1984 World Series MVP Award.

In the 1980s **Cal Ripken Jr.**, the dream team shortstop, was the best power-hitting shortstop since Ernie Banks. Originally a third baseman, he was switched to short in 1982, his first full year with the Orioles. When Ripken slugged 28 home runs and batted in 93 runs, he was named AL Rookie of the Year. His second season was even better. He led the AL in hits with 211, doubles with 47, and runs with 121. He batted .318 with 27 homers and 102 RBI. The Orioles were 1983 World Champions, and Ripken was named MVP.

Ripken has been chosen for the AL All-Star team every year since 1983. His value to the Orioles was evident as his batting average and RBI totals mirrored the Orioles' up-and-down slide in division standings during the eighties. Ripken's consecutive game streak is approaching that of Lou Gehrig.

Dream team alternate shortstop Ozzie Smith, the acrobatic Wizard of Oz, may be the best defensive shortstop of all time. The back-flip he used to do on the way to his position at the start of a game was just for show, but it showed the kind of defensive plays he could make. Smith's range was exceptional, and while his arm was not, his ability to make accurate, off-balance throws made up for any lack of strength. No shortstop has ever made more assists in a season than did Smith in 1980 (621). He helped take the Cardinals to three World Series, in 1982, 1985 and 1987.

Originally a good-field, no-hit player, Smith turned himself into a valuable offensive performer. He became adept at drawing walks, held his strikeout total low, and moved his batting average up. The Wizard hit .303 in 1987. Although without home run power, his ability to steal bases somewhat makes up for that. He hit a rare and dramatic home run that won a game against the Dodgers in the 1985 National League Championship Series.

Right: *The Orioles' Cal Ripken at bat. This dream team shortstop started out in 1982 as Rookie of the Year, and followed that up with a brilliant 1983 MVP season that helped Baltimore win it all. A perennial All-Star selection, Ripken holds a consecutive inning streak of 8243, extending from June of 1982 to September of 1987.*

Far right, above and below: *The Cardinals' Ozzie Smith, at the plate and in the field. "The Wizard of Oz" began his career with the Padres in 1978, and went to St. Louis in 1982. This alternate dream team shortstop added offensive ability to his bag of tricks afield when he batted a career-high .303 in 1987, with 75 RBI, 40 doubles, 43 steals and 89 walks.*

Left: *A slugging Jim Rice at the plate. Alternate dream team left fielder for the second consecutive decade, Rice contributed to Boston's 1986 bid for the World Championship with a .324 season batting average and a .333 Series batting average. After a couple of injury-plagued seasons at the decade's end, Rice was released by the Red Sox.*

Right: *Montreal's Tim Raines slaps one up the middle. Dream team left fielder of the eighties, Raines led the league in stolen bases four consecutive seasons, and can also hit for power and average from both sides of the plate.*

# LEFT FIELD

Speed and power reigned supreme in left field during the 1980s. The dream team selection list includes Vince Coleman of the Cardinals, George Bell of the Blue Jays, Tim Raines of the Expos, and Jim Rice of the Red Sox.

Vince Coleman is the heir apparent to Ricky Henderson's mantle as the leading base-stealer in the major leagues. In only five seasons, 1985-1989, the Red Bird thief swiped 472 bases and scored 493 runs. If Coleman ever learns to hit, NL opponents are in deep trouble.

George Bell, the moody, misunderstood slugger, has yet to achieve the sustained greatness that was predicted for him. Bell's 1987 season won him the MVP Award and would be considered excellent for most players. That year he hit 47 homers, scored 111 runs, knocked in 134 runs and batted .308. On opening day of 1988, Bell hit three home runs off Bret Saberhagen of the Royals.

**Tim Raines** is the dream team left fielder. He may be the top player in the NL in the 1980s. A compact switch hitter,

Raines' main weapon is blinding speed, but he also occasionally hits with power. As a rookie in 1981, Raines stole 71 bases in only 88 games. He led the NL in steals in his first four seasons, with a high of 90 in 1983. Still going strong, he had the best base-stealing percentage in history for players with 300 or more steals; for the decade he went 583 for 673, for 87 percent. Raines led the league in runs scored in 1983 and 1987. In 1986, he topped the NL with a .334 batting average.

Raines opted for free agency in 1987, but no team made a legitimate offer. It was an absurd situation that was later ruled to have resulted from collusion on the part of owners. Raines eventually re-signed with Montreal, but he missed spring training and the first month of the season. When he returned to hit .330, he made a lot of people wonder about the need for spring training.

Jim Rice, the dream team alternate, cut his strikeout totals and concentrated on RBI as a maturing slugger. He had 868 of them in the 1980s. His other achievements include 734 runs scored, 224 doubles, 210 homers and a batting average of .291. Rice's foible is his foot speed; once a decent runner, late in the decade he often grounded into double plays.

# CENTER FIELD

If you could run and catch the ball at a major league level, you had a chance to play center field in the eighties. If you stayed in center, it meant that you could also hit.

The dream team candidates for center field are Willie Wilson of the Royals, Andre Dawson of the Expos and Cubs, Tony Gwynn of the Padres, Kirby Puckett of the Twins, Rickey Henderson of the Yankees and A's, and Dale Murphy of the Braves.

The talent in the center-field position during the 1980s was prodigious. Willie Wilson, third in hits for the 1980s, was the decade's sixth-best center fielder. Wilson was the only batter to hit 100 or more triples during the 1980s. He won a batting title in 1982 and stroked 230 hits in 1980.

Andre Dawson, the NL slugger who decided to beat the owners at the collusion game in 1987, offered the Chicago Cubs a blank contract. Dawson wanted to play at Wrigley Field and the Cubs could fill in the amount of pay. It was a deal the Cubs could not refuse. Dawson rewarded them with 49 homers and 137 RBI. He won an MVP Award, the first ever for a

player on a last-place team. For his services, the Cubs paid $700,000 counting bonuses.

Tony Gwynn was the 1980s' version of Rod Carew. Base hits rained from his bat; he closed in on his third consecutive batting title, and fourth during the eighties. Gwynn has a decade average of .331.

Kirby Puckett may soon be rated the best player in baseball. The Gold Glove outfielder is built like a Mack truck, and he can hit and run. Puckett led the league in hits in 1987, 1988 and 1989, and has a decade average of .320. After years of trying, he finally captured the AL batting championship in 1989.

**Rickey Henderson** is the 1980s dream team center fielder. He is the greatest offensive catalyst in the game today and ranks with the best of all time. Dale Murphy is the alternate. Murphy's slugging average, .491, is nosed out by Dawson's .497, and Murphy scores runs, walks frequently and provides more to his team's total offense. He is a Golden Glove outfielder as well.

Rickey Henderson is known as the greatest thief since Willie Sutton. He demolished the single-season stolen base record in 1982, when he swiped 130 for Oakland. Three times he

Above left: *Rickey Henderson at the plate. This dream team center fielder began his impressive career in 1979 with Oakland, went to the Yankees in 1985, and rejoined the A's in the middle of the '89 season. A consummate base stealer who at times during the eighties has led the league in hits, runs and walks as well, Henderson's bright '89 performance helped the A's win it all.*

Above right: *The Braves' Dale Murphy slides into second. A steady performer for Atlanta since 1976, Murphy led the league in RBI in 1982 and 1983, winning consecutive MVP Awards. The big Gold Glove outfielder and dream team runner-up has led the league more than once in round-trippers.*

has gone over 100, and he led the AL in steals 11 times. After only 14 years in the majors, Henderson ranks first in stolen bases, with well over 1,000, surpassing Lou Brock and Ty Cobb in recent years.

An ideal lead-off man, Henderson usually bats in the .290-.310 range, draws plenty of walks (led the league three times), and scores plenty of runs. He has averaged over 100 runs scored per season for his career and he has a career on-base percentage of .400.

Henderson also hits with occasional power. He has more than 50 leadoff home runs in his career, tops in the major leagues.

Dale Murphy has not had much luck in NL pennant races. In 11 seasons as a Braves' regular, the best Murphy's team has ever done is one appearance in the 1982 NLCS.

Murphy came up as a catcher but switched to first base in 1978. Two years later he moved again, this time to center field, where he became one of the best, and has five Gold Gloves to prove it. He also has a powerful bat. He won back-to-back MVP Awards in 1982 and 1983, leading the NL in RBI and slugging average both years. In 1984 and 1985, he led in homers.

# RIGHT FIELD

Nothing in baseball is as awe-inspiring as the right fielder's throw to third to stop the runner from taking the extra base. The ability to make that throw is the criterion upon which great fielders are judged. Most managers, however, prefer a strong hitter in right.

Dream team competitors for right field are Harold Baines of the White Sox and Rangers; Dave Parker of the Pirates, Reds

Below: *Big Dave Winfield is safe at second. Dream team right fielder of the eighties, Winfield played for the Padres from 1973 through 1980, then joined the Yankees as a free agent. The speedy Gold Glove outfielder is a perennial All-Star and a consistent RBI man.*

Opposite: *The powerful Dave Winfield breaks his bat. Winfield had five consecutive seasons with 100 or more RBI – the longest stretch by a Yankee since Joe DiMaggio's seven from 1936 to 1942.*

and Athletics; Dave Winfield of the Padres and Yankees; and Darryl Strawberry of the Mets.

Harold Baines, an underrated player, is a solid .288 hitter with an average of 19 home runs and 84 runs driven in per year. He is a good player, but not the slugger most managers and the dream team want in right field.

Dave Parker has shaken off the effects of cocaine dependency to re-establish himself as one of the premier players of the game. Emerging as a star once again, first with Cincinnati and then with Oakland, Parker lost too many unproductive years to make the dream team.

**Dave Winfield** is the 1980s dream team choice for right field. He has produced consistently, whereas Darryl Strawberry has yet to achieve his vast potential. Winfield, a seven-time Gold Glove outfielder, is probably the best all-around athlete in the majors in the last quarter century. He was drafted in all three major professional sports.

Frustrated at playing for the losing Padres, Winfield signed an estimated $25-million contract as a free agent with the New York Yankees in 1981. He drove in 899 runs in the

decade's 10 years that include the strike-shortened 1981 season. In addition to being a good hitter, Winfield is considered an outstanding fielder and team leader, and has conducted himself as a model citizen. The Winfield Foundation, funded by his baseball earnings, is known for its charitable work with underprivileged youth.

Darryl Strawberry, the dream team alternate right fielder, has yet to reach his prophesied greatness, but he has a decade slugging average of .520, a figure surpassed only by those of Mike Schmidt and George Brett during the eighties. After only seven seasons, Strawberry had 215 homers with 570 runs scored, and 625 runs driven in for the decade.

*Below: The Mets' Darryl Strawberry at the plate. This alternate dream team right fielder began his career with a 1983 Rookie of the Year performance. The long and lanky "Strawman" is the first National Leaguer to be an All-Star starter in each of his first four full seasons.*

*Right: Don Baylor at bat for the Angels. The versatile Baylor made the switch from outfield to designated hitter in the early eighties. Dream team DH of the decade, Baylor played with four clubs during the eighties, three of which made it into post-season play. He supplements power at the plate with an uncanny ability to get on base as a hit batsman.*

# DESIGNATED HITTER

The DH position has evolved into that of a hired gun. Don Baylor typified the 1980s DH as the man who is brought in to drive the team over the top. He played on division-winning teams in Boston, Minnesota and Oakland in 1986, 1987 and 1988.

There were only two real candidates for the dream team spot because many teams were still reluctant to establish a full-time designated hitter. Instead, owners wanted to put aging superstar sluggers in the position to pacify the fans. Managers sometimes used the DH spot in the lineup as a place to rehabilitate injured position players. The choice for 1980 designated hitter was between Hal McRae of the Royals, and Don Baylor of the Angels, Yankees, Red Sox, Twins and A's.

Hal McRae, who won the dream spot in the 1970s decade, opted to hit for average rather than go for home runs, possibly because it is so difficult to hit home runs at Royals Stadium. Don Baylor, on the other hand, has truly become a hired home run bat. Since he best typified the evolved role of the DH, and because he out-slugged McRae, .477 to .457, **Don Baylor** is the decade top choice at DH.

Don Baylor was one of the most effective DHs of all the American Leaguers who have tried it. He was even the AL MVP in 1979 when he decorated his .296 batting average with 36 homers and league highs of 139 RBI and 120 runs scored.

All told, Baylor officially played nearly 1300 of his more than 2200 games at DH. Except for six seasons in California, he has been a big bat on the move. His willingness to travel pushed him into rarefied sluggers' air; he hit more than 300 homers and nearly 1300 RBI in his career. Although he was always hired for his bat, he also has had an admirable reputation as a team leader and steadying influence in the clubhouse. While such things are not subject to statistical evaluation, most of the teams he hit for were winners.

Hal McRae was named the top DH in the AL five times. He was another disciple of the Charlie Lau school of hitting, and managed to combine power (308 extra-base hits) with a good batting average (.290). McRae's 133 RBI in 1982 were the most ever by a DH, and won him the nickname "Mr. Ribbie" among teammates.

McRae hit more than .300 four times during the eighties, and tossed in two seasons of more than 40 doubles. McRae could still hit at the end of his career, .313 in 1987.

LEFT FIELD

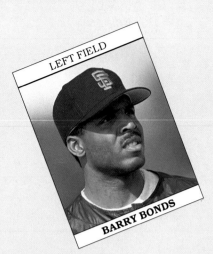

**BARRY BONDS**

CENTER FIELD

**KEN GRIFFEY, JR.**

SHORTSTOP

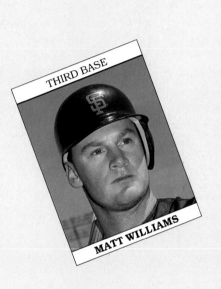

**JAY BELL**

SECOND BASE

**ROBERTO ALOMAR**

THIRD BASE

**MATT WILLIAMS**

PITCHER (LH)

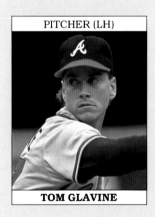

**TOM GLAVINE**

PITCHER (RH)

**JACK MCDOWELL**

DESIGNATED HITTER

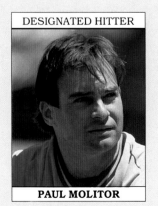

**PAUL MOLITOR**

CATCHER

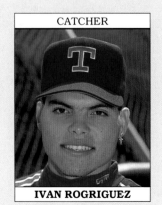

**IVAN ROGRIGUEZ**

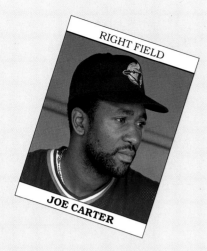

RIGHT FIELD

JOE CARTER

FIRST BASE

FRANK THOMAS

# THE GREATEST PLAYERS OF THE
# NINETIES

## ALTERNATE DREAM TEAM

| | | | |
|---|---|---|---|
| **Pitcher** | Greg Maddux (rh) | **Shortstop** | Travis Fryman |
| | Steve Avery (lh) | **Left Fielder** | Albert Belle |
| **Catcher** | Mike Piazza | **Center Fielder** | Devon White |
| **First Baseman** | Fred McGriff | **Right Fielder** | David Justice |
| **Second Baseman** | Ryne Sandberg | **Designated Hitter** | Tony Phillips |
| **Third Baseman** | Robin Ventura | | |

## HONORABLE MENTION

| | | | |
|---|---|---|---|
| **Pitcher** | Jose Rijo | **Third Baseman** | Dean Palmer |
| | Roger Clemens | | Wade Boggs |
| | Kevin Appier | | Chris Sabo |
| | Juan Guzman | | Terry Pendleton |
| | Aaron Sele | **Shortstop** | Ozzie Smith |
| | Pat Hentgen | | Cal Ripken, Jr |
| | Jason Bere | | |
| | Jimmy Key | **Left Fielder** | Juan Gonzalez |
| | Wilson Alvarez | | Ron Gant |
| | Mark Langston | | |
| | Randy Johnson | **Center Fielder** | Kirby Puckett |
| | | | Lenny Dykstra |
| **Catcher** | Darren Daulton | | Andy Van Slyke |
| | Mickey Tettleton | | |
| | Chris Hoiles | **Right Fielder** | Tony Gwynn |
| | | | Larry Walker |
| **First Baseman** | Don Mattingly | | |
| | Cecil Fielder | **Designated Hitter** | Manny Ramirez |
| | Rafael Palmeiro | | Troy Neel |
| | Mark Grace | | Danny Tartabull |
| **Second Baseman** | Carlos Baerga | | |
| | Harold Reynolds | | |

# THE SETTING

Retrenchment became the order of the day for the nineties. Club owners reeled from losses in three collusion lawsuits. Older players frequently found themselves out of a job, while younger stars were the object of lavish pursuit by the owners. The players' union fought hard to retain advances made in the 1980s. Barry Bonds, who as a child played practical jokes on his father's teammate, Willie Mays, signed the most lucrative contract in baseball history: $46 million for five years. National League expansion put teams in Denver and Miami in 1993. The Denver franchise, called the Colorado Rockies, drew more than four million fans to converted Mile High Stadium, surpassing even the Toronto Blue Jays in attendance. Toronto opened its new stadium with a retractable dome about the same time that the Montreal Expos finally finished their Olympic Stadium (begun in the mid-1970s for the 1976 Olympic Games).

The biggest news of the 1990s was the ouster of the commissioner of baseball. After having invoked the "best interests of baseball" clause during a confrontation with the National League, Commissioner Fay Vincent found himself regarded suspiciously by owners who were preparing for the toughest Basic Agreement negotiation yet. The owners wanted give-backs from the players' union, and worried that Vincent might step into the Basic Agreement negotiations in order to prevent a lockout or strike.

The office of the commissioner was vacated in September 1992, and the Executive Council, headed by Bud Selig, owner of the Milwaukee Brewers, ran baseball. In its first months, the Council concentrated mainly on its search for a new commissioner. Its most notable actions were the suspension of Reds majority owner Marge Schott for repeatedly using racial slurs, and the reinstatement of George Steinbrenner of the Yankees in 1993.

# GAME STRATEGY

On-base percentage became the watchword of the 1990s. In the 1993 World Series between the Toronto Blue Jays and the Philadelphia Phillies, the two best leadoff men of their day – Rickey Henderson and Lenny Dykstra – got on base almost at will. The other teams took a lesson from the performance and began a frantic search for the best leadoff man available. The main strategy of the 1990s was using the free agent market to fill gaps in defense or fine tune offense. Offensive game strategy continued a trend started during the 1980s when individual performance became the catalyst to outstanding team performance.

Pitchers adopted the two-throws-to-first defense. Research showed that runners were more successful in stealing bases when there were no throws from the pitcher to first base. Base stealers were less successful with one or two throws, yet the effectiveness of the throws to first diminished after the second throw. Pitchers also employed the slide-step delivery to prevent would-be base stealers from getting a running start.

Defensively, managers placed a great deal of hope in the strikeout. The emphasis on hitting caused managers to use infielders and outfielders who were good with a bat, but less than polished in the field; they made errors and lacked judgment. The pitcher striking out batters covered mistakes in the field.

Relief pitching was a fine art. The Cincinnati Reds rotated their trio of Nasty Boys – Randy Myers, Rob Dibble and Norm Charlton – in the 1990 World Series to shut down the opposition from the seventh inning on, rather than going with the traditional ninth inning closer. Teams with outstanding closers began searching for the "set-up" man, the fellow who would toss the eighth inning. As a result, baseball statisticians began counting "holds," and relief pitchers were rewarded for them.

# FACTORS INFLUENCING PLAYER PERFORMANCE

Baseball experienced no rule changes during the first part of the 1990s, though there was a structural change. Beginning in 1994, the American and National Leagues were broken into three divisions. Since this made two more opportunities to win, winning became paramount. The concept of being a first-division or second-division team, prevalent from 1900-1960, and common thereafter, no longer satisfied. Winning has become everything, and every team except the World Championship team could be considered a loser. This pressure to win it all has become a major factor affecting performance during the decade.

Pressure from the news media, pressure from fans, and pressure from million-dollar salaries, act in concert to isolate players from the public and the sportswriters. The game has become incredibly popular, rotisserie leagues remain in vogue, baseball call-in talk shows proliferate, and the public has become acutely aware of every penny a baseball player makes. As a result, professional ballplayers have become more aloof than ever before. Constant tension surrounds the major league player of the 1990s, both on and off the field. Every activity, every word is scrutinized. The players' agents get them bigger and bigger contracts, thus adding to the building pressure. The teams' common foe is becoming the public at large, causing teammates to band together, resulting in more closely knit clubs than at any time since the 1950s. Many of the triumphs during the decade will truly be team efforts.

# THE POSITIONS

## PITCHER

A premium was placed on control in the 1990s. New ways of analyzing baseball statistics – runners per inning, runners per game, on-base percentage – proved the truth of George Stallings' deathbed lament: "Boys, bases on balls put me here today." The 1990s teams that gave up the most walks finished their seasons in the sub-basement of baseball. Strikeouts, on the other hand, covered up a multitude of sins. Thus managers during the 1990s sought and demanded pitchers who struck out many, and yielded few free passes.

White Sox ace **Black Jack McDowell**, the 1993 Cy Young Award winner, is the right-handed dream team starter. Contenders were Greg Maddux of the Cubs and Braves, with two Cy Young Awards and four Gold Gloves; the Reds' Jose Rijo, with a 58-33 record in the 1990s; and Boston's Roger Clemens, who has three Cy Young Awards and holds baseball's all-time single game strikeout record (20). A host of good young hurlers – Kevin Appier of the Royals, Juan Guzman of the Blue Jays, Aaron Sele of the Red Sox, Pat Hentgen of Toronto and Jason Bere of the White Sox – are notable.

Black Jack McDowell, who plays in his own rock-and-roll band between starts, won 20 games in 1992 and 22 in 1993. His toughness on the mound is signified by the fact that he led the AL in shutouts, won 22 games and won the Cy Young Award despite a 3.37 ERA, a fairly high mark for such a winning performer. In other words, this decade's dream team pick is tough when he has to be. McDowell is difficult to steal on; he gives up just over two walks per game.

Greg Maddux, the dream team right-handed runner-up, won the NL Cy Young Award in 1992 and 1993, pitching for two different teams. He won 55 games while leading the NL in innings pitched three consecutive years, 1991-1993.

Below left: *White Sox ace Jack McDowell, while a college student, pitched Stanford University to the NCAA championship in 1987. McDowell led the AL in complete games, 1991-1992.*

Below: *Black Jack McDowell was the first draftee in the class of 1987 to make the majors, playing in September of his first pro season. The big right-hander led the AL in wins and shutouts as he took Cy Young Award honors in 1993.*

Left: *In June 1984, Tom Glavine was drafted by both the Atlanta Braves and the Los Angeles Kings of the National Hockey League. The dominating left-hander won 20 games in 1992 following his 1991 Cy Young Award-winning year, when he captured 20 victories with a 2.55 ERA.*

Below: *Tom Glavine was the first NL pitcher since Warren Spahn to lead the league in wins for three consecutive years. When he started the 1992 All-Star Game, he also became the first NL pitcher since Robin Roberts in 1953-1955 to start two consecutive years in the midseason classic.*

The left-handed choices were among Atlanta Braves teammates Tom Glavine and Steve Avery – who led Atlanta to three straight division titles – and Jimmy Key, who became a hired lefty as he pitched the Blue Jays into the 1992 World Championship, then went to New York, hoping to achieve the same for the Yankees. Rounding out the left-handed starter talent pool are Wilson Alvarez of the White Sox, who tossed a no-hitter in 1991; Mark Langston of the Angels with five Gold Gloves, three strikeout crowns and nearly 150 career wins; and big Seattle Mariner Randy Johnson. At 6′ 10″ Johnson is the tallest player in baseball history. He found a semblance of control during his no-hit season of 1990. That and his blinding speed made him very effective. His dominance may have hastened the retirement of several aging and left-handed batting superstars.

The dream team lefty choice is **Tom Glavine**, who at the age of 27 has three consecutive 20-win seasons, 1991-1993. He has won a Cy Young Award and finished second in Cy Young voting twice to Greg Maddux. Glavine led the NL in wins for three consecutive years. The last NL pitcher to do that was all-time great lefty Warren Spahn, who led in wins five straight seasons, 1957-1961.

The alternate dream team left-handed choice is Steve Avery, who was a more highly ranked prospect than Glavine as the two made their ways through the Braves' farm system. Avery seldom plays second fiddle to anyone. He tossed two 1-0 shutouts in the 1991 NLCS over the Pirates, allowing only nine hits and four walks in more than 16 innings.

Right: *Nineteen-year-old Ivan Rodriguez's wedding was postponed several days when the Rangers sent for him during an emergency. The talented backstop won Gold Glove Awards and was selected for the All-Star Game in 1992 and 1993.*

Below right: *Ivan Rodriquez played 211 big league games before his 21st birthday. The 5' 9", 165-pound dream team catcher hails from Puerto Rico.*

# CATCHER

Catcher is a position that seldoms changes because the demands are always the same: catch the ball, throw out runners, then hit the ball. The new wave of post-Johnny Bench receivers finally learned how to catch by 1990. The new receivers arrived in the big leagues as youths, loaded with batting power.

The dream team selection pot includes the Phillies' Darren Daulton, the one with the best stats 1990-1993; Texas Ranger Ivan Rodriguez, with two Gold Gloves and two All-Star Game starts; Mike Piazza, the Dodger who was the 1993 NL Rookie of the Year; Mickey Tettleton, who had so much power that the Tigers switched him to left field; and the Orioles' Chris Hoiles — a fearsome AL slugger.

In one of the most controversial picks, **Ivan Rodriguez** is selected as first catcher for the dream team. He arrived in the big leagues in a big hurry (The Rangers' 1991 call-up by telegram literally disrupted his wedding in Tulsa, where he had been playing on their Double-A Texas club.) at age 19. He began catching regularly from that moment. Awarded Gold Gloves and selected for the All-Star Game in 1992 and 1993, Rodriguez is the best catcher in the AL.

Mike Piazza is the alternate catcher on the dream squad. The selection is based on the tremendous potential he showed in his 1993 NL Rookie of the Year season, when he hit .318 and slugged .561 with 35 homers and 112 RBI.

# FIRST BASE

First base is still considered a power position, but recent studies show that nearly as many grounders are hit to first as to third base. Every team knows that a good fielder at first is necessary to win. The top candidates for dream team first baseman were Frank Thomas of the White Sox, Don Mattingly of the Yankees, Cecil Fielder of the Tigers, Rafael Palmeiro of the Rangers, Mark Grace of the Cubs, and Fred McGriff of the Padres and Braves. Mattingly is the finest fielder of his era. He was awarded eight Gold Gloves and the 1985 AL MVP Award. Cecil Fielder is the top slugger of the group, smacking 160 homers and driving in 506 runs in the first four seasons of the 1990s – both figures are top marks for the decade. Before the Cubs sent Palmeiro south to Texas, he and Grace were two peas in a pod, both outstanding at their positions. Grace has won two Gold Glove Awards. He batted .303 and Palmeiro batted .301. Raffy outslugged Grace but Mark reached first more often – 15 times more often.

Among these contenders, the choice for dream team first baseman is **Frank Thomas**. Only once in an era does a player come along with the skills and talent of this youngster. His percentages are phenomenal – a .321 batting average, a .444 on-base percentage, and a .561 slugging percentage. Thomas hits consistently well in the clutch and was instrumental in Chicago's 1993 American League West division title. Only 23 years old in 1993, Frank Thomas has the brightest future of any dream team player.

Fred McGriff, despite his relative youth, is already an established star who has played for the Blue Jays, Padres and Braves. McGriff is the dream team alternate. He swatted 35 homers to lead the NL in 1992, becoming the first player since turn-of-the century stars Sam Crawford and Buck Freeman to lead both the AL and NL in homers. McGriff has averaged more than 34 homers per season, and still has potential.

Above: *Superstar Frank Thomas used his well-trained eye to average more than 100 walks per season since coming to the majors in 1990. He led the AL in walks and on-base percentage in 1991 and 1992, and also hit 56 homers in those two years.*

Left: *Frank Thomas played tight end as a freshman for the Auburn University Tiger football team. Breaking into the majors on August 2, 1990, Thomas hit in 45 of his first 60 games, including a 13-game hitting streak for a .330 average.*

# SECOND BASE

The keystone position has come full circle since 1901. Originally a slugger's position, it has become so again in the 1990s. Teams with weak sticks at second tended to finish out of the money. The top candidates for the dream team squad were the Blue Jays' Roberto Alomar, Cleveland Indian Carlos Baerga, Ryne Sandberg of the Cubs, and Harold Reynolds of the Mariners and Orioles. Reynolds, who buys 1,000 seats for underprivileged youth for almost every game, is a real asset to the community as well as to his ball club. He is another of the perennial Gold Glove winners. Baerga emerged in the early 1990s as a high-average run producer in the high-octane offense of the Indians. His shirtless billboard ads have given him high visibility, and his .300-zone bat made him one of the decade's most solid middle infielders.

The dream team selection for second base is **Roberto Alomar**. Several AL managers insist that he was the best player in the league during the first half of the 1990s. His Blue Jays won back-to-back World Series, the first time a team repeated since the Yankees did so 15 years earlier. Alomar was a key reason for the double-barrel championship. He batted .326 and slugged nearly .500 in 1993. He also stole 55 bases and won another Gold Glove that season, totaling three during the first four years of the 1990s. He has played in the All-Star Game in each of his first four full seasons. Alomar does everything well: hits in the late innings, pushes the winning run to the next

base, gets on and steals second and third in a clutch situation, or dives on defense for the game-winning hit.

Runner-up for the 1990s dream team is sure-fire Hall of Famer Ryne Sandberg. Still a tremendous player at 34, Sandberg leads all active second basemen in home runs and slugging percentage. He has won nine Gold Glove Awards, has made nine All-Star Game appearances, and was voted NL MVP in 1984. His career stats are comparable to those of all-time greatest second baseman, Hall of Famer Joe Morgan.

*Above right: Roberto Alomar and his brother Sandy, Jr. are sons of former Brooklyn Dodger outfielder Sandy Alomar. Roberto's multiple Gold Glove Awards testify to his cat-like reflexes and aggressive fielding at second base.*

*Right: High schooler Roberto Alomar was signed as a free agent by the San Diego Padres in 1988. One of the brightest young talents in the game today, he stole 247 bases and scored 548 runs in his first six seasons.*

# THIRD BASE

Above: *Matt Williams shook off a disastrous 1992 season to post career highs in runs, home runs and batting and slugging averages in 1993.*

Right: *Matt Williams was drafted number one by the San Francisco Giants in 1986. The heavy-hitting third baseman led the NL in RBI in 1990, with 122.*

Play at the hot corner showed little change from that of the previous decade. Teams still want hitters at third. The 1990s dream team selection pool consisted of Dean Palmer of the Rangers; Robin Ventura of the White Sox; five-time batting champ Wade Boggs from Boston and New York; the Reds' Chris Sabo, the NL Rookie of the Year in 1988; the Giants' Matt Williams; and the Braves' Terry Pendleton, who won both the NL MVP and the batting champ title in 1991. All these dream team candidates can hit.

In a close contest, the Giants' home run slugger **Matt Williams** was selected as the third baseman for the 1990s

because of his powerful bat. He led the other third sackers in RBI, triples, home runs and slugging average.

Robin Ventura, in the runner-up spot, started to reach his potential during the early 1990s as he hit 22 homers and drove in 94 runs, walking 105 times in 1993, when Chicago won the AL West division title.

# SHORTSTOP

Clubs tried to overlook a player's tendency to make errors in their search for a heavy-hitting shortstop. Well-manicured infields took bad bounces out of the mix, leaving speed as the main criterion for a good-fielding shortstop. Perennial pennant contenders usually had big sticks at short. The dream team bevy of shortstops included 13-time Gold Glove winner Ozzie Smith of the Cardinals; Baltimore's Cal Ripkin, Jr., who was Rookie of the Year and owns two Gold Gloves and two MVP Awards; the Tigers' slugger Travis Fryman; and the Pirates' 1993 Gold Glove winner, Jay Bell.

Ripkin, who will surpass Lou Gehrig's consecutive game streak in 1996 if he stays healthy, is one of the all-time best power hitters at short. Smith, in the declining years of his career, yet arguably the best fielder ever to play the position, loses the 90s' dream team slot to the young lions, Jay Bell and Travis Fryman.

Bell has long been coveted by rotisserie league players as a shortstop with offensive numbers. He has averaged 94 runs, 166 hits, 32 doubles, 8 triples, 10 homers and 62 walks per year during the 1990s. He bats second in a lineup that won three straight division titles for the Pirates. **Jay Bell** is the choice for shortstop on the 1990s dream team.

Travis Fryman was so good at short that the Tigers moved Hall of Fame candidate Alan Trammell to third base when he came back from an injury, so that the youngster could continue at short. With a bat that keeps getting better – 22 homers and 97 RBI in 1993 – Fryman is an AL All-Star, and the dream team alternate for the 1990s.

Above: *Jay Bell was drafted number one by the Minnesota Twins in 1984, and was later traded to the Indians for Bert Blyleven, where he made his major league debut in 1986. Cleveland traded Bell to the Pirates three years later. When he became a regular in Pittsburgh, the Bucs won three straight division titles.*

Left: *Jay Bell won his first Gold Glove in 1993, beating out Ozzie Smith. One of the strongest-hitting shortstops in the NL, Bell homered in his first big league at-bat.*

Right: *Barry Bonds, who grew up in the San Francisco Giants' locker room, has been named NL MVP in three of the last four years. The son of powerful outfielder Bobby Bonds, Barry has developed much faster into a much better player than any scout imagined.*

Below right: *Barry Bonds, from Arizona State University, was drafted number one by the Pittsburgh Pirates in 1985. Bonds slugged .624 in 1992, the year he walked 127 times and struck out only 69 times.*

# LEFT FIELD

The player holding down the number seven position frequently batted third in the lineup. There were real stars in left field during the 1990s. Left field was overrun with power. Teams who did not have a power hitting superstar in left did not win during the decade. At the head of the class is former Pirate and now Giant **Barry Bonds**. Runner-up dream team member is Albert Belle of the Indians, who edged out 1993 AL home run champ Juan Gonzalez of the Rangers and Ron Gant of the Braves. Gant was a member of the 30-30 club (at least 30 steals and 30 home runs) in 1990 and 1991.

Bonds has won four Gold Gloves and three MVP Awards in the first four years of the decade. He leads all position players with a .595 slugging average. His statistics — 138 homers, 437 runs, 456 RBI and 453 walks in just the first four years of the decade — justify to some his $46 million, five-year contract, signed in 1993 with the Giants.

Albert Belle is a high-spirited youngster who led the AL with 129 RBI in 1993. The Indians built their team around him during the early 1990s, and he gave them reason to keep on going after the tragic boating accident that killed Steve Olin and Tim Crewes and injured Bob Ojeda in 1993. Belle has a career .505 slugging average heading into the 1994 season.

# CENTER FIELD

The center field garden has once again become the home of superstars, much like it was in the golden days of the 1950s, when the center fielder was the best player on the team. Gold is the operative word here. This group of center fielders has won 18 Gold Glove Awards among them. The contenders for the 1990s dream team at center field were Ken Griffey, Jr. of the Mariners, Kirby Puckett of the Twins, the Blue Jays' Devon White, the Phillies' Lenny Dykstra, and Pirate Andy Van Slyke. The slick-fielding Van Slyke, the super-aggressive Lenny Dykstra, who scored 143 runs in 1993, and highly productive superstar Kirby Puckett, all stellar performers, nonetheless lose the honor to **Ken Griffey, Jr.** and alternate Devon White.

Griffey, sometimes called Junior, walloped 45 home runs in 1993, making a total of 116 dingers for the 1990-1993 period. The young slugger, who has a .311 decade batting average, continues to improve as the Mariners surround their star with better hitters.

White is one of the catalysts of the back-to-back World Champion Toronto Blue Jays. He excels at most aspects of the game. He has averaged 31 stolen bases, 95 runs, and 76 walks per season during the early 1990s, and is a Gold Glove-caliber outfielder as well.

Above left: *Ken Griffey, Jr. was injured in his rookie season, but has hit more than 20 home runs and batted over .300 in every year since.*

Left: *Cincinnati's Moeller High School star Ken Griffey, Jr. was the first player selected in the 1987 draft. Beginning his professional baseball career at age 17, he has been a star in every league in which he has played.*

Right: *Ken Griffey, Jr. and Sr. played together on the 1990-1991 Seattle Mariners, becoming the first father-son duo ever to play together in the major leagues.*

Left: *A star at Wichita State University, Joe Carter was second draft pick of the Chicago Cubs in 1981. Overcoming constant shifting between first base and outfield while playing for the Indians and Padres, Carter gained recognition as the most prolific power hitter in baseball when he joined the Blue Jays in 1991.*

Below left: *Joe Carter led Toronto to three division titles. His dramatic home run in the last game of the 1993 World Series was the first round-tripper to end the Series since Bill Mazeroski's famous shot in 1960.*

Right: *Paul Molitor was an All-American shortstop at the University of Minnesota when he was drafted number one by the Milwaukee Brewers. After 15 seasons playing third base, DH and other positions in Milwaukee, Molitor moved his act to Toronto in 1993.*

## RIGHT FIELD

Managers in the 1990s wanted their right fielders to be able to throw. Preventing runners from taking third on singles to right was very important in the decade strategy to make runs dear. The right fielders in contention for dream team honors were Joe Carter, star of the Blue Jays; San Diego's Tony Gwynn; the Braves' David Justice; and young Expos star-on-the-rise, Larry Walker. Gwynn, despite five career batting titles and five Gold Gloves, loses to top choice **Joe Carter** and alternate David Justice. Two-time Gold Glove winner Larry Walker, who combines speed and power (80 homers and 82 steals in four years) may end up being the best right fielder of the bunch.

Carter may become a designated hitter, but he is currently the most productive right fielder in baseball. Though hitting only .256, he has averaged 89 runs, 31 homers, 33 doubles and 116 RBI during the first four years of the 1990s.

Justice, who leads right fielders in slugging percentage, appeared to have reached his potential in 1993, when he clouted 40 dingers and drove in 120 runners.

# DESIGNATED HITTER

During the 1990s, the designated hitter profile changed from that of a well-established, veteran hitter to that of the new breed of youngster who was trained at age 23 to be a DH. The Indians' Manny Ramirez and Oakland's Troy Neel fit this category. For pure performance excitement, however, you could not beat the old-timers, like Paul Molitor of the Brewers and Blue Jays, Detroit's Tony Phillips, and Danny Tartabull of the Royals and Yankees.

Tartabull signed a multi-million dollar contract with the Yankees in 1992, taking his home run and RBI bat to New York. Injuries that plagued him with Kansas City continued to haunt him in the Big Apple. Both Ramirez and Neel had great seasons, albeit many strikeouts, in their rookie years. Neel had back-to-back two-homer games in 1993, and Ramirez wal-

loped two homers and a double in his Yankee Stadium debut.

The 1990s dream team DH starter is **Paul Molitor**, who has averaged 185 hits, 102 runs, 33 doubles, 8 triples and 16 homers with a .318 batting average during the first four years of the 1990s. Molitor, who has been known throughout his career as the "Ignitor," proved that the DH does not have to be a big, slow-footed slugger whose best days are behind him. Molitor even played third base in the 1993 World Series when the Blue Jays wanted his bat in the lineup at Philadelphia's Veterans Stadium.

Tony Phillips is one of baseball's most unsung players. He fueled two Oakland division titles as a utility player. He went to the Tigers to begin the 1990s, where he became a starter for the most potent offense of the decade. Phillips averaged 103 runs and 106 walks per year from 1990 to 1993. He led the league in runs scored with 114 in 1992, and had an amazing 132 bases on balls to lead the AL in 1993.

# INDEX

## Picture Credits

**Bettmann Archive:** 11(1B); 24(2B).
**DiMaggio/Kalish Photography:** 167; 168(left).
**Malcolm Emmons:** 132, 136, 137.
**Nancy Hogue:** 140(LP, C, 2B, 3B, SS, LF, CF, DH); 144; 145(top); 146; 147; 149; 150; 151(both); 152-153(both); 154(right); 155; 156; 157; 158; 159; 160; 161; 164(LP, DH); 189.
**Ron Modra:** 162-163.
**National Baseball Library, Cooperstown, NY:** 10(CF, 3B, 2B, C, LP); 13; 14; 14-15; 16; 17(right); 18(both); 19(both); 22; 23(both); 24(C, 3B); 25(1B); 28(both); 29(top); 30(right); 33; 35; 39(bottom); 40(LP, LF); 44(bottom); 45; 46; 53; 54(bottom); 55; 58-59(both); 60(3B, LF); 64; 65; 67; 70(right); 71; 72-73; 74(top); 75; 76(left); 81; 82(C); 85; 89(left, top right); 98(top); 101(RF), 103; 104(left); 113; 120(LF, SS); 129(top); 131(right); 133(both); 140(RP); 141(1B); 143; 148; 154(left); 164(SS); 181(left).
**Ponzini Photography:** 2; 164(LF, CF, 3B, 2B, RP, C); 165(RF, 1B); 168-169(center); 169(right); 170; 171; 172; 173; 174-175(both); 176; 177(both); 178; 179(both); 181(top right, bottom right); 182; 183; 184-185(both); 186; 187; 188; 190-191(all 11); 193 (both); 194 (both); 195 (both); 196 (both); 197 (both); 198; 199; 200 (both); 201 (both); 202 (both); 203; 204 (both); 205.
**UPI/Bettmann News Photos:** 1; 4-5; 10(LF, SS, RP); 11(RF); 17(left); 24(RP, CF, LF, SS, LP); 25(RF); 27; 29(bottom both); 30(left); 31; 32; 34(both); 36; 37; 38; 39(top); 40(RP, C, 2B, 3B, SS, CF); 41(RF, 1B); 43; 44(top); 47(both); 48; 49; 50; 51(both); 52-53(top); 52(bottom); 54(top); 56-57; 60(CF, SS, 2B, C, LP, RP); 61(1B, RF); 63; 66(both); 68(both); 69; 74(bottom); 76-77(bottom); 78; 79; 80; 82(LP, RP, 2B, SS, 3B, LF, CF); 83(1B, RF); 86; 87(both); 88; 89(bottom right); 90-91(both); 92; 93; 94-95(both); 96; 97; 98(bottom); 99; 100(all eight); 101(1B); 104(right); 105; 106-107(both); 108-109(all three); 110-111; 112; 114(both); 115; 116-117(all three); 118(all three); 120(C, RP, 2B, 3B, LF, CF); 121(1B, RF); 123; 124; 125; 126; 127; 128; 129(bottom); 130; 131(left); 134; 135; 138(both); 139; 141(RF); 145(bottom).

## Acknowledgments

The author and publisher would like to thank the following people who have helped in the preparation of this book: Barbara Thrasher, who edited it; Adrian Hodgkins, who designed it; Rita Longabucco, who did the picture research; and Elizabeth McCarthy, who prepared the index.